Praise for HAVEN

"Everyone concerned about courage in a grievous time will want to read *Haven*. Compelling and moving, personal and absorbing, it raises immediate alternatives for the present, while illuminating a lonely example of activism when too few existed during the dastardly days of neglect and unconcern for refugees and Jews. Ruth Gruber, one of America's finest journalists, a dedicated woman of action, principle, and vision, has given us an enduring and inspiring gift."

—BLANCHE WIESEN COOK, Distinguished Professor, John Jay
College, City University of New York, and author of
Eleanor Roosevelt (volumes one and two)

"An important journalist's empathic account."

—CYNTHIA OZICK

"Miss Gruber combines the thorough knowledge of the insider with the writing skill of the professional. . . . It is a touching story."

—*The New York Times*

"It will be a rare reader who is unmoved by this heart-wrenching story. . . . Although largely Jewish, the group consisted of members of many faiths: all had experienced the horrors of Nazism and the stories they told Gruber are truly spine-chilling."

—*Publishers Weekly*

"*Haven* [gives] us an excruciating glimpse of what might have been done had there only been a will to save precious lives. Most readers will emerge from the Oswego experience with a sense of joy at those who were rescued by American government largesse and a sense of forlornness that this generosity was the exception rather than the rule."

—HENRY FEINGOLD, author of
The Politics of Rescue

HAVEN

HAVEN

《 》

The Dramatic Story of
1000 World War II Refugees
and How They
Came to America

Ruth Gruber

Foreword by Dava Sobel

THREE RIVERS PRESS · NEW YORK

Published by Three Rivers Press, New York, New York.
Member of the Crown Publishing Group.

Random House, Inc. New York, Toronto, London, Sydney, Auckland
www.randomhouse.com

THREE RIVERS PRESS is a registered trademark and the Three Rivers Press colophon
is a trademark of Random House, Inc.

Originally published in 1983 by Coward-McCann, Inc. This edition published by
arrangement with the author. For this edition, chapter 26 has been substantially
revised and chapter 27 is entirely new.

Printed in the United States of America.

Book design by Helene Berinsky

Library of Congress Cataloging-in-Publication Data
Gruber, Ruth.
      Haven : the dramatic story of 1,000 World War II refugees and how they came to
America / Ruth Gruber.—[Rev. and expanded ed.].
      Includes index.
      1. Gruber, Ruth, 1911–   2. World War, 1939–1945—Refugees.   3. World War,
1939–1945—Civilian relief—United States.   4. World War, 1939–1945—Personal
narratives, American.   5. World War, 1939–1945—New York (State)—Oswego.
6. Oswego (N.Y.)—History.   7. Refugees—United States—Biography.   I. Title.
D809.U5 G77   2000
940.53'086'91—dc21   99-087897

ISBN 0-8129-3301-X

9 8 7 6 5 4

To my four young grandchildren

Michael Philip Evans,
Lucy Jennifer Evans,
Joel Philip Michaels, and Lila Sarah Michaels

FOREWORD

Unlike the eighteenth-century sailors I wrote about in my book *Longitude,* the one thousand refugees who shipped with my Aunt Ruth aboard the *Henry Gibbins* out of Naples knew exactly where they were: in a war zone at precise coordinates on the Atlantic Ocean, surrounded by enemy submarines. Having lost their homes and many of their family members, they were running for their lives from a scene of devastation in Europe, bound for an uncertain, temporary future in the United States. During that 1944 crossing they learned to love and trust the young Jewish-American woman who had come to their rescue, who walked among them on the decks, taught them the rudiments of English, and wrote down their horror stories in Yiddish and German. To this day, when they embrace her at reunions, they call her "Mother Ruth."

The historic journey of the *Henry Gibbins* ended in the port of New York before I was born, so the Aunt Ruth of my childhood was already a war veteran with the honorary rank of general. Her apartment in Manhattan resembled a small museum. The long corridor from the front entry to the back bedrooms was lined, even down to my height, with plaques, tributes, and photos of Ruth posed with the leaders of numerous countries, including David Ben-Gurion, Golda Meir, President Harry S Truman, and Eleanor Roosevelt.

A large glass-enclosed case in the dining room exhibited the artifacts of her career in statesmanship and journalism; it contained, for example, bits of Eskimo carved ivory figures she acquired as special assistant to the Secretary of the Interior, and gold nuggets she panned in the Soviet Arctic. Perhaps the most curious item was a prosthesis of ugly false teeth, intentionally decayed and decrepit-looking. Young male survivors of the Holocaust, displaced and detained on the island of Cyprus, had worn these to help disguise themselves as old men, in the hope of escaping their captivity and joining the Haganah to fight in Israel's War of Independence.

My earliest Aunt Ruth memory is of the birth of her daughter, Celia, in 1952, when I was five. Ruth is only two years younger than her sister, my mother, but she waited seventeen years longer to start having children: she was forty-one by the time Celia arrived. In this postponement of motherhood, as in so many other areas, Ruth pioneered without even realizing that she was spearheading a movement. Her brother Harry, a physician, warned her that she courted disaster by becoming pregnant at her age, but my father, as Ruth's obstetrician, delivered Celia—and David two years later—without encountering the slightest complication.

Whenever my family drove down from the Bronx to visit, Ruth would always answer the door in something floor-length and fur- or feather-trimmed. I loved those flamboyant housecoats she wore (and still wears), because they were (are) just as characteristic of her as her U.S. Army uniform with "war correspondent" emblazoned over the left breast pocket like a battle ribbon. Even when she rode in a military convoy with a machine gun in her lap, Ruth had her nails polished and her lipstick in place.

Ruth's writing life was an inspiration to me. Or rather, it made traveling around the world and being an author seem an acceptable, accessible pursuit. At the same time, I was very glad my own mother had not chosen such a path, which would have required her to go off for weeks or months at a time, as Ruth did, and perhaps leave my brothers and me in the care of our iron-jawed, big-bosomed Grandma Gussie, who forced Celia and David to drink milk.

I lived in Ruth's home briefly during my student years at the City College of New York, and wrote a couple of term papers on her typewriter. It was an early electric model that printed only capital letters. There were two television sets in Ruth's kitchen, so she could watch the news on two channels at once while eating breakfast and reading *The New York Times*. At least one radio also broadcast simultaneously, and of course everyone in the room was talking.

In my twenties, when I held my first job as a newspaper reporter, Ruth visited the upstate New York town where I lived, and I got the assignment to cover her lecture of March 1, 1970. As I later wrote in my article, Ruth had already made twenty-one trips to Israel and written five of her seven books about the birth and growth of that country, but she counted as her most important tribute a high school classroom in the Israeli desert town of Dimona that had been named in her honor.

Alone with her in her hotel room that morning, as she paced through her yoga exercises, we were just family. But at the breakfast presentation I met her public persona for the first time. With no prepared speech or notes, she stood up before the audience of several hundred and closed her eyes. When she opened them a moment later, she began reciting her recalled visions in a trembling voice: "You speak to Moshe," she recounted of a child she'd met in Israel, "whose parents came from Yemen, and ask him what he wants to be when he grows up. 'I want to be a schoolteacher.' David, whose parents came from Morocco, 'I want to be a pilot.' You ask Sorella, whose parents came from Poland, what she wants to be when she grows up. 'I want to be prime minister.' And little Yonkel, whose parents came from Auschwitz and Bergen-Belsen, 'I want to be alive.' "

By the time she finished talking she had brought nearly all the people in that room to tears and to their feet. Since then I have seen her create this same spell in any number of other banquet halls and auditoriums. And even though I know what's coming, I can never inure myself to the emotion of her impact. Nor would I want to.

All the cousins of my generation laughed a little at Ruth when Celia joined a CBS news crew to report live from Beirut on the war in Lebanon, because General Ruth seemed suddenly—finally!—alert to the concept of personal danger. But I can tell, as she prepares now to travel alone on a twelve-city publicity tour for her fifteenth book, *Exodus 1947,* that she still has absolutely no idea how old she is.

Like its author, the story you are about to read in these pages has lost none of its poignancy, immediacy, or relevance over a period of fifty years.

Dava Sobel
October 1999

CONTENTS

Foreword by Dava Sobel   ix

Introduction   xv

《》

PART ONE
THE STRUGGLE IN WASHINGTON   1

PART TWO
THE VOYAGE OF THE *HENRY GIBBINS*   51

PART THREE
THE OSWEGO ADVENTURE   117

PART FOUR
AFTER THEY CROSSED THE RAINBOW BRIDGE   249

《》

Appendix   297

Index   327

INTRODUCTION

THIS IS A TRUE STORY.

Few people are aware, and those who knew have largely forgotten, that nearly one thousand refugees were brought to the United States as guests of President Franklin Delano Roosevelt during World War II.

Transported on an Army Transport Ship with wounded soldiers from Anzio and Cassino, hunted at sea by Nazi planes and U-boats, brought to haven in Oswego, New York, they were to know the exquisite relief of freedom from bombings and terror. Refugees from eighteen countries Hitler had overrun, they tried to rebuild their lives inside an internment camp on American soil.

As special assistant to Harold L. Ickes, secretary of the interior, I was sent by our government to escort them from war-torn Italy and help resettle them in Fort Ontario, a former army camp on Lake Ontario. Thus I became witness and participant. I experienced their joys and pain, rejoicing in their marriages and love affairs, sharing pride in their children, mourning those who died by their own hand or by acts of God.

Stowed away in the bottoms of filing cabinets were more than forty notebooks I had filled during the eighteen months my life was interwoven with theirs. These notebooks, together with copies of the reports, letters, and documents I had prepared for the government, were the major source for the events recorded in this book. Invaluable, too, were the diaries that Cabinet members frequently keep, made public by their heirs. When the Ickes family opened Secretary Ickes's secret diaries to the world, I spent fascinated hours in the Library of Congress discovering the personal, often intimate details of his years in office, his battles, both epic and small, and his discussion of the assignments he gave me.

In Hyde Park, I dug into the voluminous diaries of Secretary of the Treasury Henry Morgenthau, Jr., and the papers of Eleanor and Franklin Roosevelt, all of whom played character roles, sometimes larger than life-size, on the Oswego stage.

Luck was with me. In the National Archives I uncovered the confidential log of the *Henry Gibbins*, the Army Transport on which I sailed with the refugees, and succeeded in persuading the government to declassify it.

Across the years, as I balanced my life as writer, wife, and mother, I continued my friendship with many of the refugees, who gave generously of their time and their memories. To all of them I give my heartfelt gratitude.

I have tried to write the story of the only group of refugees b.rought to America by the government during World War II with some of the humor I learned from them, with anger and passion and honesty, and with love.

Part One

—《 》—

THE STRUGGLE
IN WASHINGTON

ONE

THE WORDS LEAPED at me from *The Washington Post.*

"I have decided," President Franklin Delano Roosevelt announced, "that approximately 1,000 refugees should be immediately brought from Italy to this country."

One thousand refugees.

Europe was burning. It was June 1944, the middle of the war.

For years, refugees knocking on the doors of American consulates abroad had been told, "You cannot enter America. The quotas are filled." And while the quotas remained untouchable, like tablets of stone, millions died.

Suddenly, one thousand refugees were to be brought in *outside* the quotas, by order of the President himself. Until now I had felt helpless, frustrated, enraged. Noble speeches were made each day about saving refugees before they were swept into the fire, but the deeds belied the words. Our doors had been slammed shut. Now suddenly there was hope.

At my breakfast table, air-conditioned against Washington's summer heat, I continued to devour the article. The thousand refugees, I read, would be selected by the War Refugee Board, transported to America by the Army, and housed in a "temporary haven," a former army camp called Fort Ontario, in Oswego, New York. The camp would be administered by the War Relocation Authority of the Department of the Interior. Only a few months before, the President had placed WRA, soon to be disbanded, under

Harold L. Ickes, the secretary of the interior. I was Ickes's special assistant, his field representative for Alaska.

Ickes would know what lay behind this sudden humanitarian gesture.

At E Street I jumped out of a cab and looked up at the handsome gray stone Interior building with its great bronze doors and modern columns. Interior—the vast grab-bag department of Indians, wildlife, Alaska, Puerto Rico, Hawaii, the Philippines—would now be in charge of Europe's refugees too.

In my office, I telephoned Ickes's appointments secretary and arranged a meeting for 11:55 A.M.

Ickes sat behind a huge desk littered with papers. His head was lowered as I began the long walk across the huge blue-carpeted office. He was writing with the thick scratchy pen I had seen him use countless times.

"Sit down," he said briefly, and continued to write.

I sat in the armchair at the side of his desk. Behind him was a long table carefully stacked with books, newspapers, magazines. *The Nation* and *The New Republic,* to which he frequently contributed, were on top.

He finished his writing and buzzed for his secretary, who took the papers and disappeared.

Now he turned his full attention to me. "Yes?" he asked quizzically. "I understand it's urgent."

"It's about the thousand refugees that President Roosevelt is inviting to America."

He nodded. "The President sent me a copy of his cablegram to Robert Murphy in Algiers announcing it."

"Mr. Secretary," I said, "it's what we've been fighting for all these years. To open doors. Save lives. Circumvent the holy quotas. What's behind it? How did it happen?"

He leaned back in his chair. His eyes looked weary. "It came up in a Cabinet meeting with the President. It seems that Yugoslavian refugees and others are finding their way into Italy at the rate of about eighteen hundred a week. It's a problem for the military in Italy."

Was it Army pressure, then? The Allied armies were just now pushing up the boot of Italy. The papers were filled with the bloody battles of Anzio and Cassino. We had lost thousands of troops in the hills of southern Italy. I could see refugees fleeing into Italy on the heels of the Army. Clogging roads. Needing to be housed and fed.

"Someone at the meeting," Ickes went on, "I don't remember who, proposed that refugees be brought to this country. The President was still in favor of finding havens for them in Europe, Sicily, or parts of North Africa like Libya. I suggested, if any were brought to this country, that instead of coming to the mainland they be sent to the Virgin Islands. There's plenty of room on the island of St. Croix, where the weather is mild, like southern Italy. Instead, they're putting these people in New York State, near the snow belt around Lake Ontario."

"But surely it's not only because of the Army that we're taking them in? It has to be more. It has to be humanitarian."

"Of course it's humanitarian." His eyes blazed through his gold-rimmed glasses. "And it's about time, too. We've been trying for years to open the door to refugees. Look what happened to the Alaskan Development Bill we prepared here in the department."

I nodded. In November 1940, a year before Pearl Harbor, a bill was introduced to bring ten thousand settlers to Alaska: half of them were to be Americans; the other half would be European refugees who would promise to stay in Alaska for five years. Then they would be allowed to enter the United States under the existing quotas.

The bill was to do two things at once: help open Alaska for settlers and provide a haven for refugees. But the opposition was so great, from Alaskans as well as from isolationists who wanted no refugees at all, that it died in committee.

"I'm sure there'll be opposition again," Ickes said, "the restrictionists on one side and the damn fools on the other who'll scream that one thousand isn't enough. They don't realize, with all the opposition to immigration in general and Jews in particular, that you can't take in more than a thousand at a time."

I thought of the millions of Jews waiting to be rescued. There were frightening rumors that several million had already been murdered in Germany, Poland, and other countries Hitler had overrun, though most of us still did not know how. But there were millions more—in Hungary, Romania, Italy. Maybe we could rescue them, snatch them from Hitler's jaws.

Of all the Cabinet members, Ickes, who told me he had never met a Jew until he was sixteen, was the most passionate in denouncing the Nazi atrocities against Jews and the angriest that the doors of America were sealed.

"Mr. Secretary." I heard the urgency in my voice. "These people coming here—they must be frightened, bewildered, coming to a strange land. Somebody has to be with them. Somebody has to take their hand."

"You're suggesting . . . ?" His eyes began to sparkle; the weariness was gone. "Of course. It's a great idea. I'm going to send you. You're the one to go over and bring them back."

Ickes was a man of instant decisions. He called his operator. "Get Dillon Myer on the phone."

Myer was the head of the War Relocation Authority; his agency would administer the camp.

"Myer," I heard him say, "I want to send someone over to Italy to bring back those refugees. . . . What? You've already selected someone? . . . A man? You send your man, I'm sending her. . . . That's right. It's a woman. A young woman. . . . What's that?" His jowls trembled with anger.

I felt my stomach knot.

"What has being young got to do with this job? Being young didn't stop her from getting a Ph.D. in literature when she was twenty, the youngest in the world. And she took it in Germany—as an exchange student from America. I know her capabilities. She's been working for me now"—he turned to me—"how long is it?"

"Three years." I could hardly hear my own voice.

"Three years. With all kinds of jobs. And this one is right for her. Those refugees are from the Balkans and Central Europe. They probably speak mostly German. She speaks German and Yiddish. There'll be a lot of women and children. She'll know how to reach them; she'll understand them. You better come in at two-thirty today; I want to talk to you about her."

Midafternoon, I was summoned to Ickes's office. "Myer has just left," he said. "I told him I couldn't think of a better person to send."

I sat upright in the chair.

"I told him it's a unique job and you've got unique qualifications. You can communicate with the refugees. With your background, they'll trust you."

I waited for him to go on.

"What's more, I assured Myer that you could be of great help to us by writing and speaking about the refugees when you get back. I told him how you are always asked to lecture on Alaska. Also, your press contacts are important. I made certain he knew that the *Herald Tribune* sent you to the Soviet Arctic. I told him I have full confidence in you, that you understand these people, and you can write."

He was still not telling me Myer's decision.

"It's not settled, then?" I asked.

Myer, I knew, was an old-school government official who had come up through the ranks of the Agriculture Department. Instinctively, I sensed he would be dubious about sending a woman to do this job.

"Myer says there are problems," Ickes went on. "Interior is not in overall charge of this project. The War Refugee Board is."

The War Refugee Board had been created by the President five months ago—to save war refugees.

"Myer will have to check with WRB to get approval for you. I told him to see you first before he checks with them. He'll see you at eleven tomorrow morning. I have to tell you, he's hesitant about you."

"He's never met me."

"I have the feeling he thinks you're a big buxom social worker."

I was neither big nor buxom nor a social worker.

"It's these bureaucrats," Ickes said. "They get in a niche and then they're afraid to do anything unusual, anything that takes courage and imagination. Come back tomorrow after you've seen him."

That night I replayed the scenes in Ickes's office in my head. I walked to my desk and read again the President's message to Congress. It was dated June 12, 1944.

> This nation is appalled by the systematic persecution of helpless minority groups by the Nazis. To us, the unprovoked murder of innocent people simply because of race, religion, or political creed is the blackest of all possible crimes. . . . The fury of their insane desire to wipe out the Jewish race in Europe continues undiminished. This is but one example. Many Christian groups are also being murdered.

I leaned my head on my desk. There had been so many false starts to save them, so many conferences, so many hopes dashed. In July 1938 the United States had convened the Evian Conference in France on the shores of Lake Geneva. Thirty-two nations had sent representatives, most of whom stood up, one by one, to explain why they could not accept refugees. All that came out of Evian was a new committee, the Intergovernmental Committee on Refugees, which did little more to save refugees than the League of Nations had done before.

Meanwhile the two world leaders we loved, Roosevelt and Winston Churchill, made eloquent speeches about refugees even as they barred them. England closed the doors of Palestine, and the

United States closed the doors of America. To be sure, individuals were brought into our country. Albert Einstein had been helped to escape; Thomas Mann had been invited as an honored guest. But now at last Roosevelt was inviting not famous men but a whole group of "common" people.

After World War I, America had pulled back between its two oceans, isolationist, largely antiforeign. The idea of taking in large numbers of refugees—especially Jews—was unpopular. The specter of anti-Semitism was in our country, to be evoked by any overt gesture. So FDR, along with many others, was careful not to show too much sympathy for beleaguered Jewish refugees. Besides, the time-honored distaste for Jews—if not outright hatred—was still a hallmark of the upper echelons of some government agencies, particularly the Department of State. I knew it firsthand working in Washington. Ickes was a different breed of high officialdom; there were not many like him.

That was why I was so excited, why Roosevelt's decision to bring in even one thousand seemed to me such a triumph. One thousand, out of the millions being slaughtered and more millions without homes or refuge. It could be the beginning of a mass rescue movement. And for at least a thousand people, it would mean life, not death.

At eleven the next morning, I entered the seedy and steaming-hot Barr Building on Seventeenth Street and rode the elevator to the executive offices of the War Relocation Authority. Unlike the cool marble halls and broad corridors of Interior, the narrow halls and small offices seemed out of another era. I waited in the small room.

"Mr. Myer is free now." His secretary pointed toward the door.

My instincts were right. There was no warmth in his greeting. A tall man with steel-rimmed glasses and steel-gray hair, he stared down at me as I entered. He looked like the engineers I had seen on construction projects in Alaska, hard-driving men who seemed closer to machines and mortar than to people.

"So," he said coldly. "You're even younger than I thought."

I said nothing.

"I can't understand why, for such an important, unprecedented mission, Ickes should want to send a young woman. Do you realize what this job means? You'll be going over in the middle of war. You can be shot down. That's all we need, to have a young woman from our department shot down by a Nazi plane."

I wanted to tell him that I had been in the Aleutians when they were invaded, that I was a fatalist, that I would die when my number was up. Instead, I said, "It's a danger I'm prepared to face."

"Do you realize you'll be dealing with a thousand people—with men as well as women and children? Don't you see that after what they have gone through, they would have more respect for a man? They would pay much more attention to a man than they would to a woman."

In a corner of my mind I thought, Maybe there is validity in his arguments. Maybe refugees would have more respect for a man who was old and wise and experienced. I pushed the thought away, opened my purse, and pulled out copies of the President's message to Congress and the cablegram he had sent to Ambassador Murphy in Algiers. I had underlined some of the President's phrases; I read them now to Dillon Myer:

"The Nazis are determined to complete their program of mass extermination. . . . We have made clear our determination to punish all participants in these acts of savagery. In the name of humanity—"

"In the name of humanity." I repeated the words. "Mr. Myer, what have age or sex to do with *humanity*?"

He stood up abruptly. "It's not up to me. I can't make the decision. I must speak with John Pehle; he's executive director of the War Refugee Board. I'll call you back after I've talked with Pehle."

Two hours later, my office phone rang.

"I've talked with Pehle." Myer's voice seemed a shade less cold.

"He did some checking himself in Interior. You got some pretty good recommendations. Pehle agrees that you can go."

"Thank you, Mr. Myer," I breathed into the phone.

"You know, of course, I'm sending my own man over, Ralph Stauber. He'll be getting the statistics we need, where the people came from, et cetera."

I listened silently.

"You are Ickes's personal representative. But you can help us gain insight into the makeup of the people, so that we can develop policies. You must make it clear to them that they are coming here to live inside a camp where they will have food, a place to live in, and enough to keep them warm."

"What about leaving the camp?" I asked. "What if they have relatives? Will they be able to visit them? Will they be able to go outside to work?"

"That's a policy decision to be made later, in thirty or sixty days after they arrive. Be very careful. Don't make any promises we can't fulfill. We don't want to raise their hopes too high. That happened in our other camps."

The "other camps" were the Japanese-American internment and relocation camps, where over 100,000 Japanese were then incarcerated under Myer's administration. After Pearl Harbor, after the "date of infamy" on December 7, 1941, the country had exploded with hysteria against the Japanese. Innocent men, women, and children were pulled from their homes, businessmen from their shops, farmers from their land. In one of his darkest hours, the President, describing them as "potential fifth columnists," ordered the Japanese segregated in isolated camps. They were fenced in with barbed wire, patrolled by soldiers. To run the camps, Roosevelt created a special agency, the War Relocation Authority, WRA, headed by Milton Eisenhower, who recommended Dillon Myer as his successor when he resigned. Two years later, in February 1944, the President ordered WRA transferred to Interior.

Ickes recorded his reaction to his new responsibility in his secret diary. "This is something I distinctly do not want, but I told the President that I would take it and do the best I could."

Ickes was determined to close the camps swiftly and resettle the internees as humanely as possible, a task Eisenhower and Myer had already fought to achieve. He held a press conference to announce his decision. Since he was the liveliest Cabinet officer they covered, most of the Washington corps of journalists and radio commentators filled the auditorium. They loved his quips, his sardonic wit.

Ickes revealed that 23,000 Japanese had already been resettled. He had even talked with Mayor Fiorello H. La Guardia about relocating them in New York. "La Guardia," Ickes said, "is perfectly willing to have the Japanese resettled in New York City, but not if they are still banned from the Pacific Coast." Ickes wanted the ban "lifted right away—the sooner the better."

Some of the reporters applauded. I joined in the applause, knowing that at last innocent people, whose only crime was the color of their skin and the slant of their eyes, were to be freed. I thought of the Jews that Hitler was murdering, whose only crime was that they were Jews.

Ickes looked up as I approached his desk. "Myer has agreed," he said. "I can tell from your face."

"The War Refugee Board gave the OK," I said triumphantly, and told him that Myer had admonished me to keep the mission secret and promise the refugees nothing.

"That's not bad advice," Ickes said. "But I don't want them to hamstring you. You're to feel free to do what you want, go where you want, see what you want, and report to me. I'm giving you full rein."

That was what I needed to hear. "Mr. Secretary, this is going to be the most important assignment you've ever given me—maybe the most important thing I've ever done in my life."

"I'm sure you'll do an excellent job. Myer is lucky to be getting you. You can reassure those refugees, make them feel better than some official just doing his routine duty. I know that this whole thing, saving refugees, means a lot to you, as it does to me. You're going to be my eyes and ears. I'm depending on you."

That evening I called my parents in Brooklyn. "I'm going to Europe," I said.

"What?" my mother screamed into the phone. "Are you crazy? Every day I read how they sink ships and shoot down airplanes. And my daughter has to go to Europe to get her head shot off."

"Mom, don't worry."

"Don't worry, she says to me. It's enough your brother Irving is in the Army and I pray to God every night that he should come home safe. He has to go to war, he's a captain. But you're no soldier. What do you have to go for? What kind of *mishegaas* got into you now?"

"I can't tell you, Mom. It's a secret. But it's very important."

"Important. It's always important. Ever since you were a little girl you started running. Do I know where you went? Germany. Siberia. Alaska. I never knew if you were alive. What normal girl goes to Siberia and Alaska? Now she has to go to Europe."

"I'll be all right, Mom. Don't worry."

My father, on the extension phone, said quietly, "Will you come home to say goodbye?"

I could see his handsome face—the wide-set eyes, the tall sturdy body—the father who always had faith in me.

"I'd love to come home before I go abroad, Pop," I said, "but I won't have time. I've got to go through a whole process of briefings before I go."

"Then I'll come to Washington to see you off," my mother announced.

TWO

I SPENT THE NEXT WEEKS in a maze of bureaucratic briefings.

The refugees were even now being selected in southern Italy. I had to reach them before their convoy sailed.

I was completely bureaucratized—at the War Relocation Authority, where my official travel orders had to be drawn up; at the State Department, waiting interminably for a special passport; at the Public Health Service, where a battery of doctors pummeled, stethoscoped, X-rayed, and bled me and, with ominously prophetic voices, handed me a card with my blood type "in case you're shot down and need a transfusion."

Vaccines against typhus, typhoid, tetanus, smallpox, and plague were shot into my arms, my buttocks, my stomach. I reacted with a high fever and was told to stay in bed. I refused, hoping to speed up the briefings. It was useless. The bureaucracy in Washington moved on slow interminable wheels, each agency guarding its own authority, feeding upon its own red tape.

Marking time, I occupied myself trying to discover why Roosevelt was acting now, after all those years of a closed-door policy. I spent daylight hours in the Library of Congress reading newspapers and evenings talking with my friends in government, asking, "Why are the quotas being circumvented now?" In restaurants and in the privacy of our apartments we told one another, "It's Congress and the State Department who bar refugees. Roosevelt can't act alone. He can't have his New Deal labeled the Jew Deal."

There were other factors too, we reminded each other. Long before Hitler, Europe was an anti-Semitic continent. In America the quota system, under the fitting racist title National Origins Quota, had become law in the early 1920s, largely to bar Orientals and immigrants from Eastern Europe, many of them Jews.

Changes in the quota were unthinkable. The labor unions were opposed, fearing that refugees would take their jobs. The isolationists in Congress rode high. All this left the American Jewish community, scarcely 3 percent of the population, powerless to save the Jews of Europe.

"Trust Roosevelt," one faction exhorted us. "Roosevelt saved us from a Communist takeover during the Great Depression. Now he will save the world from Hitler. Don't make waves. Silent diplomacy is the safest route to rescue Jews."

Saying, "No, silence is the enemy," a small group denounced silent diplomacy. Their leader was Peter Bergson, a young Palestinian; only an aroused public opinion, he insisted, could save refugees. Even the Zionists, united in one goal, to open Palestine, were divided on whether this was the time to fight for a Jewish state.

Ben Hecht, the brilliant playwright and journalist, wrote full-page ads with venom in his pen. One of them, a long ballad, carried the refrain

> Hang and burn, but be quiet, Jews,
> The world is busy with other news.

In the end, it was clear that only the President himself had the power to break the ironclad quotas and to begin rescuing Jews. Who had reached him?

"It was the cables," a friend in Treasury told me one day.

"What cables?"

"The ones that told everything—how Jews were being murdered."

"Why didn't we know about them?"

He shrugged and was silent.

"You mean they were suppressed?"

"For two years."

Two years in which we were kept in darkness. Two years when public opinion might have galvanized our leaders into action.

Only later could I put together the pieces of the story that led from those suppressed cables to FDR's belated announcement and then to a shipboard odyssey and a haven in America, while war and holocaust raged in Europe.

In the summer of 1942, a German industrialist visiting Switzerland on business brought shocking news. Hitler was planning to exterminate all the Jews of Europe with a new device: prussic acid, the deadly compound of Zyklon-B gas. The news was delivered to Gerhart Riegner, a thirty-one-year-old refugee from Berlin working for the World Jewish Congress in Switzerland.

Riegner, whom I was to meet two years later in Geneva, told me, "At first I wouldn't believe it. Deportation of Jews—this we knew. Killing Jews, torturing them, shooting them in graves—this we knew." His eyes clouded over. "But this was a whole, total, embracing plan. It was *Vernichtung*."

Vernichtung. Annihilation.

"I had to verify it," he said. "I had to find out: Were the Germans capable of total *Vernichtung*?"

Fair-skinned, blue-eyed, Riegner looked and sounded like the students I had known in Germany.

Riegner had promised the industrialist he would never reveal his name. He kept his promise, even though research later pointed to Eduard Schulte, a banker and industrialist from Upper Silesia who loathed the Nazis. With friends in high places in the Nazi government, Schulte was able to alert the Allies to Hitler's plans for annihilating Jews.

"I needed eight days to investigate the German industrialist and to convince myself," Riegner said. "Finally convinced, I wrote a cable and took it to the American and British consuls, asking them to transmit it in code. In America it was to be sent to Rabbi Stephen S. Wise, who was president of the American Jewish Congress and was my boss in America. In Britain it was sent to Sydney Silverman, a Member of Parliament and chairman of the British section of the World Jewish Congress."

The cable, dated August 8, 1942, read:

RECEIVED ALARMING REPORT THAT IN FÜHRER'S HEADQUARTERS PLAN DISCUSSED AND UNDER CONSIDERATION ACCORDING TO WHICH ALL JEWS IN COUNTRIES OCCUPIED OR CONTROLLED GERMANY NUMBERING 3½–4 MILLION [excluding Jews in the Soviet Union] SHOULD AFTER DEPORTATION AND CONCENTRATION IN EAST BE EXTERMINATED AT ONE BLOW TO RESOLVE ONCE FOR ALL THE JEWISH QUESTION IN EUROPE STOP ACTION REPORTED PLANNED FOR AUTUMN METHODS UNDER DISCUSSION INCLUDING PRUSSIC ACID STOP WE TRANSMIT INFORMATION WITH ALL NECESSARY RESERVATION AS EXACTITUDE CANNOT BE CONFIRMED STOP INFORMANT STATED TO HAVE CLOSE CONNECTIONS WITH HIGHEST GERMAN AUTHORITIES AND HIS REPORTS GENERALLY SPEAKING RELIABLE STOP RIEGNER

The cable was never delivered to Rabbi Wise. The State Department decided the information was "unsubstantiated" and summarized the report as "a wild rumor inspired by Jewish fears." Undersecretary of State Sumner Welles, one of the few State Department officials considered friendly to Jews, signed the order to suppress the cable.

Three weeks later, Riegner was informed that Wise still knew nothing. "I went through the worst period of my life," Riegner told me. "There I was in my office looking out at the lake and Mont Blanc, and there was such peace in those snow-capped mountains. And the Jews were trapped in Europe."

Fortunately, the British did not suppress the cable to Silverman, in which Riegner had carefully inserted the words INFORM AND CONSULT NEW YORK. Silverman sent a copy of the August 1942 cable to Rabbi Wise by ordinary Western Union.

In New York, Rabbi Wise read the cable over and over. He knew Riegner well. He knew how cautious he was. It had to be true.

He rushed to Washington to see Sumner Welles. Had Welles seen this cable? Did he know these facts? Welles, of course, had seen the original cable weeks earlier. Now he prevailed on Wise to keep the cable secret until State Department representatives in Switzerland could confirm Riegner's charges.

Finally, in November, Welles telephoned Wise. "Come to Washington immediately."

Welles showed the rabbi documents and affidavits from his own men in Switzerland confirming everything Riegner had reported. He would no longer hold Wise to his promise of secrecy.

Wise released the terrible information. But three months had already elapsed. No one knew if the Nazis had begun their *Vernichtung*.

On January 21, 1943, Leland Harrison, our minister in Bern, ordered another cable from Riegner to Rabbi Wise coded and transmitted through the State Department.

It was Cable 482, a file number that was to become famous. In four horror-filled pages, Riegner described the terror that had been decimating Jews in two lands: in Poland, where the Germans had been killing 6,000 Jews each day; in Romania, where 130,000 Jews had been deported to Transnistria in the Romanian-occupied Ukraine. The clothes had been ripped off the refugees' backs; everything they owned was stolen. Of the 130,000 deported to the Transnistrian "reservation" for Jews, 60,000 had already died and 70,000 were starving to death.

Welles himself forwarded Cable 482 to Rabbi Wise. Wise immediately began arranging for a Stop Hitler Now mass rally to be held at Madison Square Garden in New York on March 1, 1943.

On February 10, 1943, the State Department sent an unusual message to Harrison in Bern. It was Cable 354, and it opened by referring to Riegner's Cable 482:

YOUR 482, JANUARY 21. IT IS SUGGESTED THAT IN FUTURE REPORTS SUBMITTED TO YOU FOR TRANSMISSION TO PRIVATE PERSONS IN THE UNITED STATES SHOULD NOT BE ACCEPTED UNLESS EXTRAORDINARY CIRCUMSTANCES MAKE SUCH ACTION ADVISABLE. IT IS FELT THAT BY SENDING SUCH PRIVATE MESSAGES WHICH CIRCUMVENT NEUTRAL COUNTRIES' CENSORSHIP WE RISK THE

POSSIBILITY THAT NEUTRAL COUNTRIES MIGHT FIND IT NECES-
SARY TO TAKE STEPS TO CURTAIL OR ABOLISH OUR OFFICIAL SE-
CRET MEANS OF COMMUNICATION.

In the strangulated language of diplomacy, this meant, "Stop sending any more messages about Nazi atrocities."

Sumner Welles again signed the cable. In Welles's defense,
many people, including Henry Morgenthau, Jr., the secretary of
the Treasury, believed that he was too busy to inquire what 482 re-
ferred to.

For Harrison and Riegner in Switzerland, however, Welles's
cable was an enigma. Only two months earlier, the Allies had announced that Nazis would be punished as war criminals for their
atrocities against Jews. America would need eyewitness accounts
from Riegner to build its case against war criminals. Why now this
order from the State Department to stop all information? And why
specifically the order to stop further cables disclosing Nazi atrocities, when hundreds of commercial cables for private businesses
were being transmitted?

Fortunately the cable to cease and desist was sent too late to
halt the Stop Hitler Now rally.

It was a blustery first day of March 1943 in New York. The
streets around Madison Square Garden were clogged. The Garden
held 21,000 people, but at least 75,000 more were outside, unable
to enter.

We kept each other warm, no longer strangers. We belonged together, a wall of Americans—Jews and Christians—shouting with
one voice, "Stop Hitler now!"

We listened to loudspeakers as our leaders pleaded with the Allied governments to act swiftly, before it was too late.

"The world can no longer believe that the ghastly facts are unknown and unconfirmed," Dr. Chaim Weizmann, the eloquent
leader of the Jewish Agency, the shadow Jewish government in
Palestine, declared. "At this moment expressions of sympathy

without accompanying attempts to launch acts of rescue become a hollow mockery in the ears of the dying.

"The democracies have a clear duty before them." Weizmann's voice rang through the night air. "Let them negotiate with Germany through the neutral countries concerning the possible release of the Jews in the occupied countries."

Negotiate with Germany through the neutral countries to release the Jews in the occupied countries? Sweden was neutral. Switzerland was neutral. In fact, Switzerland was far more. It was a giant ear, the listening post for diplomats, provocateurs, spies, mysterious travelers. It was in Switzerland that Riegner was getting much of his information from German travelers.

"Let havens be designated," Weizmann went on, "in the vast territories of the United Nations,* which would give sanctuary to those fleeing from imminent murder."

Havens! The word became symbolic in my mind. America had been one great big haven since its birth. We could have hundreds of havens—if only we opened our doors.

Weizmann was pleading for a haven in Palestine. "The Jewish community of Palestine will welcome with joy and thanksgiving all delivered from Nazi hands."

A man near me shouted, "Tell it to Churchill!"

But Britain, with a mandate from the world to turn Palestine into a homeland for Jews, was even now sending crucially needed warships to the Palestine coast, not to fight the Nazis but to prevent Jews from entering.

We heard Cardinal Hinsely, the Roman Catholic Archbishop of Westminster, denouncing both England's Foreign Office and our State Department. "We need cold deeds and speedy deeds, not the rhetoric behind which governments are still hiding."

The wind grew stronger. More people kept thronging the streets

---

* The United Nations Organization was not created until 1945, but the term had already come into the language.

around us, pushing, shouting, shoving, while police sought to keep some semblance of order.

Now at last the voice we were waiting for swept over us. The President was talking from Washington. I could see the patrician face, the strong jaw exuding optimism and strength. The night air grew warm again, embraced by his words.

"The Nazis will not succeed in exterminating their victims. . . ."

He's talking now about the Jews, I told myself, he's going to tell us how he'll save them.

"The American people will hold the perpetrators of these crimes to strict accountability in a day of reckoning which will surely come."

Was that it? Were we to wait until the war ended? Why couldn't he act now? Why not open havens in the empty valleys, the hill-tops, and the deserts of America?

This was March 1943. Our soldiers were battling in North Africa. The Russians had driven the German Sixth Army back from Stalingrad, but Hitler still controlled most of Europe. I knew the argument; it was implicit in the President's words: First we must win the war. Then we will take care of the refugees.

But how many, I thought in despair, would still be alive?

"We have adopted a resolution"—Rabbi Wise's voice rolled through the loudspeakers like the music of an organ—"a resolution which we will forward to Secretary of State Cordell Hull to protest against the continuing failure to act against the strange indifference to the fate of five million human beings."

I clutched my arms, shivering in anger and frustration. We were 75,000 people—and all we could do was send a protest to Cordell Hull.

No havens were suggested. The doors to America and Palestine remained tightly sealed.

As the clamor in the country to save refugees grew into a groundswell, the State Department called a conference in Bermuda specifically to discuss rescue. The conference opened on the day the Nazis launched their final attack on the Warsaw Ghetto. It was also the week of Passover.

The Bermuda conference was a fiasco. "Palliatives," *The New York Times* described it, "designed to assuage the conscience of the reluctant rescuers rather than to aid the victims."

Not one country offered to take in a single refugee.

Months passed. Hundreds of thousands of Jews were murdered, and still no havens were provided.

Then, late in 1943, the suppressed cables were discovered.

The World Jewish Congress in Switzerland had cabled Washington that they could ransom the lives of thousands of Jews in Romania and France. They could raise the money themselves; they knew the officials to be bribed; all they needed was the license to send dollars abroad.

Both Treasury and State had to approve the license. Treasury agreed to issue the license immediately. State did nothing. Half a year was lost.

Outraged, Secretary of the Treasury Morgenthau called in Josiah E. DuBois, Jr., a young assistant general counsel working with Treasury's Foreign Funds Control. "I want you to investigate the whole thing. Get to the bottom of it."

Joe DuBois was a large canvas of a man with a generous spirit, disheveled eyebrows, and tousled hair. He went through all the files in the Treasury Department to dig up correspondence with State and found a copy of the cable from Harrison in Bern dated April 20, 1943, which opened by referring to Cable 354 (the cable of suppression). He telephoned the State Department. "Please send over a copy of your Cable 354."

"Sorry," he was told. "This cable does not relate to Treasury. Only a few people have seen it even in State. We cannot furnish it to Treasury."

"Knowing the State Department as I did," Joe told me later, "I became very suspicious. If State said it was none of Treasury's business, I was pretty sure it *was* our business. I decided I had to see it."

Joe knew the head of Foreign Funds Control at the State Department, Donald Hiss. He telephoned Hiss asking for a copy of Cable 354. Briefly he told Hiss of Morgenthau's determination to get the license issued so the rescue from France and Romania could begin.

Hiss, sympathetic, promised to look for the mysterious cable.

Several times Joe called Hiss's office, only to be told, "Joe, I'm having a hard time getting that cable."

Finally, in desperation, Joe called Hiss at home; the cable was still missing.

On the morning of December 18, 1943, Hiss's secretary called Joe's secretary. "Please ask Mr. DuBois to be at our office at two-thirty this afternoon." No reason. No explanation.

Before two-thirty Joe was in Hiss's office. On the desk were two cables. "I've been warned," Hiss confided to Joe, "that under no circumstances should these cables be shown to Treasury. If anyone finds out that I'm showing them to you, I might lose my job."

Courageous and fearless himself, Joe knew that Hiss was risking his career to save thousands of lives.

"I can't let them out of my office, Joe," Hiss said. "I can't even give you copies."

Joe read of the terror in Poland and Romania since 1941. "Can I copy these cables?" he asked.

Hiss nodded silently.

Joe pulled several small slips of paper from his pocket, copied the full text of the cable of suppression, and made notes of the longer horror cable.

Back in his office, he dictated a "memorandum for the files" and marked it confidential. For the first time it told the full story of the cables, "so shocking and so tragic that it is difficult to believe."

"I am physically ill," Morgenthau said when he read the memorandum. He then asked Randolph E. Paul, his counsel, to prepare a complete background paper describing the State Department's delays, subterfuges, and suppression.

Paul turned the writing over to Joe DuBois. With the help of Paul and John Pehle, head of Foreign Funds Control at the Treasury—both, like Joe, non-Jews—he began working on the report. He dictated drafts to his secretary during the day and worked evenings at home. He spent Christmas morning with his wife and family, then went back to his desk and continued writing. Finally, on January 13, 1944, he submitted his report to Morgenthau. Though it was signed *R.E.P.* (Randolph E. Paul), Joe had written it out of his guts. He called it "Report to the Secretary on the Acquiescence of This Government in the Murder of the Jews."

It began with an impassioned denunciation of the State Department. "One of the greatest crimes in history, the slaughter of the Jewish people in Europe is continuing unabated." Officials in the State Department

have not only failed to use the Governmental machinery at their disposal to rescue Jews from Hitler, but have even gone so far as to use this Governmental machinery to *prevent* the rescue of these Jews.

They have not only failed to cooperate with private organizations in the efforts of these organizations to work out individual programs of their own, but have taken steps designed to prevent these programs from being put into effect.

They have not only failed to facilitate the obtaining of information concerning Hitler's plans to exterminate the Jews of Europe, but in their official capacity have gone so far as to surreptitiously attempt to stop the obtaining of information concerning the murder of the Jewish population of Europe.

They have tried to cover up their guilt by:
(a) concealment and misrepresentation;
(b) the giving of false and misleading explanations for their failures to act and their attempts to prevent action; and
(c) the issuance of false and misleading statements concerning the "action" which they have taken to date.

DuBois pointed the finger directly at Breckinridge Long, the assistant secretary of state who was in charge of the Visa Division, which decided who could enter the United States—in effect, choosing who would live and who would die.

Breckinridge Long, in DuBois's report, was the archvillain in our government's "acquiescence in the murder of Jews." The report quoted a speech by Congressman Emanuel Celler of Brooklyn. "Frankly, Breckinridge Long, in my humble opinion," Celler had told Congress, "is the least sympathetic to refugees in all the State Department. I attribute to him the tragic bottleneck in the granting of visas. . . . It takes months and months to grant a visa, and then it usually applies to a corpse."

Congressman Celler blasted the misleading and fraudulent statements Long had made in testimony before the House Committee on Foreign Affairs. "We have taken into this country," Long had told the Committee, "since the beginning of the Hitler regime [1933] and the persecution of the Jews until today, approximately 580,000 refugees. The whole thing has been under the quota—except the generous gesture we made of visitors' and transit visas during an awful period."

Celler nailed Long's lie:

In the first place these 580,000 refugees were in the main ordinary quota immigrants coming in from all countries. The majority were not Jews. His statement drips with sympathy for the persecuted Jews, but the tears he sheds are crocodile. I would like to ask him how many Jews were admitted during the last three years in comparison with the number seeking entrance to preserve life and dignity. . . . One gets the impression from Long's statement that the United States has gone out of its way to help refugees fleeing death at the hands of the Nazis. I deny this. On the contrary, the State Department has turned its back on the time-honored principle of granting havens to refugees. The tempest-tossed get little comfort from men like Breckinridge Long. . . . Long says that the door to the oppressed is open but that it "has been carefully screened." What he should have said is "barlocked and bolted." By the act of 1924, we are permitted to admit approximately 150,000 immigrants each year.

During the last fiscal year only 23,725 came as immigrants. Of these, only 4,750 were Jews fleeing Nazi persecution.

If men of the temperament and philosophy of Long continue in control of immigration administration, we may as well take down that plaque from the Statue of Liberty and black out the "lamp beside the golden door."

Morgenthau read DuBois's eighteen-page report with mounting rage. He changed the title to the simpler "Personal Report to the President" and cut the document to nine pages, but kept most of its evidence and accusations, even adding his own charges:

There is a growing number of responsible people and organizations today who have ceased to view our failure as the product of simple incompetence on the part of those officials in the State Department charged with handling this problem. They see plain anti-Semitism motivating the actions of these State Department officials and, rightly or wrongly, it will require little more in the way of proof for this suspicion to explode into nasty scandal.

On a rainy Sunday morning on January 16, 1944, Morgenthau went to the White House with his young assistant, John Pehle. Morgenthau had easy access to the President, who affectionately called him "Henny-Penny." On this Sunday morning, Morgenthau was no Henny-Penny. He had become a committed, anguished, passionate Jew. The suppressed cables had touched ancient roots. He told his friend the President that if these cables became public the whole world would know of the anti-Semitism in his State Department. The scandal, he said, could reach into the White House itself.

Six days later Roosevelt created the War Refugee Board, WRB, composed of the Secretaries of State, Treasury, and War—Hull, Morgenthau, and Henry Stimson. Of the three, neither Hull at State nor Stimson of the Army was enthusiastic.

Rescuing Jews was withdrawn from the sabotaging hands of Breckinridge Long and given to the War Refugee Board. Pehle, a slim, circumspect thirty-five-year-old lawyer, became its executive director. Cables would no longer be suppressed. Ships would be leased in Sweden to smuggle refugees out of the Balkans. Ira Hirschmann, an executive of Bloomingdale's department store in New York, would be sent to Istanbul to rescue, if he could, the sixty thousand still alive in the Romanian concentration camp in Transnistria. Raoul Wallenberg, a young Swede of a distinguished family, would be sent to Hungary and single-handedly save seventy or eighty thousand.

But time was running out for nearly 1 million Jews in Hungary and another 800,000 in Romania. Letters flooded the White House. "Mr. President," a man in Los Angeles who signed himself "Not a Jew" pleaded, "do all you can to save the Jewish people of Europe. Establish rescue centers for temporary detention and care until we've knocked the hell out of Hitler."

On March 6, 1944, Joe DuBois drafted a memorandum for the President urgently recommending temporary havens of refuge. Under his proposal the refugees would be treated "in effect as prisoners of war," for whom no quotas were required.

Peter Bergson and the young Palestinians who worked closely with the War Refugee Board began a massive propaganda campaign to establish temporary havens. "In the eleventh hour of the reign of death," they suggested, let "twenty-five square miles of rescue camps be set aside in five temporary mercy reservations in Palestine, Turkey, North Africa, and some of our own abandoned military training camps in the United States." One of their full-page ads carried the headline 25 SQUARE MILES OR . . . 2,000,000 LIVES: WHICH SHALL IT BE?

But bringing refugees into the United States outside the quotas was the political roadblock. How would the isolationists in Congress react? Samuel Grafton, the widely read columnist for the *New York Post* offered a brilliant solution. Free ports! Why not, he asked in his column of April 5, 1944, "have a system of free ports for refugees fleeing the Hitler terror?"

Obviously we need a place where we can put refugees down without making final decisions about them, a place where they can be stored and processed, so to speak, without creating legal and political problems. . . . Of course, I am a little ashamed to find myself pandering to anti-refugee prejudices even to the extent of saying yes, pile the legal disabilities on them, give them no rights, store them like corn, herd them like cattle—but the need is so sharp, the time is so short, our current example to the world is so bad, that it is necessary to settle for whatever can be done.

In a cordial meeting in the White House, Pehle recommended that an executive order be issued establishing a free port as a temporary haven in the United States. Roosevelt seemed receptive, though he told Pehle he preferred the term "emergency refugee shelter" to Grafton's "free port." The word "emergency" would show that it was temporary and shelter was "honest," since little more than shelter would be offered the refugees. Pehle, who had expected to rescue unlimited numbers, was startled when Roosevelt ended their meeting with the promise to consider opening one camp to rescue one thousand people.

"Roosevelt was a politician first," Joe DuBois told me later, "and then a humanitarian."

Still, one camp for one thousand could be the beginning. If the isolationists in Congress lay quiescent, then perhaps more camps could be opened and more refugees saved. At least this was what others and I hoped.

At a Cabinet meeting on May 24, 1944, Morgenthau introduced the resolution, drafted by WRB, proposing that one thousand refugees be brought from Italy to the United States. He admitted to the Cabinet members that the President was still "a little afraid."

Only Ickes expressed complete support. Ickes was now the honorary chairman of Bergson's Emergency Committee to Save the Jewish People of Europe. Even Attorney General Francis Biddle opposed the resolution on legal grounds, though it was known he loathed Breckinridge Long's policies on refugees.

In Europe the trains roared toward Auschwitz. The Nazis had occupied Hungary toward the end of March. On April 27, 1944, the first transports of Jews were shipped from Hungary. Scarcely three months later, Adolf Eichmann had already packed 520,000 into cattle cars headed for the gas chambers.

On June 6, General Eisenhower issued his order of the day: "Soldiers, sailors, and airmen of the Allied Expeditionary Force! You are about to embark upon the great crusade. . . . The eyes of the world are upon you." The invasion of Normandy began. At the same time seven members of the House introduced resolutions urging Roosevelt to open "free ports."

The time, at last, was right. On June 12, the President sent the formal message to Congress—the message I had read in the press—that one thousand refugees would be brought to a safe haven in Oswego, New York.

On Friday, July 14, Ickes called me to his office.

"The Army just phoned," he said. "You're leaving tomorrow. Are you ready?"

"I've been ready for weeks. The longest weeks of my life."

He swiveled his chair, turning his full face toward me. "You're going to be made a general. A simulated general."

"Me? A general?"

"You'll be flying in a military plane. If you're shot down and the Nazis capture you as a civilian they can kill you as a spy. But as a general, according to the Geneva Convention, you have to be given shelter and food and kept alive."

I laughed at the idea of my being a general.

"I'm coming in to work tomorrow," Ickes said. "Come see me before you take off."

THREE

I WAS PACKING my bag in the early evening when the doorbell rang. My mother burst in, carrying a huge brown grocery bag tied up with a cord.

"Tell me the truth."

She wasted no time as she walked into my studio apartment, headed straight for the kitchen, and untied the cord around the grocery bag. She pulled out her nightclothes, a roast chicken wrapped in wax paper, a small jar of gefilte fish, and a larger jar of prunes marinated in my father's best scotch.

"The truth, now," she repeated. "Do you really have to go?"

Before I could answer, she twisted open the cap of the jarful of fat, inebriated prunes.

"Eat one now." She jabbed a fork into the jar, speared a prune, and put it into my mouth. "It will do you good."

Food, second only to her husband and her five children, was intimacy; food was survival; food was the tribal memory of all the countries Jews had wandered through. Food, she was convinced, Jewish food, kept the family together.

Outside the window, dusk was settling on the Washington streets. She looked at her watch. "It's nearly eight o'clock. Time to light candles."

I brought out my grandmother's brass candlesticks that she had given me when I moved to Washington. We walked to the raised dining area, placed a freshly laundered white tablecloth on the Swedish table, and set it, with the candlesticks in the center.

My mother draped her hand-crocheted white scarf around her mass of curly white hair, struck a match to the Shabbat candles, and with outstretched hands drew circles over the flames. Then she covered her eyes and murmured the Shabbat prayer in the Hebrew she had learned as a child, and in Yiddish she added a special message to God. I was sure she was begging Him to keep me safe. Shabbat magic flooded the room.

"What do you need to go to Europe for?" she asked, as we sat opposite each other.

I put my hands to my mouth, showing her it was so full of her delicious fish that I could not speak.

She waited impatiently for me to answer, her gray eyes penetrating and shrewd.

"I'm not going to have one night's rest all the time you're away. Honest, I can't figure you out, you have such a nice place here— and you keep it pretty good." It was a rare compliment. In fact, so rare were her compliments that I knew she was desperate tonight.

"You have a good job. You could be—God forbid—killed."

I leaned across the table and took her gnarled, work-worn hands in mine. The fading light and the burning candles softened the lines on her face. She was in her early fifties, but hard work from the time she was eight had grooved sharp creases in her cheeks.

"Mom, remember when I went to Poland just before the war and saw your relatives and Pop's relatives?"

She nodded.

"Remember I told you the story of how your cousin Yankel came to the railroad station in Warsaw to meet me, though it was midnight? He had a horse and carriage with hay. He made me lie on the hay and covered me with a big horse blanket while he whipped his poor horse like crazy."

Her eyes narrowed as she watched me.

"He was afraid someone would kill me. Bandits maybe. Even the gendarmes. The Poles were suspicious of any traveler—especially somebody like me. I was carrying a typewriter and a camera, and Yankel was afraid the gendarmes would think that maybe I wasn't a journalist, maybe I was a spy."

She stared at me, pulling herself up in the chair. She was barely five feet tall, full-bosomed, wide-hipped. "What has this got to do with you going off—" she began.

I was determined not to let her interrupt. "It was two o'clock in the morning when we finally reached your shtetl. We drove into the courtyard. 'Wake up, everybody!' Yankel shouted, so loud you could have heard him in Brooklyn. '*Zie iss gekimmen* [she has come].' Suddenly I saw an elderly woman put her head out of the window. It was your Aunt Mirel, screaming '*Gnendel's tochter iss du*' [Gussie's daughter is here]."

In the Shabbat-filled room in Washington, I saw again the small brick courtyard coming alive with aunts, cousins, neighbors embracing me in the darkness, laughing, crying, drawing me into one of the little poverty-stricken wooden houses.

My mother's face grew animated. "We thought you were crazy when you went off on that trip. We were so worried because you were going to all those dangerous countries, and there wasn't even a war then like now."

"What I never told you, because I didn't want to scare you, is that about five o'clock in the morning two gendarmes knocked on the door with their nightsticks. They demanded to see my passport, opened my suitcase, held everything, even my underwear, up to the light, looking for something, examined my typewriter and camera, and told me that if I didn't get out in an hour I would be arrested."

"My God." My mother's face blanched. "What happened?"

"Some of the relatives said, 'Don't pay any attention. They can't be serious.' But some of the others said, 'Leave right away. They could throw you in jail and, who knows, torture you, maybe kill you. Nobody like you ever came to our shtetl before.' I knew there was danger. I kissed all the relatives goodbye and climbed back into Yankel's wagon. The relatives stood wringing their hands, worrying. Yankel covered me all over again, this time even my face. Then he drove his horse like a madman back to Warsaw."

"And we never knew," my mother said, shaking her head. "They wrote us letters after, never telling us about the gendarmes. And when you went to Odessa, all the relatives told us how you left all your clothes with them, and how you went home with only the dress and coat on your back."

A cloud of sadness darkened her face. She stared across the studio. "Then the war started and we never heard from them again."

Once again I leaned across the table to touch the gnarled hands. "I might find your Aunt Mirel and your Aunt Sima and your cousin Yankel and their daughters."

Tears formed in her eyes. I could not comfort her.

Early the next morning we closed my apartment, put my suitcase in a cab, and drove to my office, waiting for the call from the Army. It came just before noon.

"This is Captain Hester. Would you like to take a little trip this afternoon? Be at National Airport at three."

At two o'clock we entered Ickes's office, my mother still clutching her brown grocery bag. It was smaller now, with only her nightgown, robe, and hairbrush inside.

Ickes stood up at his desk as I led her across the blue carpet.

"You look worried, Mother," he said, shaking her hand, his face crinkled into a warm, almost comforting smile.

"It's very dangerous, Mr. Secretary, what she's doing, flying to Europe in the middle of the war."

I was struck by the instant rapport between the short man of power and the short woman of Brooklyn, both self-confident, both unintimidated, both with jutting jaws.

My mother was completely underawed by power. The fact that she was in the office of a Cabinet member did not faze her.

"Mr. Secretary," she said, "you are sending my daughter to Europe in the middle of the war? Every day I read that airplanes are falling out of the sky. Ships are blowing up in the ocean. How do I know she'll come home safe?"

He stood up, walked around the desk, put his hand on her

shoulder, and said, "Don't worry, little mother, she's going to come home safe. We're making her a general."

How little we know of our leaders, I thought. To allay my mother's fears, Ickes was revealing something he had told me in strict confidence. It was the part of his character he allowed few people, and certainly none of his critics and enemies, to know. The inner Ickes, unlike the old curmudgeonly outer Ickes, had a heartfelt sensitivity to human suffering. His words and unexpected action calmed my mother.

"It is dangerous, but Ruth will come home safe," he assured her.

"I pray to God," she said.

He turned to me and shook my hand. "Good luck," he said.

He sent us down to the garage with instructions to his chauffeur to take me to National Airport and then drive my mother to Union Station. At the airport I showed her I was carrying the jar of alcohol-soaked prunes in my handbag. "See, I won't get hungry on the plane." I kissed her goodbye. "Don't cry, Mom."

"Who's crying?" She wiped her eyes. Then, unexpectedly, she asked, "Should I tip the chauffeur?"

"Mom, you don't tip a government employee."

Later she told me how she felt—a little woman with a grocery bag in the back of a limousine half a block long. "I gave the chauffeur a dollar. You should have seen how glad he was to get it."

National Airport swarmed with men and women in khakis, stiff whites, summer grays, and olive greens and serious-faced civilians carrying briefcases, rushing to catch planes.

Exhilarated that at last I was taking off, I moved swiftly through the airport routine: passport control, currency control, baggage inspection.

"You carrying any letters?" a long-faced intelligence officer asked me as he examined my suitcase, my hatbox, my battered typewriter, camera, and purse.

"Letters?" Ickes had given me several letters of introduction to officials in Casablanca, Algiers, and Naples. "Be sure to pay your respects, especially to Ambassador Robert Murphy in Algiers," he had said. "Murphy is the President's personal representative. I want you to tell him how we feel about this project."

"Do you have a diary?" The intelligence officer was still interrogating me.

"Not yet. But I'll be starting one in the plane. I've got a lot of empty notebooks."

He waved me through.

A young second lieutenant in summer uniform approached me. "Sit down over there with those men."

Some twenty-five American and French officers, most of them one- and two-star generals with bands of colored ribbons on their breasts, sat in an open enclosure in the airport. They stared at me so curiously that I pulled my skirt over my knees and glanced swiftly to be sure my blouse was buttoned. I had dressed carefully for the trip, in a blue silk suit, a small mauve hat with a mauve veil, and brand-new white gloves.

"Follow me." The young lieutenant shepherded us through the milling airport and up a flight of stairs to a small dark room with no windows and almost no air.

At one end of the room a panel of army officers sat behind a table; in front of them was a huge collapsed lifeboat.

"Gentlemen—I mean, lady and gentlemen," one of the officers began, "the first thing we are going to do is show you what to do if the plane is shot down over water and you ditch." He stepped forward and showed us step by step how to open the collapsible lifeboat, inflate the Mae Wests, and operate the radio.

I listened intently, though I wondered how long anyone could survive in the shark-infested waters of the North Atlantic.

A public health officer moved among us, teaching us how to apply a tourniquet if we were wounded. His voice became ominous. "You are going to be landing at a port in the Azores that has plague. You're never to go off the military reservation at the airport. There are rats outside; they carry lice that can infect you with plague.

"There's malaria too." As he continued the litany of peril,

he walked around the table and handed each of us a bottle of mosquito-repellent fluid. "Use it constantly," he said.

A third officer passed out mimeographed sheets headed MEDICAL BRIEFING. "You're to carry this in every area you enter."

I held the sheet up in the dim light and read, "Eighty percent of the natives are infected with one or more tropical diseases. Avoid personal contact with them. Body lice, flies, mosquitoes may infect you. Avoid personal contact with them too."

Army humor!

Capitalized words shouted at me:

NATIVES in most countries FERTILIZE their fields with HUMAN FECES. They CONTAMINATE EVERYTHING THEY TOUCH. NEVER EAT UNCOOKED VEGETABLES OR FRUIT. Thick-skinned fruits can be eaten if they are soaked in Clorox (1% hypochlorite solution) for thirty minutes.

My mind balked. Soak fruits and vegetables in Clorox? If the bugs didn't kill me, the Clorox would.

I forced myself to read on in the semidarkness.

Venereal diseases are rampant in the tropics. Almost 100%. Staying away from all "Pick Ups" is your best insurance against serious venereal disease. So-called controlled prostitutes are almost 100% infected with Syphilis, whereas with Gonorrhea, their annual rate is 40% to 60%. The natives of tropical countries are filled with all types of disease. THE WOMEN ARE HUMAN CESSPOOLS. KEEP AWAY FROM THEM.

As our engines revved, I opened my notebook. *Six o'clock, Saturday, July 15, 1944, departing Washington.*

The sturdy prop-engined C-54 flew over the great dome of the Capitol glistening in the July sun, past the stark obelisk of the Washington Monument, and then, most beautiful of all, over the monument with the great brooding figure of Lincoln on whose steps I had so often taken refuge.

A bank of clouds enveloped us; about an hour later we were in the open over my own city, New York, which looked like a toy town with miniature cars speeding on its highways. The light shimmered gray-gold; a ball of flame sank into the Hudson.

Boston, then Bangor, Maine, and then as the North Atlantic spread below us the captain's voice came through the loudspeaker. "We're flying north to Newfoundland. We'll be landing there to refuel and leave you. A new crew will take you on to the Azores, and from there to Casablanca."

I peered into the night sky. It was almost midnight when we landed at Stephenville on the west coast of Newfoundland.

An army bus drove us to a nearby army camp. In the mess hall, soldiers piled hotcakes and scrambled eggs in front of us. But I could not eat, for around us were enlisted men, some sullen, some angry, some depressed. All were bandaged, several were without arms, those without legs were in wheelchairs, ready to be flown to hospitals in America. At eighteen or twenty, to be disabled, crippled forever!

One of the generals approached me. "May I join you?"

"Of course."

He was a white-haired one-star general with a leathery face and a midwestern accent. "I'm an opera buff," he said, "and my favorite opera is *Aida*. Every time I get to New York, I try to make the Metropolitan Opera."

I wondered why a general at midnight in Newfoundland would talk about opera. Still depressed by the sight of the wounded soldiers, I tried to listen, until I heard the general say, "We're all so curious about you. What are you doing on this plane?"

Heeding Dillon Myer's admonition, I said, "I'm sorry, General, I can't tell you. My mission is a secret."

"Are you Lily Pons?" he asked. Lily Pons, the Metropolitan Opera singer, and her husband, André Kostelanetz, the conductor, were touring army installations.

I assured him I could not sing.

It was midmorning Sunday in Washington, 1440 GMT (Greenwich Mean Time), when we flew over the Azores, so low we could watch the ocean pounding the islands' cliffs.

A small contingent of American soldiers in shorts came running toward us as we landed, and some entered the plane. "You are not to go off the reservation," a sergeant commanded. "There's plague here, and it's bad."

I felt less hostile about the shots I had been given in Washington.

A stocky lieutenant whose walk and talk were straight off the sidewalks of New York escorted us to the mess hall with a rapid-fire patter. "This here's a secret base. We ain't here, see. We don't know from nothin'. The Krauts don't know we're here. Only the Portuguese know. They own the goddamn place. We don't even know there's a war. In France our guys are chasin' bullets. Here we're tracin' dust."

Back in the plane, we headed for Casablanca. I felt I would know it from the Humphrey Bogart movie, but from the air it was a giant, sprawling rock pile of white stone houses.

After we were loaded into a bus, an army officer told us, "We're billeting you in the Atlantic Hotel, and you mess in the Excelsior."

I wondered for a moment why we couldn't mess and billet in the same hotel, but I knew better than to question the Army.

Unlike its name, the color of Casablanca in the early evening light was brown. The air was brown, the streets were brown, the people, the camels, the horses, the donkeys, the dust—all seemed brown and centuries old.

The next morning, I walked to the American embassy. Arab men in white djellabas, Arab women, their bodies and faces hidden inside voluminous gray robes and hoods, peering at the world through narrow slits, moved in an aura of mystery, while not-so-mysterious women in tight Western dresses and frizzled hair clattered down the sidewalk on the arms of French or British or American soldiers.

At the embassy, I paid my respects to the consul general. "I'd like to get to Algiers and Naples as soon as possible," I told him. "Is there any way of flying out today?"

He pressed a button, asking an assistant to bring him the flight schedule. He shook his head. "I see nothing flying to Algiers today."

My spirits slumped. The refugee ship might sail without me.

"But you're in luck. There's a plane tomorrow morning at nine. It's probably all booked, with a long waiting list, but we'll get you on it."

"I do appreciate this."

He smiled. "Anything special you'd like to do today?"

"Yes, I'd like to see the medina and the mellah." The medina was the ancient Arab quarter; the Jews lived in the mellah.

"You can't go alone," he said. "It's not safe for a woman, especially a young woman like you. I'll give you a car and an English-speaking native driver."

Both the medina and the mellah were netherworlds of labyrinthine streets filled with the smells of poverty and dirt and goats and human beings. Maimed beggars pulled at my skirt. Naked children sat lethargically on stones, pus running out of their opaque blind eyes. Gaunt women showed me their babies, their little faces like masks of death. Bells clanged, donkeys brayed, camels moved past hovels with ten and twelve people crowded into a single dark, dank space. The smell of goats was everywhere.

"Had enough?" the driver asked me. "You look white. Why don't you go back to the hotel, get some lunch, and have a rest?"

"Let's drive to the Anfa Hotel," I said. Roosevelt and Churchill had met at the Anfa in January 1943 to plot the course of invasion.

This was a different Casablanca we were driving through, with spotless white streets, palm-lined boulevards, and elegant shops. European men and women pedaled near us on bicycles; others sat at corner cafés sipping *café noir* from demitasse cups; water boys in colorful rags clanged little bells, hawking water, which they poured out of sheepskin bags into a metal cup.

Surrounding the stately forty-bedroom hotel on a promontory high on the Anfa hill were luxurious white villas. The sweet smell of tropical flowers and the salt air of the Atlantic cleansed my lungs. I breathed the air deeply to wash away the dark smells of the medina and the mellah.

Tomorrow I would be flying along the very route our troops had wrested from the enemy, first Algiers and then Naples, where I would join the refugees.

Long before nine the next morning, I was already in the plane. The DC-3 with a five-pointed white star on its wings had none of the comfort and, I was sure, none of the emergency lifesaving gear of the C-54. My U.S. Army companions from our overseas flight greeted me like old friends. They told me they had spent most of yesterday swimming on the beach.

We sat on the tarmac in the desert heat, our motors roaring, but we did not move. Suddenly a small armada of fighter planes came out on the apron, tore down the runway, and zoomed up in the air. The invasion of Normandy had already begun.

At ten-twenty Casablanca time we finally took off. Once again the city spread below us. In the morning light the houses had line and form and pattern, elegant white tier upon tier. But the odor of the goats was still with me. Casablanca would forever have a goat smell.

"Ambassador Murphy is expecting you." A young man ushered me to an embassy station wagon at the airport in Algiers. "I'm taking you right to him."

Even the roads seemed to be boiling as we drove into town. I was sticky and queasy and apprehensive.

Suspecting that Robert Murphy, who came out of the State Department, might not be enthusiastic, Ickes hoped I could convince him of the importance of this first haven. It would be a message to the world that America was now assuming responsibility for refugees. A few countries—Sweden, Switzerland, England—had been taking in refugees, though, God knows, not enough. Now others too might follow our lead.

Murphy was the most important official I was scheduled to meet; Roosevelt's personal representative, he had limitless power in the Mediterranean theater of war. I expected a middle-aged if not elderly career diplomat. Instead, rising from a cluttered desk to shake my hand was a tall, blond, youngish man with electric-blue eyes and an appraising smile.

"So you've come about the refugees."

I nodded and handed him Ickes's letter of introduction.

Murphy looked up from the letter. "You know, of course, we're building a huge refugee camp here in Algeria, in Philippeville, to house as many as forty thousand."

I nodded. The consul general in Casablanca had mentioned it.

Murphy began to describe this huge camp the United States was building east of Algiers, near the Tunisian border. I listened, wondering if he was trying, obliquely, to show me that a haven in America was unnecessary, that Philippeville, soon to be completed, could take in thousands of refugees without circumventing quotas.

I told him of Ickes's hopes for the haven in Oswego.

"It's a very important step and an excellent move," he said.

I was startled. Perhaps he was really convinced Oswego was a good step; perhaps we had all misjudged him.

"The first thing I did when Ickes gave me this assignment," I told him, "was to have the President's cable to you translated into twelve different languages. I plan to hang these cables all over the ship, so the refugees will be sure to read them."

Murphy looked pleased; his mouth broadened into a smile. But the blue eyes squinted and turned hard.

"I hope the refugees read that cable very carefully," he said, "especially the line that says they 'will be brought into this country outside of the regular immigration procedures and will return at the end of the war.' "

I said nothing. He had confirmed my suspicions.

Four

WHILE I MULLED over Murphy's words, a chauffeured American car drove me through the streets of Algiers to the Aletti Hotel. I wondered if Murphy was powerful enough, even at this late date, to stop the project.

The late-afternoon sun burned long shadows on the hot Algerian streets. Well-dressed Europeans, Arab men in burnooses, and veiled Arab women walked down the broad French boulevards; the air was serene and peaceful. It was hard to believe that north of us, across the Mediterranean, tanks were clashing, planes were dive-bombing, human beings were burning to death.

The veranda of the Aletti Hotel looked like the porch of a resort hotel as people watched each other, studying newcomers. At the registration desk I was signing my name when a suntanned young man came toward me.

He held out his hand. "Pardon me. I'm Jimmy Saxon, Treasury Department representative in Algiers. Treasury alerted me to your coming."

"How do you know who I am?"

"I had a full description of you. Besides, not many American gals are floating around Algiers. Are you free for dinner tonight?"

"How soon?"

"In an hour."

An Arab in a djellaba and a red fez led me upstairs to a spacious room with a double bed, a huge tiled bathroom, and French windows. I stepped out on the terrace and looked down at a geometric jigsaw of white Arab houses, flooded with sunlight. Back inside, I soaked luxuriously in the large bathtub and changed into a white halter dress with a white stole.

In the lobby, Jimmy looked at me approvingly. "You're a breath of America. Come on. We're off for the Allies Club."

The club was set in a tropical landscape of waving palms and sweet-smelling flowers. We sat in a tiled garden sipping a long cool drink, then entered a dining room crowded with American, French, and British officers. Arab waiters set before us platters of fish and filled our glasses with chilled French wine, while Jimmy talked about how our Army and diplomats saw the refugees—a massive nightmare, clogging roads, blocking the path of tanks and troops, needing shelter, food, medical care.

"Lots of opposition to the whole refugee problem is being stirred up here," Jimmy said. "The British don't want them—never did want them, especially the British military—and the Colonial Office types are trying to keep them out of Palestine. Our own military don't want them either. It was only direct pressure from the President on all the boys here—State and War—that got this whole Oswego thing started."

Suddenly he looked at me.

"We're here making plans for after the war—what to do with the property of the Nazis, indemnities for people who suffered, like the Jews. But you're transporting refugees right now, with the war on. That's some assignment. I wonder if I could handle it." He downed his glass of wine. "I don't envy you. You're in for some rough waters. Don't sink."

The plane for Naples was due to leave at two. I spent most of the morning at Allied Forces Headquarters with Major Sam Goldsmith, a small tense social worker I had met on trips to Chicago. Sam, scarcely a military type, his army uniform drooping on his slightly hunched shoulders, had been assigned to Philippeville.

"We hope to start with ten thousand refugees," he said, "but we're putting up enough housing for thousands more. Nobody here knows how many refugees we're going to have to take care of." Deep grooves etched into his forehead. "As soon as we liberate an area, we're overrun. The refugees have no papers, except maybe some false documents to help them survive. An order just came to establish another camp at Tripolitania. We're making plans to set up tents and huts, but we don't know who'll be living there—or how many thousands."

He stopped talking and stared out past the terrace as though he were seeing an avalanche of refugees. Then he went on.

"Tomorrow another operation may start and uncork another area, and we'll be overrun with thousands more stateless people. It's no good, I tell you. We're supposed to be working with the British on the refugee problem. But the snippety Britisher I'm to work with, Major Griffin-White, is disgusted with me, disgusted with all these refugees, so that right now very little is being done. I hope you have more success at that camp in Oswego."

I listened to his foreboding as I had to Saxon's. "We don't know," Goldsmith said, as though he were talking to himself, "how many tens of thousands, maybe hundreds of thousands, of refugees we may have to take care of. Right now it's still a trickle. Europe is bottlenecked. Jews especially can't get out. We don't really know what's happening to most of the Jews in Europe. All we know is that they were sent to Poland to build roads and fortifications—and died."

"But we do know more. The cables told us."

Goldsmith looked mystified. "What cables?"

It took me a few moments to realize that Goldsmith, a major in G-5 for displaced persons, working with refugees in liberated Algiers, knew as little about the death camps as did most Americans back home. Even Army Intelligence had not been privy to the secret cables.

Briefly I told him some of the things I had learned in Washington.

"My God." The lines in his forehead etched deeper. "When will the country learn the truth?"

Broiling inside a life jacket and strapped into an iron bucket seat in a cargo DC-47A, I looked down at the turquoise waters and the magnificent geography of the Mediterranean. Officers and soldiers sat silently, lost in thought. They were on their way to the Italian front.

Five hours out of Algiers, and Naples spread before us, a city of white rimmed with green water and green hills, with Mount Vesuvius penciled against the horizon. Naples was circled red on my map and in my consciousness. Here I would meet the refugees.

"Welcome, Ruth, welcome, welcome." Bob Neville smothered me in his huge embrace. He looked like a football player in army uniform, but he was editor in chief of the GIs' *Stars and Stripes.*

Bob helped me scramble up into the truck.

"I want to hear everything—about New York, about Washington, about all our friends, everything."

But I could not talk. Naples, so beautiful from the air, was a lunar landscape. Buildings hung like rags. Whole streets were ripped up. Houses were sliced down the front, with staircases that led nowhere and curtains flying insanely in the wind.

"And people go on living," I murmured.

He nodded. "Without water, without plumbing, without food. Starving. The Germans blew up the water supply. They even blew up the whole sewer system before they ran."

He paused while the truck bounced over a giant crater. We were covered with ashes and dust.

"The Nazis blew up every hotel in Naples except the one you're going to, the Parco. They destroyed the whole waterfront. They mined the buildings at the port. They put a twenty-one–day bomb in the post office, so innocent people would get killed weeks after the Germans were gone. To add to the madness, they even emptied the prisons and insane asylums." I shut my eyes for a moment in horror.

The truck pulled up before the Parco, elegant and white. In the lobby Bob greeted American officers, while I dropped my bag in a huge room filled with massive furniture and phoned the Peninsular Base Section. My orders were to call military headquarters immediately on arrival.

An American voice with a Texas drawl answered. "We've been expecting you, ma'am."

I told him I needed to know three things: Where were the refugees right now? When could I see them? Were my orders to sail with them ready?"

"Sorry I can't answer your questions on the phone. Come in tomorrow morning. Do you need a vehicle tonight?"

"Not tonight, but tomorrow morning at eight."

"Yes, ma'am."

I hurried downstairs and climbed into the truck again to have dinner with Bob and his night crew. They were turning out *The Stars and Stripes* in a once-luxurious complex of shops, arcades, and opulent apartments. Their suite, the home of a fascist judge, was high-ceilinged, with red lace curtains and heavily carved furniture, overstuffed sofas and armchairs upholstered in pink moiré. We joined the crew for a supper of turkey sandwiches and coffee, supplied and served by the Army. The men, having just put *The Stars and Stripes* to bed, filled the judge's dining room with invasion fever.

Bob spread a map on the table to show me where the Allied troops were pushing north of Rome, battling Germans under Nazi field marshal Albert Kesselring. More areas would be liberated; more refugees would be on the run. I kept hearing Sam Goldsmith's words: "Tomorrow another operation may start and uncork another area, and we'll be overrun. . . ."

After midnight, I turned on the radio in my hotel room. The words bolted me out of bed. From somewhere in Germany an announcer screamed hysterically against "this assassination plot, this criminal attack against the Führer."

Hitler's voice, high-pitched, barked into the dark hotel bedroom. "We will catch these traitors," he raved. "Their stupidity is enormous. They plot for the slavery of our people. They planned a terrible fate which our people will live through." His voice and his madness felt like snakes crawling on my skin.

I stopped listening to the words, catching only the German rhythms, when I heard the announcer end, with a sob in his throat, "Long live our Führer. Heil Hitler."

I switched off the radio and lay in the dark Italian bedroom. What would have happened if the assassination had succeeded? Whole areas of Hitler's Fortress Europe would have been un-corked. Hundreds of thousands of refugees would have raced to safety. We could be saving not one thousand but millions.

The assassination attempt showed that not all the Germans were mesmerized by Hitler. Later we learned it was a young Ger-man officer, Colonel Klaus von Stauffenberg, who had plotted the attack at Wolfsschanze (Wolf's Lair), Hitler's headquarters in East Prussia. No one searched Stauffenberg's briefcase, in which he had hidden a time bomb; he was highly trusted; he had lost an eye and his right arm in the western desert.

Carefully Stauffenberg had maneuvered his briefcase next to Hitler and left the meeting. A suspicious officer kicked the brief-case away. The bomb exploded. Hitler escaped with a concussion, burns, and shock.

Still shaken and heavily bandaged, the Führer asked his aides to bring in Mussolini. The Duce had invited himself to Germany and had arrived at four o'clock that afternoon. Mussolini had left Italy in a state of depression and despair. The Allied armies and Italian partisans were routing not only his fascist followers but the Ger-man divisions in the north.

Hitler's escape bolstered Mussolini's spirits. "After this miracle," he assured the Führer and himself, "it is impossible that our cause should know defeat."

In Naples, food was the obsession.

"It's only because we have special privileges that we have pow-dered eggs," a young red-haired lieutenant assured me at breakfast in the Parco.

The eggs tasted like sawdust.

"This is a real delicacy," he went on. "The Allied personnel have been warned not to buy any food from the Neapolitans. First of all, there's damned little food, the Italians need it for themselves. But with no water and no sanitation, everything is filthy, and we can all pick up typhus. Even in the Parco, in all this splendor, we get little for supper except canned peas and beans. I'd give a dollar right now for a glass of fresh milk or one egg."

I lost my appetite and took off in the army car for the Peninsular Base Section. People were everywhere—in the alleys, in the rubble—gesticulating, screaming, laughing, weeping. Life was on the street in this ravaged city. Life was the one commodity you held on to with passion, with ferocity.

Most of the people were in rags, children were barefoot, but some of the Neapolitan women looked as lovely as Renaissance madonnas. Others had bleached their hair blond, and their dark roots were showing. For a while, Naples looked like a city of big-bosomed sexy women with two-colored hair and high platform shoes, a city that seemed to redefine itself in the bright Italian morning sun.

Now it looked like a military melting pot. Soldiers from the whole world seemed to be strolling down the rubbled streets, looking the girls over or standing at pushcarts buying up the city's meager rations of fresh fruit and vegetables. I had never seen such a hodgepodge of uniforms: American, British, French, Italian, Senegalese. There were Gurkhas from Nepal and black mercenaries from North Africa hired by the French, dressed in khaki GI uniforms, army boots, and the dashing profile hats of Australia.

The Peninsular Base Section was a noisy confusion of men and women in uniform, opening and closing doors and rushing through corridors. Telephones rang. Typewriters clacked. Washington had been transplanted to Naples.

Captain L. C. Sutton, Jr., the assistant adjutant general, stood up from his desk as I entered. I had already learned from my chauffeur that Sutton was "a big wheel," in charge of all official correspondence, personnel records, and the preparation and distribution of orders.

"Sit down." Sutton motioned to a hard chair opposite his desk. "I'll get your orders ready right away. Any questions?"

"The refugees? Where are they now?"

"They're aboard a troopship in the bay."

Thank God. I said a silent prayer of thanks. Murphy had done nothing to abort the mission.

"When do we sail?"

"Tomorrow at five."

"Tomorrow! Can I go aboard now to meet them?"

"Once you're on the ship you won't be able to disembark again. If you have work in Naples, I recommend you do it today and go aboard tomorrow."

I was torn. A whole day and a half before I could meet the refugees. But there were people I wanted to see and government officials I had promised Ickes and others in Washington I would call on.

"I'll go tomorrow," I said. "What kind of ship is it?"

"It's an Army transport," Sutton said, "and it's packed full. The thousand refugees are in the forward holds, and about a thousand wounded soldiers from Anzio and Cassino are in the stern. We use every inch of space on every ship to get those wounded men back to stateside hospitals. A lot of them are in pretty bad shape emotionally. Battle fatigue. There are others too, doctors and nurses to take care of the refugees and the wounded."

He stood up.

"And now, unless you have more questions, I'd like to get your travel orders ready."

Part Two

—⟨ ⟩—

THE VOYAGE OF THE
HENRY GIBBINS

FIVE

THE NAPLES SUN streamed into the barren office, turning particles of dust into diamond sparkles, as Max Perlman came around the small wooden desk to greet me.

"What a stroke of luck to find you in Naples," I said.

I had learned that Max was one of the team that had screened the refugees. They had first been selected by Leonard Ackerman of the War Refugee Board, who, working day and night until he was no longer able to "go on playing God," had asked Max to help. Max was a natural, a representative of the Joint Distribution Committee in Italy. The JDC was the overseas arm of the American Jewish community, financing rescues through the underground, paying off officials to save Jews in Romania and Hungary, and sending men like Max to rescue and feed homeless Jews.

"I was only a small part of the team," Max said. "Captain Lewis Korn became head of the group after Len Ackerman took ill. You'll meet Lew; he's already aboard the ship. Trying to select some of those thousand refugees for America was the toughest assignment of my life. Word of that invitation from the President spread like a brushfire. Day and night, people were knocking on the doors of all the offices taking applications—in Naples, Bari, Rome. Women and men weeping, people fainting from emotion, parents holding their children up in the air so we'd notice them. It was a lousy job, Ruth. We were all playing God to a group of desperate people. Three thousand applied—"

"Three thousand!" I cried. "It would be so easy to bring three thousand into America!"

I remembered Joe DuBois's comment on the number of refugees. "It was the President himself," he had told me, "who fixed the figure at one thousand. He's a politician first and then a humanitarian."

Max leaned forward. "There's this tiny village in the mountains called Campagnia where Jews had been hiding out. I went up there by truck with Captain Moscovitz—he's with the Palestinian Jewish unit of the British Army. When the refugees saw our truck with the blue-and-white Star of David painted on both sides, they began embracing the two of us. They couldn't believe it—Jewish officers, one from America, one from Palestine.

"We went on to an old monastery built in the Middle Ages— the fascists had turned it into an internment camp for about a hundred and fifty refugee Jews. Some of them looked eighty; they were in their forties. I told them of the President's invitation to come to America. You can't imagine the excitement. Some of the men made whole speeches telling me how many years they had been dreaming about going to America. Others just wept openly."

His voice, usually a rich tenor, suddenly cracked. "They filled out the applications and then bombarded me with questions. 'When will we know if we're accepted? When will the transport leave for America?' I felt awful, leaving them with such anxiety. I couldn't tell them if they'd be accepted or not. These men were all alone; they had seen their entire families wiped out."

His voice broke again. "Ruth, the pain in their faces is still with me."

My throat went dry.

"But then there were things to make you happy. The best part for me was arranging the trucks to transport the people from Bari to the ship. I decided not to use British army trucks, even though the British offered them to us. It's a long trip from Bari to Naples—five or six hours, crossing the mountains. I figured these people had been through so much that British military trucks might frighten them. I went back to my Palestinian friends, Major Bar Shmorak, a kibbutznik, and Captain Moscovitz, and asked them to lend us their trucks with the Star of David. Picture the sight. Refugees crossing Italy in a convoy of trucks with the Star of David painted on their sides, heading for a ship to America."

I stood up in the bare office, walked behind the desk, and kissed Max's cheek. "I think these refugees will never forget what you did. Nor will I."

In Hungary, Jews were being selected for death. In southern Italy, a precious few were being selected for life.

Not allowed to board the ship until noon the following day, I decided to spend the afternoon and the next morning paying courtesy calls on the officials whose names were in my notebook.

At eight in the morning, the GI chauffeur stacked my suitcases, camera bag, and typewriter in the car. I had dressed for the protocol visits in a white suit, white gloves, and a big red straw hat to protect me from the sun.

We finished the rounds and then sped down to the waterfront. Barbed wire barring unauthorized civilians and potential spies circled the entire port. A huge sign hung near the entrance gate: KILL HITLER. KILL MUSSOLINI. The sense of war was in the water, on the docks, in the sky. Planes zoomed above us, army vehicles sputtered and choked, soldiers and sailors blocked already-snarled traffic.

In the harbor, giant cranes lifted huge military equipment from cargo ships onto the docks. Young soldiers, some baby-faced, all loaded with gear, marched down the gangplanks of troopships, leaped into trucks and personnel carriers, and headed north to the battlefront.

The GI driver took me to a launch where a young navy lieutenant in a white uniform helped me jump into his motorboat. Soon we were chugging past wall-to-wall ships. Even the sun seemed to be searching for space in the harbor to cast silver shafts of light.

"There's your convoy." The lieutenant pointed to a flotilla of cruisers, troopships, and cargo ships, some sleek and elegant, some dowdy, but all riding high as if they controlled the water. They were anchored in the Bay of Naples, waiting like soldiers to begin a parade of war.

How many thousands, I wondered, are aboard those navy escort vessels—soldiers, sailors, gunners armed to the teeth? My nerves tightened with the sense of danger and the awesome beauty of this seawall of war.

"You'll be picking up more escorts in the Med," the navy officer was saying. "The Med is a bad spot for U-boats. Bombers."

I hardly listened. "Which is the ship with the refugees?"

"Over there. It's an Army transport—the *Henry Gibbins.*"

The ship, rigged with graceful steel cables, lifeboats, elevated tubs with gun emplacements, dwarfed our launch. Its decks were lined with people staring down at us, some waving.

The lieutenant stood up to signal the crew on the *Henry Gibbins,* who dropped a rope ladder down the side. A sailor in the launch held the ladder as I reached for the first rung. Suddenly the lieutenant stared at the white suit, the gloves, the big red hat as if he were seeing them for the first time.

"You can't climb the Jacob's ladder in that outfit. Not with a thousand refugees and a thousand wounded soldiers watching." He ordered one of his sailors to go below. "Take off your pants and hand them up to me."

The lieutenant gave me the sailor's pants. I pulled them over my skirt, handed him my hat, and once more began climbing the ropes. The ladder swung and pitched against the hull; I clutched each rung so tightly I could feel the rope digging into my skin. The water below looked menacing. Finally, near the top of the ladder, a sailor leaned over, placed his hands under my armpits, and lifted me onto the main deck. The refugees surged forward.

"It's Eleanor Roosevelt!" a man shouted.

I laughed with relief.

Waves of bodies crowded around me, men in tattered shorts, naked to the waist, women in ragged and rumpled skirts and blouses, sad-eyed children in torn sandals or without shoes. Some of the people had cloth and newspapers tied around their feet. Several stared at me as if they were seeing an apparition.

A slender man broke through the crowd and extended his hand. "I'm Captain Lew Korn."

He was in army uniform, a thin bony man who looked sad even when he smiled, as though the weight of having selected most of these refugees was an enormous burden to carry.

"This is Miss Gruber," he told the refugees. "She's a representative of the government."

Two officers, army and navy, came forward, extending their hands. They introduced themselves: Major Judson W. Allen, transport commander and head of the army escort, and Lieutenant Donald M. Martin, commander of the naval armed guard.

"Captain Shea would like to see you on the bridge," Allen said. I recognized his Brooklyn accent.

The people opened a path on the cluttered deck. We entered the midship house and climbed a narrow steel ladder to the bridge deck.

Captain John Shea, a jovial Irishman in a spanking-white uniform, smiled broadly. "Glad to have you aboard. Feel free to come up here at any time. If we can be of any help, don't hesitate. This ship has been in a lot of convoys in the Atlantic and the Med, but it's the first time we're transporting refugees."

It was a first for most of us.

"We've divided the ship," Captain Shea continued. "The refugees are all down in the forward holds, the wounded soldiers in the stern. They're not to have any contact. We're not looking for trouble. Of course, you're free to go anywhere you like. Nothing's off limits to you."

He grinned, looking at the sailor's pants I was still wearing. "I guess you want to get to your cabin."

I grinned too.

"You have a few hours before we sail. We're weighing anchor at five this afternoon."

He called to a midshipman to escort me to my cabin. There two army nurses in summer uniforms lay on neatly made bunks reading magazines.

"Hi, I'm Mary Toum." The attractive blonde put down her magazine.

"And I'm Caroline Haltiwaner," said the other, a slender nurse with a southern accent.

I introduced myself while I pulled off the sailor's pants and changed into slacks and a cool blouse.

"I know why Mary and I are on this ship," Caroline drawled. "We agreed to take shifts in the ship's hospital, so we could get home on rotation. What are you doing aboard?"

"To help with the refugees."

Mary lit a cigarette. "You've got your work cut out for you. Some are already seasick down below, even before we sail. They're going to need all the help you can give them."

I prowled the ship to find Ralph Stauber, the man whom Dillon Myer had sent as his representative. I found him in the wardroom, a chunky man with heavy eyebrows, thin well-shaped lips, and rounded shoulders. He was in a white short-sleeved shirt, drinking coffee and writing on a long sheet of paper. The wardroom was filled with army and navy officers talking across wooden tables welded onto the deck.

Stauber tried to rise.

"Don't get up." I put my hand out. "I'm glad to meet you."

He settled back, his manner correct. "Well, you made it. For a while it looked as if the convoy would sail without you."

Later I learned that someone in the State Department in Naples had sent a cable to Ickes that I had missed the ship.

"Am I interrupting you?" I asked Stauber, obviously a man of paper and statistics. Even the yellow pencil he held so tightly seemed an integral part of his fingers.

"It's OK. I'm working up a statistical table on the number of refugees, the countries they came from, their sex, religion, and so forth. Would you like a breakdown?"

I nodded.

"Number of refugees, nine hundred and eighty-two."

"I thought the President invited a thousand." *Three thousand applied.*

"What happened to the other eighteen?" I asked. The figure one thousand had become a fixture in my mind. It was a nicely rounded figure that you could cope with. You could touch it. It seemed to me it danced, it pirouetted. One thousand refugees. It was like a song.

"That's all that came aboard. I'll start with religion. Most people think all refugees are Jews. The greatest number on the ship, to be sure, are Jews, but this is by no means a Jewish project." His yellow pencil pointed to the figures. "Eight hundred and seventy-four are Jewish, seventy-three are Roman Catholic, twenty-eight are Greek Orthodox, and seven are Protestant."

Roosevelt had cautioned that the camp not be known as a Jewish camp; he wanted refugees of all denominations.

"Here's the breakdown now by sex: five hundred twenty-five male, four hundred fifty-seven female. Lots of children and old people—the range is from an infant to an eighty-year-old man, Isaac Cohen, from Salonika, Greece."

"And the countries they've come from?"

"Eighteen different countries."

I went back to the deck and began walking among the people. I joined a group sitting in a line on the ledge of the covered hatch.

"You haven't told us yet who you are," a slim professional-looking man said.

"I've been sent by the secretary of the interior—"

"The secretary of the interior! Are you a policeman?"

"No. In America the Interior Department has nothing to do with the police. It's not like Europe."

"Are you FBI?"

I put both hands to my head. "Me? FBI? Good heavens, no."

"To us, everyone in government looks suspicious." Another voice came from the crowd. It belonged to a tall dark-haired young man about seventeen, with clear dark eyes and an air of strength even in his round adolescent face. His name, he said, was Adam Munz. "They don't tell us anything. Even when they invite us to come to America, they put us on this ship and they still don't tell us anything. You're not a policeman. You're not FBI. So what *are* you doing on this ship?"

More and more people left the spots they had staked out for themselves to join the circle around us.

"When we get back to America—" I began.

"*If* we get back," someone interrupted. "If the Nazis don't sink this ship."

I went right on. "I will have to report to my boss, Harold Ickes—he's the head of the Interior Department—and he will report to the President, the Cabinet, and Congress. I would like them to know who you are, what kind of people you are. What you've gone through to survive."

"You'll find out soon enough." Otto Presser spoke up. He was a small man, full of broad theatrical gestures that reminded me of Eddie Cantor. "We're all kinds of people. Big and little, some once rich, some not so rich, and now all the same—poor."

The people smiled at Presser, who was obviously a popular figure. Later I learned he had been a song-and-dance man in Vienna.

"I want to spend as much time as I can with you," I said. "People in America are just beginning to learn what Hitler has done to you. You will be the first group of refugees the people of the United States will see."

They were listening intently now.

"You are the living witnesses. Through you, through the experiences you tell me, I can report to Ickes and he can tell the people of America what has been happening and surely is still going on now."

They sat in silence on the hatch combing, staring far off into the sea. A few wiped their eyes.

"You're a woman," one of the men said. "How can I tell you the things they did to me—the dirty, filthy, obscene things?"

"Forget, if you can, that I am a woman. It's your story, it's your experiences, that are important, not how they affect me. Maybe if the world learns what you suffered, maybe we'll be able to rescue more people."

Tuck, the bos'n, a grizzled old tar with a rubbery face, followed by a few deckhands, made his way through the milling refugees toward the bow. We heard the clang of metal on metal and watched the huge chain come up through the hawse pipe to the anchor windlass.

"We're sailing!" some of the refugees shouted.

We rushed to the rails. Some of the people hugged and kissed each other, some held up their babies to wave goodbye to the Italian shore. Several wept. The convoy was moving, ships were streaming white foam. Naples lay behind us golden in the afternoon sun as warships maneuvered around us in formation, ensigns flying. The Mediterranean opened, wide and blue and fraught with danger.

SIX

A CLANGING BELL announced dinner.

The sun was still riding high, dappling the water with silver. Leaving the deck, I followed some of the people into the galley and stopped at the door. Soldiers standing behind the steam tables were filling the refugees' aluminum mess kits with mountains of food.

Major Allen, the head of the army escort, joined me. "Anything wrong? You look startled."

"I never saw so much food dished out in my life."

Most of the refugees, unable to talk to the soldiers, pointed to the food they wanted—goulash, frankfurters, boiled potatoes, cooked onions. There were piles of salmon salad, long loaves of sliced white bread, platters of cookies, bowls of Jell-O. "Is this to make up for the years they starved?" I asked.

"Not at all. This is the way the Army feeds. Remember, an army moves on its stomach."

I joined him as he made his inspection.

"It looks like a lot," he agreed, "but by now they're pretty hungry; most haven't eaten anything since breakfast. We serve twice a day: seven-thirty in the morning, five-thirty at night."

There were no chairs, only long counters at which the people stood eating. Three little Greek girls had been propped up by their mother, who fed them first and then dug into her own mess kit.

I saw some of the children secrete frankfurters in their shirts and vanish. Was it hunger—or fear that there would be no more food?

A young teenager picked up a slice of white bread and eyed it curiously. "It's cake," he told the girl behind him. "Imagine eating cake with frankfurters."

"And what's this?" A young woman tasted the Jell-O. "Yech, it tastes like horse glue."

But most of the people ate silently, wolfing down the food until their kits were empty.

A man whose pale skin seemed stretched across his protruding cheekbones caught me looking at him. "I still can't believe all this food. In the camp they gave us dirty hot water with something swimming in it, and they called it soup. What a country America is!"

A few men walked out of the galley carrying mess kits. "That's for people too sick to come up," Major Allen explained. "Some were on K rations before they came aboard. They ate so much the first days while we were anchored in the bay, they had to be put back on K rations. Now they're eating regular, but they still feel so lousy they can't come up from the holds."

I walked through the companionway and descended the narrow steep ladder to the first hold, clutching the iron rail. There was no air and only dim light. Stretching across the entire beam of the ship were canvas bunks squeezed together in tiers of three with narrow passageways.

An elderly woman with a wet handkerchief on her head called out to me.

"Can I bring you something?" I asked her.

She shook her head. "I can't hold anything." She put her hand on her stomach. "Maybe you know how long we will be on the water?"

"We don't know yet. It depends on how fast the convoy sails. It could be two weeks."

She moaned.

"Perhaps you'd feel better if you came up on deck. I'll help you up the stairs."

"Another day. Today my legs won't hold me."

By eight the next morning, people were already sitting and lying on the deck. They had breakfasted in the galley and now were staking out places for themselves amid the machinery.

Within minutes a group encircled me.

"Tell us what it is going to be like in America. How are we going to live?" Otto Presser, the song-and-dance man, assumed his Eddie Cantor–like expression of doleful laughter.

"I don't know what the quarters will be like. All I can tell you is that you are going to a former army camp."

"A camp in America!" Leo Mirković waved his arms in disbelief. A skeletal figure in once-white silk pajamas, he had been the premier baritone of the Zagreb National Opera.

"I haven't seen the camp," I said, "but I know it's being completely remodeled so that family groups can live together."

Presser put his hand on my arm. "*Liebes Fräulein,* don't tell me you're taking us to a concentration camp in America."

"Be realistic." A young man in his twenties limped toward us. He was Fredi Baum, from Yugoslavia. "They'll put us in a camp when we arrive, and then we'll find out where we go from there."

"We *are* realistic," a middle-aged man with a sagging paunch, wearing black-and-white striped concentration-camp pajamas, shouted angrily. "We have a right to know. Are we or are we not going to a concentration camp?"

"Why are we throwing all our anger at this young woman?" a bald man with broken glasses intervened like a judge. "Why do you jump to such terrible conclusions? The Americans are not going to put us into a concentration camp. I'm sure the Americans are doing this whole thing for the best reasons: to save refugees. But I think they are also doing it a little bit for publicity. We know they are geniuses at publicity. After all, this is a wonderful thing. We are the personal guests of President Roosevelt."

Mirković permitted himself a dimpled smile. "Maybe we are put on this crowded ship with no place to sit and those terrible bunks downstairs because somebody wants to embarrass President Roosevelt. My own feeling is that a great man like Roosevelt would want us to sail on a luxury liner."

"Oh, sure," a young woman interjected. "In Rome that Englishman who chose us—what was his name?"

"Sir Clifford Heathcote-Smith," I said. He had taken over the selection in Rome when Leonard Ackerman of the War Refugee Board fell ill.

"That's the one. He practically told us we'd have a swimming pool on the ship. Some of us even went all over Rome looking for fabric to sew bathing suits."

"There are always complainers." Manya Hartmayer, a young woman in a man's shirt far too large for her, shook her head. "After so many times close to death, to me this ship is better than the *Queen Mary.*"

She turned to me. "Don't listen to the complainers. They're just a few, but they'll make you crazy."

She stood before the group, her dark hair framing her face and falling to her shoulders. "Look how lucky we are. We are the chosen thousand."

Major Allen threaded his way through the refugees. "Can you come to the wardroom? I need your help."

I sat on the red banquette facing Allen.

"I worked up a list of orders for the people. I'd like you to translate them into German and announce them on the loudspeaker so everyone on the refugee deck can hear."

We took his list to the radio shack. "Ladies and gentlemen," I said in German, "Major Judson Allen, our transport commander, has asked me to announce the orders of the day. Please listen carefully. If you have any questions, you can discuss them with me later.

"One, everyone must police his or her own bunk and the area around it.

"Two, everyone must be out of quarters by nine A.M. or until such time as the daily Army inspection is over. It should be over no later than ten A.M.

"Three, Major Allen would like to have three men on each of the four holds, or a total of twelve men, to mop the four decks.

"Four, he would like to have eight or ten women to clean the women's latrines on D Deck, and five men to clean the men's latrines on C Deck.

"Five, he needs additional men and women to clean the public showers.

"All of this, cleaning your own areas, the decks, latrines, and showers, must be finished by ten A.M. After that you are free to do anything else for the rest of the day.

"Six, we will have an air-raid drill every morning. Everyone must be on deck except those too sick to leave their bunks. Every bunk has a life jacket. Wear it each day for the air-raid drill. Curfew must be strictly obeyed. No one is allowed on deck after dark. If you even light a cigarette after dusk, the Nazis can spot us. You must be in your bunks from dark to dawn.

"Seven, the mess lines. Everybody who comes through the line with a meal ticket will get food. After you've had your food and the line is finished, you can come back for seconds. Provisions are ample for fighting men. They should be ample for civilians.

"Eight, in each section an army doctor will make morning rounds. The Army has assigned three army doctors and six army nurses to this escort: some are on special orders, some on rotation. We are also using refugee doctors and nurses who'll be working in the hospital.

"Nine, the Army has assigned three line officers just for this escort: Lieutenant Colonel Daniel Talbot, Captain Geher, and Captain Lewis Korn."

I had promised Ambassador Murphy that I would post multi-lingual copies of Roosevelt's cable to him that I had had translated in Washington. I nailed them now on the walls of the holds, where the refugees could read the words in Serbo-Croatian, German, French, Greek, Slovenian, Polish, Albanian, Bulgarian, Hungarian, Romanian, Yiddish, and Czech.

Back in the wardroom, I joined Ralph Stauber and Captain Korn. We had decided to meet every day.

"What criteria did you follow," I asked Korn, "when you selected the people?"

"There were several," he said. "First, we tried to take people in family groups. Then we chose those in greatest need, as many as possible from concentration camps and slave-labor camps. Third, we took no families with contagious or loathsome diseases." He smiled a little. "Sometimes I think a cold is a loathsome disease. And, finally, we tried to choose people with a cross section of skills to make the Emergency Refugee Shelter as self-sustaining as possible."

Stauber pulled out his yellow pad. "You got a cross section, all right: doctors, dentists, pharmacists, opticians, artisans, merchants, bookkeepers, tailors, dressmakers, teachers, lawyers, singers, actors, painters, writers, sculptors, engineers, and two rabbis."

It's a whole community, I thought, a microcosm of a small town.

"One of the first questions they ask me," I said, "is about housing. I guess when you've been on the run so long, when you've been homeless, housing becomes an obsession."

"What do they want to know?" Stauber asked.

"Right now they want to know if they'll be put in houses according to their nationalities. The Yugoslavs especially seem to want to keep together."

"I'm getting the same question," Korn said.

"What do we tell them?"

Korn's sad face grew even sadder. "You have to tell them we just don't know."

"Education is another obsession," I said. "Some of the teenagers haven't been in school for five years, and some of the ten- and twelve-year-olds have never been in school at all."

A shadow crossed Korn's face. "Housing and education are hard questions but soluble. The toughest question of all is what's going to happen to them when the war is over. They all signed a release they would go back as soon as the war was over. But who knows if they believed it or not? What's more, I gather from the refugees who were selected in Rome that Heathcote-Smith told them it was simply a form—to pay no attention to it."

"They better believe it," Stauber said. Anger edged his words. "That's the promise the President gave Congress."

SEVEN

A YOUNG AMERICAN in a white undershirt and chinos approached me on deck. "My name is Abe Tauber." He thrust out his hand. "I'm with the Red Cross, assigned to the wounded soldiers on the ship."

His face was freckled, his hair copper red in the sun.

"We stood on the deck watching you as you came up the rope ladder in that fascinating and, I must say, highly unusual attire." He spoke with precision, each word rounded, before he sent it forth with a kind of Huckleberry Finn chuckle. "Every man on the ship wanted to know who you were, especially when the brass marched forward to welcome you aboard." He paused. "Now, my dear young lady, we know."

He handed me the ship's newspaper, a white mimeographed sheet called "Gibbins' Gab." My eye glanced down the page through the news summary.

His voice broke into my reading. "I'm sure the news fascinates you, a former foreign correspondent."

I looked at him quizzically. How did he know?

"Turn the page over. You're on the other side." He pointed to the bottom of the sheet.

Meet Your (Mysterious) Shipmate

Comes out in a special launch while we ride at anchor in Naples.

Boards the ship, treated with great courtesy by full colonels!

Walks around in a daring red turban and GI pants, since changed to lovely red slacks, lugging camera and photometer. Confers with big shots and ordinary guys alike. MPs bow at her as she passes to and from the sacred portals forward and speaks to the folks in their own (7) languages.

Is she a psychiatrist? Obstetrician? Newspaper reporter? FBI man? Here's the lowdown.

The lady is Miss Ruth Gruber; she is here to help out with the movement of the civilian group. Special representative of Sec. of the Interior Harold L. Ickes, whose department is handling the problem. A former correspondent with the NY *Herald Tribune,* traveler in prewar Europe and Alaska. Author of many articles and a book on the Arctic. Nice gal, too—green eyes, soft voice, ready smile—and a good head.

Won't it be nice to get home to our own gals again??

Laughing, I reread the line "Is she a psychiatrist? Obstetrician?" I turned to him. "And what do *you* do?"

"I've just spent a year abroad with the Red Cross. Now I'm going back to teach the two subjects I love, English and speech, at the Bronx High School of Science." His freckled face grew serious. "If I can be of any help with the refugees, it would be an honor. A privilege."

I thanked him. I would need all the help I could muster.

Whatever skills I had acquired as a journalist seemed inadequate. A journalist is supposed to see, observe, stand apart, straining for objectivity, searching for truth. Now I would still search for truth, but I did not want to stand apart, nor could I. I wanted to feel as they felt, through every cell in my body.

They were the first witnesses coming to America in one single mass movement. Through them, through their faces, their bodies, their experiences, their fears, their bravery, their flight, their survival, America would learn at last the truth of Hitler's crimes.

Theirs would not be secondhand or thirdhand stories, nor even the eyewitness accounts of trained observers. Their stories would be personal histories. They were the victims available at last to prove the crimes. I had to win their confidence without invading their privacy.

Pacing the deck, staring into the Mediterranean, I hit upon a scheme.

They talked in a babel of languages. We used German as the lingua franca only because the majority understood German or Yiddish. But there were many who spoke no German and no English. I would teach them English. I would set up classes on deck. Even with a few words in English, we could begin to make contact with one another.

Major Allen approved. "Good idea."

"I'll need a blackboard."

"The bos'n will fix it up for you on the main deck."

On the loudspeaker I announced we would have a class in English in half an hour.

Tuck, whose face was screwed up like Popeye's, hung a blackboard above the covered hatch, and immediately a crowd of men and women left their places on the deck. They took positions sitting, even lying close together, on the hatch cover. The rest spilled over, sitting on the deck itself. I had expected a handful, perhaps twenty or thirty, but not the hundreds who sat, faces uplifted, some smiling, some serious, all waiting for the lesson to begin.

"How do you feel?" I asked them, and then wrote the words in chalk on the board.

Those who spoke no English shrugged their shoulders. Others shouted, "Fine."

" 'I feel fine,' " I added the words to the blackboard. "Let's repeat. How do you feel?"

In unison, in all accents, they called out, "I feel fine." Some at the rim of the ship, clutching the rails, bending over in case they had to throw up, still mouthed the words:

"How do you feel?"

"I feel fine."

Most were smiling, laughing. We were making contact.

Abe Furmanski of Warsaw, a short barrel-chested thirty-five-year-old man with the face and muscles of a fighter, sat beside me on the cover of the hatch.

"You want to know our stories. I will tell you what the Nazis and the Vichy French did to us in France."

I opened my notebook. "Do you mind if I write your words down?"

His eyes narrowed. "You must write it down. The world must know. I hear people say that the things they did to us—it's all propaganda. Like the propaganda in the Great War. What I tell you is no propaganda."

I began to write in my own long shorthand. I could write while I watched his face. He looked like a man who would kill before he was killed.

"I was in France when Germany marched in on June sixteenth, 1940. A twenty-six-year-old German captain, his name was Captain Danniker—he was the Nazi commissar in Paris for Jewish affairs—sent for Rabbi Julien Weill, the Grand Rabbi of Paris.

"Danniker gave an order: 'Rabbi, I demand you set up a Jewish Council of seven men, French and foreign Jews, to collaborate with the Germans.' "

His face grew dark.

"We did not collaborate. We sabotaged every way we could. All of us with Rabbi Weill were ready to pay, with our heads and our lives. And many of us did. We created our own underground and brought together all the Jewish political and religious organizations. It was the first time, I think, in history we all came together in our struggle. We began to smuggle Jews to the free zone in unoccupied France. But unfortunately most were captured by the Vichy French gendarmes. Whenever the Nazis caught one of us, there were terrible reprisals. Rabbi Weill was thrown into prison. I don't know if he survived the torture."

He stopped to light a cigarette.

"August twenty-second, 1941. I will never forget that day. The Nazis took sixty-five hundred Jews—children, men, women nursing their babies—and threw them into the terrible concentration camp at Drancy, near Paris. Then they shipped them to Poland. There were some good French, like the Gaullist groups who helped Jews flee to Spain and Switzerland and gave them false documents and money. But most of the French"—he puffed the smoke from his cigarette—"ugh. I cannot look at French people anymore. They built the concentration camp at Gurs near the Spanish border where they killed thirty to forty thousand Jews."

"I know Gurs," I said.

"You—you have been to Gurs, an American?"

"No. But Lion Feuchtwanger, the novelist, was in Gurs. He was one of the lucky ones who got out. He described it to me when he came to New York."

"One lucky man. A writer. In the underground we kept trying to get hundreds out of Gurs. We got out a handful." He ground his cigarette out on the sole of his shoe. "Then the worst blow fell. All of France was occupied by the Germans. The mass murders began."

He went on swiftly.

"In closed trucks that were meant to hold twenty people, the Germans pushed one hundred and more. Quicklime was placed on the floor ten inches high. The doors were sealed tight so no air could escape. The people had to urinate—that started the lime cooking. The gas and fumes came up and choked them to death."

Abe stopped a moment, and his hands went to his throat. "The bodies were thrown into special ovens and burned."

I thought I could not listen anymore, but I listened.

"The Nazis said all the time, 'Kill Russians with bullets. Kill Jews with lime.' "

The noonday sun rode high over the convoy, the ships before us breaking foam in the green sea. My notebook lay open on my lap. I saw faces milling around me, but they were the faces of people in trucks, clutching their throats as lime turned into gas and fumes. I walked to the rail and clutched it, sucking in the air and the smell of the sea.

Had I heard enough for today? Could I absorb any more?

"Excuse me, but I think you must know what happened to us— in Yugoslavia."

I turned from the rail to see a distinguished-looking man. His open shirt revealed a wide gauze bandage on his chest.

"We Yugoslavs are not the majority on the ship," he said, "but we're about a third; there are over three hundred. I cannot speak for all of us. But my own story may give you some picture of what happened to us in March 1941 when Hitler issued his orders about Yugoslavia. I can hear them saying to each other, 'Beat them down as fast as possible. Destroy Belgrade from the air.' "

Pressing my notebook against the rail, I took down his words. He was like a man possessed.

"Yes, yes, write it down. You have people here from eighteen countries that Hitler captured, burned, tried to destroy. Get all our stories. Get all of the terror. We lived it. We will live with it for the rest of our lives. But you are the first one we can tell it to. Yes, write it down, so the world will know."

He interrogated himself for my benefit. "My name? Henry Macliach. My age? Forty-four. My profession? Doctor of medicine. My rank in the army? Major. My wounds?" He pointed to the bandage on his chest. "I am still not healed from the things they did to my body."

His hand trembled. "I tell you to write it. But no notebook and no pencil can describe what they did to us.

"Our army could not resist the Nazis. Every day the Germans would line up the people who still had the courage and the strength to defy Hitler. Jews, nationalists, Communists, radicals, professors, schoolteachers, intellectuals—everybody was a suspect. Every single day five hundred people—I saw this with my own eyes—were shot by machine guns. Every day for six months! After the shooting they strung demolitions to each dead body and blew them all up.

"Maybe you do not believe this, young woman from America. And why should you? What do you, in America, thousands of miles away, know what the Germans did to us? Why should you believe that children not old enough to go to school were included among the five hundred? Why should you believe that in the hospital where I worked as a physician seventy men were locked for eight days in a tiny closetlike room without food or air? They did not need food or air when their bodies were picked off the ground."

I wanted to whisper above the noise of the ship and the milling people and the calm sea, *I do believe.* But no words came.

"And what was the crime committed by two thousand men?" he asked. "They were selected in December to go out in the woods to cut wood for the Germans, to keep them warm. They chopped and sawed every day and kept the Germans warm in that hard winter. In January, they were sent out in a terrible snowstorm and not allowed to come back at night. Two days later, when the storm stopped, all two thousand were found, frozen stiff in the snow. What was their crime? They were Jews."

He was a doctor now, examining my face. "I see in your eyes you are asking, How did I survive? How did all of us on this ship survive when most of the Jews of Yugoslavia were shot in mass graves or on riverbanks or deported to death camps?"

He spat out the words.

"We survived by running."

He turned on his heels and disappeared in the swarm of people. I closed my notebook.

Now perhaps I could go back to my cabin, throw off the clothes sticking to my back, take a shower. Even the open-stall cold saltwater showers seemed like a luxury. But more people were pressing around me on the deck.

"Belgium. I will tell you what happened to us in Belgium."

The sun fell in slants on Samuel Silberman's ravaged face. It was a face of sorrow and nobility. His thirty-two-year-old wife, Breindel, stood silently at his side, clutching his arm.

"We have two children," Samuel said, "a boy and a girl."

"On the ship? With you?"

They shook their heads. Samuel began their story haltingly. Small, round-faced, with the thick capable hands of an artisan, he had been a furrier in Tarnow, Poland. In 1928 they had moved to Brussels, where many Jews had settled, and in 1940, when the Germans occupied Belgium, they began the flight that was to take them ultimately to our ship.

"We tried to get out of Belgium when the Nazis came," he said. "We thought France would be safe. We left everything we owned, just taking a few things we could carry easily. We lost them too in the railroad station."

With hundreds of fleeing people, they reached Boulogne on the French coast and hid in a cellar. For three days they were without food and water. Belgian soldiers escaping the Nazis with them brought them wine for sustenance. "That was the only thing our children had—wine." On the fourth day, Boulogne fell too.

"I looked out of the cellar. German officers stood up in tanks and looked around in all the corners of the street with binoculars. Soldiers stood up in army cars pointing machine guns."

He shook his head. "We were so naïve. The Germans sounded so kind. They told us and the Belgian soldiers, 'Go home. Belgium is free.' We thought—imagine how stupid we were—the Germans have achieved such victories, maybe they'll forget the Jews."

They returned to Brussels to find that the Germans had already put in special laws against the Jews.

"Then in June 1942 the order came: All boys and girls between the ages of fifteen and twenty must go to Mechlin to work. They were told to take work clothes, food for ten days, dishes. They were warned that if they didn't come, all Jews would be held responsible."

Breindel hugged Samuel's arm, as if she were hugging her only security, the core of her life. "We thought those children were going to work," she said. "But it was a lie. Mechlin was where they assembled people and pushed them onto cattle cars and sent them to Poland."

Samuel pressed his wife's arm tightly against his body. "Every day in the railroad station, a thousand beautiful young boys and girls came, carrying rucksacks, and every day five thousand adults came with them, parents, relatives, weeping at the departure of their children."

Breindel began to sob.

"After the young people were gone," Samuel said, "they were the young men and women who could have fought against the Germans, the Germans began to snatch the older people. They closed the streets and pulled off every Jew they caught. The Jews began to hide during the day, so the Germans worked at night. They entered every house. The first night they took more than three thousand Jews."

Three thousand in Italy had clamored to come aboard our ship to get to America. In Brussels, three thousand had been captured in one night.

Samuel was still talking. "Many of us Jewish men and women joined the Brigade Blanche to do underground work. We were very active; we broke into offices and burned documents with lists of Jewish names. We sabotaged trains taking raw materials out of Belgium to Germany; we assassinated Belgian collaborationists; we even made raids on the bureaus that printed meal tickets. Each month we got about two hundred thousand food stamps. We distributed them to the underground, to the resistance movement, to the Jews."

Samuel was standing tall now, like a resistance fighter.

"And your children?" I asked in a low voice.

"We hid them in a Belgian monastery. Most of the Jews hid their children with monks and nuns and peasants. Ninety-five percent of the Belgian people were very good to the Jews. But then it became hard for the Belgians. The Gestapo broke into their homes searching for Jews. Each day articles in an anti-Semitic newspaper, *L'Ami du Peuple,* said, 'Don't tell me where a Jew lives, just tell me his phone number; we'll get him and you'll be rewarded.' It became impossible for us to stay. We decided to try to escape. But the children were too small to run with us. They would never survive. We had to make the most terrible decision of our lives."

Racking sobs shook his body.

I could no longer write. I brushed aside the tears falling on my notebook.

"We had to leave our children—in the Belgian monastery. Will we ever find them again?"

More people were pressing forward now, some urging one another, "Tell her your story. Let her know what happened to us. Let her be our witness."

A man in prison pajamas made a path through the crowd for a buxom woman with a round, jovial face and dimpled cheeks; her contagious smile was illuminated by two stainless-steel front teeth. In her fifties, she wore her light-brown hair in youthful curls down to her shoulders.

"Mathilda, tell the American lady," the pajama-clad man said, "how you ran a whole underground station and saved over one hundred families, and how they caught you and locked you up and kept you in a cellar with ice for ten days with the ice dripping on you."

Mathilda Nitsch smiled, and it seemed to me all the faces around us began to smile too.

"Why did I help all these people?" She repeated my question. "Why? Because I have belief in God."

The group shushed one another, eager to hear the story of this woman whose openness and obvious love of human beings seemed to embrace us all.

"I am a Catholic, a Roman Catholic. I could not understand why they killed Jews, who were innocent people, so I helped them escape. I stole false passports from the chief of police himself. You see, I had a boardinghouse in Susak on the northern coast of Yugoslavia, though I am Austrian by birth and a Czech citizen because I married a Czech officer. But I have not heard from my husband since early in the war."

She stopped talking, no longer smiling. The people honored her silence. Then the smile returned.

"I was very happy in Susak. I lived there for fifteen years. Then the Nazis came and began to throw people into jail. That's when I decided to help them escape. I hid them in my boardinghouse, gave them the false passports I had stolen, and then I took them to other friends in Fiume.

"Fiume," she explained, "is right next door to Susak in Yugoslavia, but it belongs to Italy. Most of the Italians—though not the secret police—are much better to the Jews than the Nazis. So at night, in Fiume, we put the people on boats that took them across the Adriatic to other parts of Italy, where we hoped Italian peasants would hide them."

The people around us did not stir, wholly absorbed as this unlikely looking heroine spun her tale of courage and faith. The Mediterranean was lake-calm.

"Finally, the OVRA, the Italian secret police, caught me. That's when they put me in the ice-storage cellar for ten days to make me talk. There was no air. Ice-cold water dripped on my face and head and the ceiling and the walls. Water was in my shoes and over my feet. Ice water was all around."

Once again the luminous smile infected us. "The OVRA wanted to know who worked with me. Some of my friends were the police themselves in Susak and Fiume. There were others, too. We all worked together to help people escape. I wouldn't give out their names. I wouldn't tell anything.

"Finally the OVRA saw they couldn't find anything out from me, so they sent me to the concentration camp in Ferramonte. I was there for four months, but I still didn't tell them anything."

"Brave woman," the gaunt man interrupted. "How many people are alive because of this one woman!"

"I don't know much about politics," Mathilda said. "I am here only because I saved others. I didn't want any other pay. God will see to it that I am taken care of in spite of the fact that I am so poor."

"God will help you." A small elderly woman embraced Mathilda. "God will help you because you saved people out of the goodness of your heart. You are a *gute neshuma*—a good soul."

Mathilda's light eyes were flecked with happiness.

"Now, going to America, my greatest hopes are being answered. Please"—she put her hand on mine—"please tell the people of America that I give them a thousand thanks."

EIGHT

OUR GREATEST DANGER lay in the Mediterranean. Nazi bombers and Nazi U-boats scouted the waters, searching for convoys like ours.

The captain's orders, which I had read out in German on the loudspeaker, were rigidly adhered to. Each morning, alarm bells rang through the ship for the air-raid drill. Swiftly we donned life jackets and hurried to our battle stations. After dusk, the *Henry Gibbins* looked like a ghost ship, with no lights, no people on deck. Even the officers stomped out their cigarettes before they emerged into the blackout. Only our engines kept their rhythmic pounding; we moved swiftly at fifteen knots.

More warships joined us. By our third day at sea, we were a flotilla of twenty-nine vessels: thirteen warships escorting sixteen troop and cargo ships.

"Those two ships running parallel to us"—the navy officer standing with me on the flying deck handed me his binoculars—"they're filled with Nazi POWs."

I felt a wave of revulsion. "Why are Nazi POWs in this convoy?"

"They're our protective covering," he said. "Any Nazi warships trying to attack us on the surface would have to attack those prisoner-of-war ships first."

"It's bizarre. Nazis protecting the refugees they created, the soldiers they wounded."

"It's a good thing the soldiers don't have guns. Those POWs might never make it to the States."

"But why do we have to bring shiploads of German prisoners to America?"

"There's a real labor shortage back home, especially on the farms. A lot of the POWs are keeping our farms and factories going. From what I hear, we've brought in over one hundred thousand POWs."

I blurted out, "We're bringing in Nazi soldiers who killed our boys on the beaches of France and in Italy. And no one complains, not one word. If I tell you—I have to tell you"—I was speaking incoherently—"we went through hell, we waited so long that millions died before we could get even these one thousand refugees into the U.S. And Lord only knows what the isolationists in Congress can still do to us after we land."

I thought bitterly:

One hundred thousand Nazi POWs.

One thousand refugees.

. . .

Sunday night, our third night at sea, I woke up with a start. Bells were ringing. Orders were coming in rapid succession on the loudspeaker.

"Enemy planes overhead. Crew and gunners to battle stations. Civilian personnel and wounded soldiers don life jackets but do not move. Remain in your bunks. Repeat: Civilians and soldiers, don life jackets but do not move. Remain in your bunks."

The orders for civilians, I decided, were not for me. My battle station was with the refugees. I looked at my watch. It was two-thirty in the morning.

I jumped out of my bunk and pulled on a pair of slacks, a warm sweater, and my life jacket. What do you save? flashed through my head. What do you take with you if the ship sinks? Passport? Ridiculous. Camera? Useless in the water. My notebooks, the most precious things I had—they would be washed out. No matter, the material in them was in my brain, my guts. The only things you save, I decided, are human lives.

Suddenly I realized that each person reacts differently to imminent death. Caroline lay back on her bunk wearing only her panties and brassiere. "Hell," she drawled, "Ah'm goin' back to sleep. Ah've been through enough air raids. If they get us, Ah might just as well be sleepin' as awake."

Mary stood up, her blond hair tousled. "Ruth, if they hit us with those damn aerial torpedoes, it will be bad. We won't have a chance. I've been in hospitals after these raids. It's god-awful what happens to people who get hit. If it's torpedoes they'll get our boat and they'll get all of us, bad."

In another cabin, one of the older nurses sat writing her will.

I hurried through the narrow causeway, holding on to the wall of the ship, groping my way to the steep ladder that led down to the refugees' holds.

Could our ship withstand a direct hit? Army transport ships had taken a terrible beating in the early Lend-Lease convoys to Murmansk. Many had been dynamited in the frozen waters of the Soviet

Arctic, in the Atlantic, in the Mediterranean. Could our thirteen escort ships protect us from bombers? Would the antiaircraft guns knock out the planes before they dropped their deadly fire on us?

Fear pulsed through my body, but I pushed it aside. No time for fear—everything in me was focused on the refugees. Were they in panic? What about the children, the women, the sick? I gripped the rail tightly as I sped down the ladder.

There was an eerie hush. In the semidarkness I looked out at the vast expanse of tiers of bunks squeezed together. People lay in their life jackets, absolutely still. Even the babies seemed to sense something so dangerous they would not cry.

Army and refugee doctors moved up and down the tight aisles, here and there handing out sugar-coated placebos to those who lay frozen. A few men stood at the foot of the ladder, ready to rush up if they had to. But there was no hysteria, no panic.

I walked through the holds talking to people in a low voice, patting some on the arm, taking the hands that some of the women stretched out toward me, stroking the foreheads of children who lay wide-eyed and still.

Manya Hartmayer, her long hair pulled back, stood beside her bunk wrapped in her life jacket. I heard her praying, "Oh, God, please don't let us go down in the water. We're so close to America and still so far. God, what it means to me, to be saved and brought on this ship from so horrible a time, those terrible years. Please don't let us go down in the water. Please, God."

The sound of antiaircraft and machine guns ruptured the silence. Some of the people began to applaud. Rolf Kuznitzki, a sixteen-year-old, called to me exuberantly, "Listen to those guns!" Even in the dim light I could see his cheeks burning with excitement. "They're shooting at the Nazis," he said. "For years now, whenever they came over us we had to run or hide. I hope the gunners get every single one of them!"

Slowly, thick black smudge filtered down into the holds. The people began coughing, choking. A few cried out in panic, but they were instantly calmed by their neighbors.

Two MPs appeared, wearing gas masks.

"What's happening?" I asked.

One of the MPs moved his mask aside. "It's a smokescreen. The escort ships have blacked us out. You know the orders—in case of attack, the warships have to close in, protect our ship first."

"That's to conceal the outside of the ship. But why the smudge inside?"

"Snafu. The boys who were supposed to close the intake vents must have panicked and run below. Now the smoke is coming through all our intake valves. We're trying to fix it, but you've got to tell the people not to move and to keep absolutely still."

They were still.

The MP added, "The rest of the ship is going crazy. Especially some of the guys who cracked up in Anzio."

I made my way back up the ladder to the deck. Gunners in the circular gun tubs pointed their weapons at the sky. I groped along the wall until I reached the ladder that led to the soldiers' holds.

At the top of the stairs, I heard men screaming, coughing. Someone shouted hysterically, "Goddamn those Jews. I made it in Casablanca. I made it in Bizerte. I made it in Anzio. Now I'm going to die."

Abe Tauber came toward me. "It's murder down here, Ruth," he said. "How is it with the refugees?"

"Absolutely calm."

"Stay here, Ruth. Maybe you can help."

Abe cupped his hands around his mouth and yelled as if he were on a football field, "Hey, you guys, listen to this."

I walked a few steps down the steep ladder, then waited. The men on the three-tiered bunks closest to me grew silent first. Then the silence moved in waves back through the blackout smudge in the hold.

"Fellows," Abe yelled, "Ruth's just come from the front of the ship with the refugees. I've asked her to talk to us for a few minutes."

I began slowly. "I've just left—"

"Louder!" a voice yelled in the distance.

"If you're all quiet," Abe shouted, "you'll hear her."

I raised my voice, trying to penetrate the hold.

"The refugees are scared—sure, all of us are scared—but they're still. Even the children are still. Even the babies. They've been through hell—"

"Hell! Who's been through more hell than we have in Anzio and Cassino?"

A soldier beat his fist against the cast that imprisoned his leg. "It's because of those lousy Jews!" he screamed. "That's why they're attacking us."

"But they're not all Jews," I said quietly.

I heard a few gasps of amazement.

"A refugee," I said, "can be anyone—anyone who's homeless, anyone who's displaced."

A young soldier leaned forward. "I'm Jewish and I'm damn glad you're bringing these people over. But it's true, isn't it, most of these people you're bringing to America are Jews?"

I was suddenly grateful to Stauber for his statistics. "Eight hundred seventy-four are Jews; the rest are Catholics, Protestants, Greek Orthodox. Let me tell you about one of them, a Catholic." Briefly, I told them Mathilda's story.

"Go on," Abe said. "We should all know what these people have been through."

I told them of the hundreds of men and women crushed into trucks, choking to death from the lime. The Yugoslav doctor who had watched five hundred people shot each day. The thousand boys and girls in Belgium deported each day. Children hidden in monasteries, their parents lying so quietly now up front, anguished; were the children alive? Would they ever see them again?

The hold was growing quieter. "This air raid is one more episode in their flight. Most of them have put their faith in God and in our AA gunners." The sounds of silence filled the hold.

I climbed back up to the deck. An officer told me, "We counted thirty planes over us so far."

"And they haven't bombed us?"

"Damn lucky. Looks as if they're on their way to another mission and don't want to waste their bombs on us."

The black smudge was disappearing. The antiaircraft guns were still. "Stand easy," came through the loudspeaker. I looked at my wristwatch. It was three-fifteen, just one hour since the ship's bells had rung.

NINE

No ONE SLEPT.

In the morning we gathered on the main deck, talking, laughing, rejoicing. Some stretched out on the iron floor, watching the upturned bowl of cloudless blue. We were alive. One more miracle of survival.

Around us, the ships in the flotilla churned up pathways of white foam while we relived our escape from death.

"I was in the toilet when the air-raid alarm was sounded," said David Levy, a dark-haired Yugoslav in his early twenties, half laughing, half still not believing his luck. "Somebody in the crew locked up all the watertight compartments, so I couldn't come out. I kept thinking, All these years everyone in my family was killed, and I saved myself; now I'm going to die in a toilet."

The air raid gave the *Henry Gibbins* a new aura, like a maritime fortress on alert. The gunners sat tense in the elevated tubs, manning machine guns, watching for planes and enemy subs. Around us sailors tested the winches and practiced swinging lifeboats from their davits into the sea.

"If only we were past Gibraltar," the MP medic on the refugee deck told me apprehensively. A soft-spoken soldier, he had endeared himself to us the first day when he ripped the back off a wooden crate, lined the box with bottles of iodine and Mercurochrome, gauze pads, and adhesive tape, and set up an outdoor clinic, bandaging children's cuts, dispensing aspirin, quinine, and good cheer.

"Once you're past Gibraltar," he said, "once you're out in the Atlantic, you're still not home free but somehow you feel safer; there's more room out there to maneuver away from the U-boats."

In the sick bay, I walked toward a middle-aged woman nursing her baby.

"Did you give birth on the ship?" I asked Olga Maurer.

She laughed. "No, he was born in an American jeep."

"A jeep!"

"Yes, on the way to the ship." Her laughter was infectious, her words spilling over each other. "I never thought I would have another baby. I'm over forty." She chuckled. "It happened like this. We escaped from Vienna to Italy, my husband, my boy Walter, and me. When the Nazis came, the Italians first hid us in a tunnel; then they ran with us to the mountains until some Canadian patrol soldiers came to tell us, No more Nazis. Such a celebration the Italians made for us in the moonshine! Such a honeymoon I had, at my age, with Leon! That's when I got pregnant."

Sitting up in her hospital bed, Olga told me how one of the men helping to select the refugees, charmed, I was sure, by her zest for life, accepted the Maurers' application to join the one thousand, although Olga was in her ninth month.

She was put into a command car and taken for the night to a women's hospital in Potenza. A doctor examined her and assured her that the baby was still high in her womb. The next morning she walked out of the hospital to see a convoy of trucks loaded with refugees from the Potenza area. The vehicles were the Palestinian Jewish trucks with the Star of David that Max Perlman had described to me in his office in Naples.

Palestinian and American GI medics made a bed for Olga in the back of a jeep, piling mattresses and khaki army blankets on top of an army cot. They joined the convoy for the hundred-mile drive across the mountains toward Naples. Sitting inside Olga's jeep were two GIs and a doctor in a British uniform with the Star of David insignia. Dr. Joseph Koehler, Olga discovered, had been born in her native Czechoslovakia.

"Doctor," she cried, "you are my *landsmann*. Until now I was afraid. Now it must go perfect."

As if on target, her labor pains began. "Doctor, Doctor . . ." she cried out.

"A few minutes," he pleaded. "Soon we'll be at the headquarters of our Palestinian unit. We have a camp there. We have supplies, everything to help you deliver. A few more minutes."

But Olga's baby began to push his way out of her body.

Dr. Koehler shouted to the driver, "Stop the jeep!" It was twelve and church bells were ringing.

The driver pulled the vehicle to the side of the road, honking his horn to alert the other drivers. The trucks in front of him and behind him slowed down; the convoy came to a halt.

The people in the trucks jumped down. There were empty fields around them. "What's happened? Are we in danger? Is there an air raid somewhere? Are we turning back? What's going on?"

Dr. Koehler leaned out of the jeep. "It's a boy!" he shouted.

The refugees embraced each other, crying, "It's an omen. It's a good omen. It's a new life on the road to the Promised Land."

One of the older men took out his prayer shawl and began to pray. Everyone grew silent. They wanted no disturbances as he offered his prayer to God. Then he turned to some of the people near him and said slowly, "Life—after all the dying. After all the murders and the shootings, after the burnings and the destruction. A baby boy, a Jew to take the place of a murdered baby, a Jew born on our way to freedom."

Together now the refugees recited the Shehecheyanu, the prayer of survival. "Blessed art Thou, O Lord our God, King of the universe, Who has sustained us to this day."

Dr. Koehler, using the water from his canteen, washed the baby and mopped Olga's face. "Your son is beautiful," he said.

He placed the baby on Olga's stomach. She lifted him up. He *was* beautiful, with full pink cheeks, large dark eyes, and dark hair. She counted his fingers and his toes and stroked his body until she was convinced she had a normal child.

Outside the jeep, one of the American GIs who had helped Dr. Koehler told the people, "We've named the baby International Harry, and we predict he's going to be a brigadier general."

I kissed "International Harry" and walked back through the ship to the yeoman's desk to type up Olga's story.

Her one request had been for orange juice. "I dream about it," she had said. A simple problem easily solved. But others had problems we might never be able to solve, raw wounds, deep scars.

I pulled the pages from the typewriter, folded them into my bag, and went back to the deck.

Leo Mirković, the opera singer from Zagreb, surrounded by a bevy of beautiful young women, came toward me.

"I've been looking for you," he said. "I would like to sing opera in America. Will it be possible?"

Mirković's dark eyes peered at me. I judged he was in his sixties. I learned later he had just turned forty. He was medium height with dark thinning hair. Deep ridges in his cheeks dimpled constantly as he spoke. He was gaunt and skeletal. "Do you think I can sing in one of your opera houses?"

"I can't make any promises," I told him. "They're making decisions right now in Washington."

"I will sing for anybody. Anytime. Singing is my life." He waved his arms as if he were on a stage.

Edith Semjen, a slender blonde with a husky voice, drew a pack of cigarettes from her pocket and lit one for Mirković and one for herself. "Leo," she teased, "why don't you tell her about your great love affairs in Zagreb?"

Before he could speak, another woman joined us. "Mirković,"

she asked, "do you want your pajamas washed today?" She turned to me, explaining, "He came aboard with one pair of pajamas, good silk ones, and we women take turns each day washing them."

"Not me." Edith tossed her thick blond hair. "I'm willing to give him a cigarette, but that's it. Go on, Leo, tell her about your girlfriends at the opera."

Mirković laughed. Briefly, still circled by young women, he told us how he, like many of the Yugoslavs on the ship, had escaped to Split, on the Italian-occupied Dalmatian coast. Italian police arrested him, put him on a boat, then a train, where the prisoners were chained together. Determined to survive, he began to sing Italian songs, and he so enchanted the Italian guards that they unchained all the prisoners. They confined him in a little town called Zibello in the province of Parma.

"We had no women with us," he said, "so I wrote a letter to the Governor of Parma, 'We are all single men; we need women.' The Governor gave us permission to go to the whorehouse once a month. I tell you, the Italians are *menschen*—good human beings."

When the Nazis began deporting Jews from northern Italy, the Zibello chief of police gave him a bicycle to escape with and the names of some people in Parma who put him on a train to Rome, where he lived as an Italian. He showed me his identity card. The face was Mirković's, but the name read ETTORE TESTA.

"For a whole year I worked in the underground, bringing food to refugees and English soldiers that we were hiding out in apartments. We were waiting for you Americans in Rome. When you came, we were so tired, so hungry and sick, we couldn't shout, 'Welcome, Americans!'"

Once again he flung his arms out.

"Now I can shout it. Now I can rest, I can eat, and maybe, in America, I will be able to sing."

He threw his head back and sang the words he could not shout in Rome.

"Welcome, Americans!"

TEN

"FOR ME," Manya Hartmayer said, "the invitation from President Roosevelt came almost too late."

The noonday sun streaked gold through her shoulder-length hair. She was tall, painfully thin, her blue-green eyes sunken in her delicately boned face. But she moved with flowing grace.

"I was in five concentration camps. I tried to escape from one of them, but a prison guard caught me and kicked me in the back. For weeks I lay in the corner of the camp like an animal. I couldn't breathe."

"How old are you, Manya?"

The blue-green eyes looked weary. "I am young, but my heart is two hundred years old. I don't know where my family is: Papa, my brothers, Sigi and Willie. They're children—fourteen and fifteen. Will I ever see them again?"

She stared into the Mediterranean as if she were conjuring up their faces from the water. "See this shirt?" A man's dark cotton shirt hung over her emaciated body. "It was Papa's. He gave it to me when we were still together in the concentration camp in France—in Rivesaltes. Every day there were transports coming and going. They put Papa on one of the transports. That's when he pulled off his shirt and gave it to me so that I would have something for the cold nights."

She turned her face away from me.

"Then Sigi and Willie disappeared. Only Mama and I were still left, and then one day we were taken away too, and we ended up in Camp de Gurs. I couldn't stand seeing the desperate faces of the people around me, so whenever I had a chance I started to sing to cheer them up. I sang all the songs I had learned and loved since I was a little girl: Yiddish, French, German. I even learned an English song—'South of the Border, Down Mexico Way.' Anything I knew. I had to stay alive! Every time a transport came in, we rushed to see who was on it. Every time a transport was sent away, all the people who were left cried. They knew they would never see those people again.

" 'Don't cry,' I said to them. 'We will make it.' And I sang more songs, and the Germans and the French went on deporting the Jews.

"One day a Frenchwoman walked through the camp looking for children whose parents had been deported. She had several permits to take them out. She had been in the camp before and heard me sing, and she knew me. There was one permit left, so she asked, 'Where is the girl who sings?'

"She told me a lot of money was being collected from French Jewish families to save some of the children and get them out of Gurs. She told me I would go to an orphanage in the *département* of Cantal. I went to Mama to tell her I didn't want to go; I didn't want to be separated from her. But she was very angry with me. 'Manya, if you stay, I can never escape. You must go!'

"The next day—it was still dark—I climbed into a truck with the rest of the children, my body shaking all over, I was crying bitterly. While I was in the orphanage, I got a postcard from Papa. He had escaped to the village of Saint-Martin-Vésubie near Nice. Somehow he found out where I was. 'Manyele,' he wrote, 'the *leichter* are coming to you.' In Yiddish *leichter* are candles. It meant the fire is burning, the fire is destroying; so we called the Nazis *leichter,* the destroyers. It was our code.

"I was in danger again. The next day, very early in the morning, I disguised myself as an old lady with a babushka around my head. I went to the railroad station without any ID papers or any permission; I knew the consequences. I took the train to Nice, but I had to get off in Marseille to change trains. The next train was delayed, so I spent the whole night in the station wandering from one place to another, hiding in dark corners. My heart pounded like crazy when I saw a uniform.

"Finally the train arrived in the morning. When I was on it, I felt a little better. But pretty soon somebody came into the compartment and said, 'The Bosch are asking everybody for papers.'

"I pulled myself together and walked out heading for the lavatory. I locked myself in. Soon loud voices shouted '*Aufmachen!*' Heavy knocks crashed against the door. I told myself, They will have to kick the door in. I won't open it. If they break in, I will jump out the window. I got ready to jump out.

"The train was moving fast. Then all of a sudden I heard nothing. Whatever took them away from that door saved me. I found Papa and my brothers in Saint-Martin-Vésubie in the mountains. We were together again. You can imagine what it was like to find each other, to be together.

"But Mama's girlfriend, Regina, wrote us that Mama was very, very ill. She contracted typhus. She lost her hair and had holes all over her body where they tried to squeeze out the pus. There was no way to help her. We prayed every day that she would get better, that she would be back with us again.

"Then we heard the Nazis were coming to Saint-Martin-Vésubie. We had to escape over the Alps."

As Manya talked, a small group assembled around us, taking turns to tell of an incredible trek from the southern French villages across the Alps to Italy.

At the beginning of the war, Mussolini had resisted Hitler's demands that he attack the French. Then, just before France surrendered, Il Duce acquiesced and attacked. As a reward, Hitler gave him control of some of the French towns and villages along the Riviera. The villages, like Saint-Martin-Vésubie, were filled with Jewish refugees who had escaped from the Nazis, from French gendarmes, from Poles and Ukrainians, and from Ustachi fascists in Yugoslavia.

Interrupting one another, the people on the iron deck talked of the climb. Young Adam Munz began the story as we seated ourselves in a small area in the bow of the ship. Manya sat beside me, listening, as Adam described the trek.

"Our flight began September eighth, 1943, the day Mussolini capitulated. The Italian soldiers took off and began to hurry home. The Germans knew that many of the Italians had been protecting us, giving us false papers with Italian names. Though we had to report to the police every day, they let us live among the peasants who took us in. Most people don't know about the Italians. They had almost no food themselves, but whatever they had they shared with us.

"The Italian soldiers fled. We knew in our bones the Nazis would be coming immediately and would either shoot us or deport us. Before dawn the next morning, all of us, all the twelve hundred in our village, packed whatever we could. We had baskets tied around with rope, knapsacks, and suitcases, and we started to climb the Alps through the famous La Madonna della Finestra Pass, over six thousand feet high.

"We were a long straggly line of people. You can imagine how far back twelve hundred people extended. We looked like a string of ants scrambling up a mountain.

"That first day, we kept climbing and climbing until at last, exhausted, we reached a cow pasture. We were still in the French part of the Alps, afraid that the Nazis would be coming right after us. Still, we had to stop. We couldn't climb in the dark for fear we'd lose our footing or lose some people. So we lit fires, wrapped ourselves in whatever clothing we had. My father gave me my first cigarette. 'It will help keep you warm.' "

"We tried to sleep a little," Manya continued the story. "Maybe Papa slept, but I didn't. I kept seeing Mama. Then early in the morning we began to climb again up the mountain, and each step I took was taking me farther away from Mama. I think I wet with my tears every stone I touched.

"There were fewer and fewer trees. When I looked back, a beautiful lake we passed glistened like a small jewel. I stopped momentarily and said to myself, 'Oh, God, so much beauty in this world and we cannot be part of it.'

"I lost the sole of my shoe. Somebody found a piece of wire and tied the sole back on. My feet were so sore, but I couldn't go bare-foot on those stones. I had only summer clothes on and I was freezing. I saw the snow peaks high above us. I said, 'Papa, I don't know how we will make it.'

"We kept on climbing. I had to hold on with my hands. There were stones and rocks. We were at the head of a long line of peo-ple. My brothers, Sigi and Willie, went back down as much as they could to help other people up again. I saw them struggling on the mountainside, pulling older people and women and children with their bare hands."

Ićak Wajs took up the tale. Ićak, a huge man with a crescent face and pouches under his chin, had lost his entire family. He had at-tached himself to the Munzes. "You know how to survive," he had told Adam's father when he learned that the Munzes had escaped from six different villages, each time just ahead of the Nazis.

"People of seventy and eighty were climbing those walls," Ićak said. "If you tell this in America, people will say it is a fantasy, but it was no fantasy. Babies suckled their mother's breasts, and when the milk gave out they suckled blood. Rabbi Rothschild carried a Torah in one arm and a baby in the other."

Ićak pointed to Adam. "Adam took the baby and climbed with it. There was a man who had been crippled by the Germans. He had such terrible fear that he took his crutches and climbed with us. A pregnant woman began her labor and still she climbed."

He shut his eyes. "We climbed with fear. But it was more than fear. It was like the wind of God leading us—the Ruakh Elohim."

The midmorning sun blistered the iron deck. But no one moved.

Young Adam went on. "We were still climbing on the French side of La Madonna Pass. The Italian side would start at the sum-mit. We had lost some people the first day. They were so frightened that the Nazis would be waiting on top of the mountain that they turned around and went back."

The ship's engines hummed as we plowed through the Mediter-ranean, keeping our place in the flotilla of speeding ships. I shut my eyes, blocking out the water and the rays of the noonday sun. I was climbing the Alps with Manya, Ićak, and Adam.

"We couldn't stop," Adam said. "We kept trying to reach the top of the mountain. We knew that the Italian border began there on the top with a military outpost. Finally, late in the afternoon on that second day, we reached the border. There was a large cement barracks; Italian carabinieri came out and greeted us. We were so happy to see them. We told them we were running from the Nazis. They understood. They knew that the Italian soldiers too were running. They told us to come into the barracks. We were shivering with cold. Hungry, thirsty, exhausted, we piled into the barracks on top of one another.

"During the night the pregnant woman gave birth to her baby, and the next day she climbed down with the rest of us. Descending was harder on many of the people than climbing up."

Adam stopped talking. There was silence. Then Ićak spoke.

"We descended into a valley. We had crossed the mountains alive. Famous mountain climbers sometimes can't make it. Not one of us died. It was a miracle. Everyone was so tired. Where should we go? We came into small Italian alpine villages—only to hear something terrible.

" 'The Germans are here!' "

Nearly five hundred were captured by the SS. Many were picked up on the streets of the little villages by Nazi patrols.

"After such suffering and loss," Ićak said, "after climbing those terrible mountains, they were deported to Poland—to die."

Manya took up the story of their new flight from the Nazis. "We were sleeping in a barn—Papa and the boys. We were together, all except Mama. As far as we knew she was still in Gurs. In the morning we heard someone yell, '*Die Deutschen sind hier.* The Germans are here.' We jumped up and ran back into the Alps. The Italian peasants were wonderful, but they were scared to death. They told us several villages had been burned because they hid Jews.

"So we hid out in the woods with no blankets, no food, no shelter. My father traded his gold wedding band for a piece of canvas, so we had some covering over our heads when it rained."

Manya put her hand over her eyes. A deep sigh rose from her body. "We ran into the Italian partisans. They wouldn't take us either; they said they didn't have enough food or ammunition. We kept wandering in the mountains until we knew it was too dangerous to stay together. We had to separate. It was a terrible decision. Somehow I ended up in Rome and the wonderful nuns hid me in a convent for nine months. If not for them, I wouldn't have made it."

She stopped talking. Her forehead was wet with perspiration. "Why is it so emotional? Why can't I talk about it? In the convent there was hardly any food, only old chestnuts for breakfast, lunch, and dinner, which the nuns shared with me to keep me alive. I don't know now where my father is. I don't know where my brothers are. I don't know if Mama is alive."

On the deck behind us, I could hear people talking. The MP medic was dispensing pills and cheer. Children were running, laughing. But our group did not stir.

ELEVEN

A SUDDEN SILENCE WOKE ME.

The ship's engines, pulsing rhythmically day and night like the heart of a man, had stopped. The ship lay immobile.

I switched on the light over my bunk. It was one o'clock in the morning, just twenty-two hours since our first air raid. Were more bombers over us? Were more Nazi planes ferreting us out?

But this time no bells were ringing, no alarms sounding, no voices piercing the ship. Only the dead silence. Someone knocked on our cabin door. I flung on a robe. Caroline and Mary sat up, startled, in their bunks.

An MP stood at the door. "It's a submarine attack. You must go below and tell the refugees to be absolutely still."

I changed swiftly into warm clothes. In the silence of the ship, my heart pounded in my ears.

I raced down to the refugees' holds. Most of the people were awake, lying frozen in their bunks. I put my fingers to my lips to show them that we must not even whisper. Some lay staring up at the narrow ledge above them, their eyes glazed with terror.

In the weird silence, my mind conjured up a picture of a Nazi U-boat homing in on us with deadly missiles, piercing the welded steel, exploding into fire and smoke and chaos. I walked the narrow paths between the bunks, hoping to allay their fears and mine with a squeeze of the hand, telling myself, Don't worry, with all the guns aboard and warships around us we'll survive the submarine just as we survived the bombers last night. I wasn't comforted. The ship lay motionless, like a cornered man playing dead.

After a while, my heart stopped thumping. Convinced that the refugees would remain silent, I went back up the ladder to the main deck.

The ships had formed a double column to sail through the Straits of Gibraltar. A searchlight from shore now swept across our deck, then traveled down the water, east to west, lighting up the doubled column. A few minutes later, an airplane, burning navigational lights, flew low along the path the searchlight had paved. It was flying west to east, from the Atlantic to the Mediterranean. Was it a friendly British plane, coming out of the airfield on the Rock, or a Luftwaffe plane flying out from Spain?

Our guns were frighteningly silent.

I climbed down the ladder to the soldiers' hold. They lay rigid. If there was panic, it was internalized.

We were like a ship of living ghosts.

Out of the stillness, a soldier in a bunk near the ladder said hoarsely, "It's because of you and the lousy Jews."

Suddenly we heard the all-clear. The silence broke, the engines churned, pulsed, breathed. We were moving.

The hold came alive. "We made it. By God, we made it." A few of the soldiers wept.

I climbed back up and paced the deck. We had been saved again. But the soldier's words, mouthed in anger, rang through my head. Perhaps it was hysteria; perhaps the thought of dying in a submarine attack had made him lose control, and he needed a scapegoat.

I leaned against the rail, tormented. The fire of anti-Semitism Hitler had lit in Germany was reigniting brushfires in other countries. And one of those brushfires was right on our ship.

The irony of it. On this one ship we had refugees running from the Nazis and soldiers wounded by the Nazis. Both were victims. Both had a common enemy. But the angry soldier could not see that we were all in the same boat, in the same war.

Lieutenant Martin joined me at the rail. "I guess you can't sleep either," he said.

"We had a pretty close call, didn't we?"

"How close we'll never know. Our sonar picked up propeller sounds. We're pretty sure it was a U-boat that caught the sound of our propellers. Thank the Lord, when we turned our engines off, the sub lost us."

Mirković's voice floated across the deck. Sitting in a circle of women and men, he beckoned me to join them. "Come sing with us."

I sat on the deck next to him, looking at some of the young women, who were seductive enough to stop traffic on Times Square. Maybe if the soldiers could see them and hear them sing, we could put out one little brushfire of prejudice.

"How would it be, Mirković," I asked during a pause, "if we got a group together like this to entertain the soldiers?"

"Entertain the soldiers! I'd love it."

"Do you mean it, Ruth?" Manya asked. "Would you really let us entertain the soldiers? We owe them so much."

"Wait here," I said. "I'll be right back."

On the bridge I found Captain Shea. "Captain, would it be possible to relax the rules against fraternization?"

He seemed disconcerted. "Do you realize what bedlam you'd create? You've got to keep the soldiers and refugees apart to run a tight ship. Some of those gals you've got are pretty . . . uh . . . uh . . . and some of our soldiers are . . . uh . . ."

"Captain, that's not what I mean. We've got some wonderful singers. Professionals. I'd like to see the rules relaxed so the refugees can go to the soldiers' deck and put on a show."

Shea's Irish face lit up. "Say, that's a first-rate idea. When can you put it on?"

"I can round the artists up right now. We can have the performance tomorrow."

"We'll give you all the help you need. I'll watch it myself."

Elated, I went down the bridge to search for Abe Tauber. Standing in the doorway, I sat him in the midst of a group of wheelchaired soldiers. Some of the men were laughing. A few looked withdrawn, morose. I waited until the laughter subsided.

"Abe." I drew him aside. "I need your help."

It took less than a minute to tell him the plan. His enthusiasm was like an electric charge.

We hurried through the ship to the foredeck and beckoned everyone toward the area in front of the blackboard. I introduced Abe, who stood in his white undershirt, his freckled face eager and smiling. He was poised for action.

"I've asked Abe to help us put on a show for the soldiers," I told the people. "We're asking for volunteers—singers, dancers, entertainers. Any of you who would like to take part, please come forward right now."

The crowd moved to make an aisle for volunteers. Mirković came forward with Manya and Edith Semjen.

"Otto Presser," someone yelled. "Where is Otto Presser?"

"He's down below," someone else called out.

Two men went to the 'tween deck and soon returned with the

small vaudevillian. Behind him came the composer Charles Abeles, also small, pale-faced, with steel-rimmed glasses, and a sixty-two-year-old violinist, Samuel Landau.

More singers and musicians approached us.

Abe flung his arms out wide. "We have enough talent here to entertain a whole army. Let's begin."

We began the rehearsal on the deck, with the refugees themselves our first audience, applauding enthusiastically.

Someone handed Mirković a white handkerchief. He folded the handkerchief into a triangle, put it into the breast pocket of his silk pajamas, and bowed to the audience. "One has to preserve the dignity of one's appearance at all times," he announced.

The refugees sat listening, their faces wreathed in delight, as he began to sing. The years of flight and hunger had not damaged his glorious voice. Yet there were some who sat hugging their bodies, so enclosed in grief that they seemed to hear nothing.

In the yeoman's office I typed an announcement of the performance and cranked it out on the mimeograph machine. Then I climbed up and down ladders distributing copies in the pilot house, the mess hall—wherever I could find soldiers, passengers, and crew.

Later that night I lay awake in my bunk. There was no air in the cabin. I knew we had talent and beauty. Still, I had no idea how the soldiers would react. Would the few who had shown their resentment to me lash out against the refugees? And what effect would that resentment have?

Perhaps it would have been better to prepare the soldiers. Perhaps I should have typed up some of the case histories for distribution among the men. Let them know of Mirković's bravery, starving himself while he helped feed not only refugees but British airmen hidden in Rome.

In the dark, I shook my head. Case histories were scarcely the kind of reading matter that wounded soldiers were looking for. They had suffered too much themselves. They might listen and even enjoy a few words about International Harry or the climb over the Alps. But as more people each day came forward, revealing the whole fabric of pain and terror, of courage and survival, I knew I could not capture their stories on a mimeograph machine.

No, the soldiers had to *see* the refugees, *hear* them, *sense* them. I finally fell asleep.

The next day dawned warm, the sea calm. We spent the morning with a dress rehearsal and at two-thirty assembled the troupe.

"Good luck! *Hals und Beinbruch*—break a leg!" some of the refugees shouted as we left our deck, opened the watertight door, and marched through the corridors toward the once-forbidden soldiers' deck.

Abe, in a fresh white shirt and chino pants, patted some of the performers on the back as he moved up and down through the corridor. "You're going to knock those GIs dead."

Through the hatch doorway, I looked out as the deck filled up with soldiers in wheelchairs, heavy casts imprisoning their arms or legs. Others hobbled out on crutches or canes, the walking wounded. Still others came, the battle-weary, the battle-shocked, the ones who, coming home with both legs and arms, would still carry the scars of war.

Behind them came pilots, navigators, bombardiers who had finished their missions, doctors and nurses, army and navy officers, and off-duty crew.

At the stroke of three, Abe stepped onto the improvised stage. Behind him, smiling radiantly as if they were on the stage of Radio City Music Hall, came six of our most beautiful young women.

Instantly the deck came alive with whistle calls and shouts. "Whoopee!" "Hubba hubba!" "Hey, good lookin', what's cookin'?"

"Ladies and gentlemen," Abe shouted, "our national anthem."

Those who could stand rose to their feet; others pulled themselves tall in wheelchairs. The strong young voices filled the deck. Inside the doorway, I sang with them. The land of the free and the home of the brave had never seemed so precious.

Abe, master of ceremonies, began the program with a Bob

Hope–like routine of off-color stories he had picked up in Italy from the troops. The soldiers laughed appreciatively, even as they kept their eyes fixed on the six young women. Feeling the excitement they engendered, the young women waved at the men, who waved back frantically.

"Now, fellows," Abe said, his high-spirited voice ringing out across the crowd, "when you get back to the States—and we're all going to make it safely"—he waved at the warships in our convoy—"I just want you to remember one thing: the language you used on this side of the ocean is not quite the same that we use on the other side, the American side. For example, when you're sitting with your family—and I hope you will soon—you don't say, 'Pass the fuckin' butter.' "

Some of the men slapped their white casts, laughing.

All eyes were on Abe. The afternoon sun burnished his red hair. "And another thing," he went on. "When you get back home, if someone talks about a 'pro' they mean a professional, like a golf pro. They don't mean a prophylaxis station."

More laughter.

"Now"—Abe ended his routine—"it is my pleasure to introduce Edith Semjen from Yugoslavia."

Edith stepped forward.

"Hubba hubba! Look at that tomato!"

Edith motioned to sixteen-year-old Ernest Spitzer. Ernest pulled apart the bellows of his accordion for the opening bars as Edith placed her hands on her hips and in a husky cigarette-coated voice sang "You Are My Sunshine."

The soldiers screamed, "More!" They slapped their thighs and their casts. "Beat me, Daddy, eight to the bar."

Stretching her arms out toward the soldiers, Edith sang the refrain again.

The whistles and shrieks caromed off the deck into the sea.

More shrieks as Manya stepped forward, slender, graceful. A breeze from the water seemed to blow through her father's shirt. Poised and smiling as if she were in a Paris nightclub, she sang an aria from Franz Lehár's operetta *Das Land des Lächelns—The Land of Smiles.*

The soldiers beat on their casts. "More. More. More. More."

"Before the war," Manya said, "before all the terrible things, I learned a Hungarian song in German called 'Pustalied.' It was from a musical comedy and we had the record. That's how I learned a lot of my songs—from records and the movies and the radio."

The soldiers listened, their eyes riveted on the tall young woman singing with a catch in her voice, as if she were singing of her own life, "*Mädel, so bist du.* Young girl, this is what you are."

This was truly what Manya was, I thought, watching the men smiling as I had not seen them smile before. How would they react if they knew that the pale, willowy young woman with the sweet soprano voice had survived five concentration camps?

The Atlantic was becalmed; our ship held its place in the convoy as Abe introduced the other entertainers. The afternoon was speeding as Otto Presser did a song-and-dance vaudeville routine. Livia Finger, a handsome star of the Budapest Opera, sang "The Last Rose of Summer."

Anny Pick, a young vivacious brunette, sang Yiddish songs, moving her hips and her rounded body with such infectious joy in life that the men guffawed.

Eva Bass stepped forward, as waiflike as Edith Piaf, with straggly black hair cut like a boy's and dark tragic eyes. In a shabby man's sweater and baggy pants she held the men spellbound.

Like Piaf, she had been a nightclub singer in Paris. Fleeing to Italy, Eva had been thrown into prison, "a victim of politics, a victim of my religion," she had told me one evening as we sat on the deck, her baby Yolanda in her arms, her son Joachim at her side. His twelve-year-old body was that of a six-year-old, his face pinched and frightened. Carrying Yolanda in one arm and, when Joachim could no longer walk, carrying him in the other, she had trekked for sixty kilometers through the fighting lines to reach the Allies.

While Eva's voice pierced the deck, I slipped through the hatch door and walked toward the rail. I stared at the troopship carrying the Nazi prisoners of war and, beyond the POWs, the convoy of warships escorting us to America.

Abe's high, hoarse voice came through the loudspeaker. "Now I have a special treat. The leading baritone of the Yugoslav National Opera. Mr. Leo Mirković."

Mirković, jaunty in his silk pajamas, drew himself tall. "Now I sing," he said, in the words he was learning in our English class, "Italian song."

The soldiers sat absorbed.

He bowed deeply from the waist. "Now in Spanish I sing 'Lolita.' "

Mirković was magic. "For end, I sing aria from *Barber of Seville* by Rossini."

Flinging his arms wide, raising his voice to the heavens, he punctured the air, the ship, the convoy, the whole microcosm of the war with the joyous words, "Fee-gah-ro. Fee-gah-ro. Fee-gah-ro."

The soldiers screamed their delight. Mirković sang encore after encore.

"Another one, Manya," the soldiers shouted. "Come on, Edith." "Eva, come back."

The afternoon sun was beginning to sink. Winds had come up; the Atlantic was growing choppy. But no one moved. Even the bell announcing dinner failed to convince the soldiers the performance had to end. They continued clapping, whistling, calling for more until Abe brought all the performers out to take final bows.

TWELVE

Euphoria and congratulations for the performers spilled over into the morning English class, where people could talk of little else but the performance.

When the lesson ended, the class dispersed, some to write their life stories, others to sun themselves wherever they could find space. I walked toward Dr. Juda Levi, a distinguished-looking silver-haired jurist from Yugoslavia, who sat surrounded by several middle-aged men. Suddenly a little Polish boy raced in front of us, tripping over Dr. Levi's feet.

Levi shouted in Serbo-Croatian, "*Polako, polako!* Go slowly, go slowly!"

But to the Polish Jews on the deck the word *polako* had only one meaning—the denigrating insult *Polack*.

A Pole rushed forward and punched Dr. Levi in the chest. A Yugoslav tackled the Pole. From all over the deck, Poles and Yugoslavs converged, bloodying each other's noses, blackening each other's eyes. New fights and arguments broke out. People hurled insults at each other. MPs, called to the deck, pulled the bruised and angry men apart.

At last calm was restored. Some of the women brought cloths to wipe the blood from the men's faces, though no one was seriously hurt.

During the air raid I had seen ugly prejudice among the soldiers. Now I was seeing ugly prejudice among the refugees.

Angry and disappointed, I went back to my cabin, hoping to be alone to sort out my feelings. The cabin was empty. I stretched out on my bunk.

Here they were, refugees fleeing murder and war, yet they were fighting their own age-old battles as patriots and even chauvinists of the countries that had tried to annihilate them. In the confines of our ship the fight mirrored the Balkanization of Europe.

Captain Korn, Stauber, and I met for our nightly conference in the chaplain's cabin. This night we knew we would have to face the problem of nationality prejudice before it exploded even more violently.

We decided to set up three committees, one representing the Yugoslavs, one the Poles, and one the Austrians and Germans, the major nationalities. Later we could have committees representing the smaller groups. Korn asked Fredi Baum, the multilingual young Yugoslav, to discuss the committees with the people and bring three representatives to meet with us in the morning.

Fredi ushered in three men who had already emerged as leaders: Dr. Juda Levi, representing the Yugoslavs, Dr. Artur Hirt, a judge representing the Poles, and Dr. Ernst Wolff, a well-known novelist who would represent the Austrians and Germans.

Dr. Levi spoke first. "Before we ask our questions, I would like to make a statement. I want to thank the three of you and the great President Roosevelt for saving our lives. Without your help, we would still be wandering, hungry, hunted, unwanted. We are deeply grateful to you for this noble act of humanity."

"Hear, hear." The Polish judge voiced approval.

Levi leaned forward. "Now you have brought us as leaders to discuss our problems. I would say our first problem is critical. How will you house us in America? Will we be thrown together, people from eighteen different countries; will it be the way we are thrown together in the bunks down below? If so, I think it would be a disaster. I strongly recommend that you keep us together according to our nationalities."

"*Behüte Gott!* Heaven forbid!" shouted Dr. Ernst Wolff. He took his glasses off and wiped them with a handkerchief. "You keep us together by nationalities, and what happened yesterday will be nothing compared to the fights that will break out. You'll have chaos."

"It is the only way," Dr. Levi argued. "I wasn't insulting that little Polish boy. It was a question of language. We don't speak the same languages. Put us all together and you will have a crisis every day. We are Christians and Jews, yet even the Jews among us don't speak the same languages. Many of the Ashkenazim who come from Germany or Eastern Europe speak Yiddish. We Sephardim, who come from the Balkans, speak Ladino. It's to Spanish what Yiddish is to Middle High German. Because we're the descendants of the Jews who were expelled from Spain, we have a Spanish background and Spanish culture. We have different values, different points of view. You can't put us together with people from Germany and Poland."

"But among the Jews there is a common bond," I said. "The bond of Jewishness."

"It is not enough," Dr. Levi argued, "to keep us living together under one roof. We can meet together in synagogue, in work, in schools, but living together under one roof—"

"Excuse me, but I disagree with Dr. Levi one hundred percent." Ernst Wolff turned toward me. "I agree with you there is a bond of Jewishness that links us all together. But I see our problem of housing in a different way. I speak as an Austrian, but I can't understand all the Austrian people. I believe you should put people together who have a similarity of interests and culture. Like writers and artists, doctors and lawyers."

Hirt, the Polish judge, curled his thin lips sardonically. "My dear lady and you two gentlemen from America, you should know you have two distinct groups here, the intellectuals and the nonintellectuals. You have the highly educated and the very simple. The wishes of one are not the same as the other. Here, packed like sardines, we are thrown into one kettle. But the two groups, I tell you, must be separated."

Anger was rising in my throat. I tried to keep my voice calm. "Gentlemen, for hundreds of years Europe has been torn by nationality rivalries. Should we be carrying these rivalries onto the ship, into America?"

"Look, madam." Hirt fixed his eyes on me. "You are the government's representative. You are the father—no, forgive me, the mother figure on this ship. You represent the President of the United States. We are talking honestly and openly with you, because we feel you want to help us."

"I do want to help—with all my heart. But you make it difficult. Why all this squabble about how you'll be housed at Fort Ontario? Why bring Europe's sicknesses to America?"

"Because that's the way it's always been—and will always be. Madam, do you think you can change people overnight? You want peace in the camp, separate us."

"By nationalities!" Levi shouted.

"By intellect!" Wolff exploded.

Stauber's cheeks grew purplish red. "We cannot tell you now how people will be assigned to their quarters. I can tell you this, however. You will be living in army buildings that housed troops in the past. They were dormitories for the most part. We are changing that. We are putting in partitions so they will be like apartment houses and families will be kept together. Single people will still be in dormitories. So far that is all we know."

Word of the morning meeting spread across the deck. Dr. Rafailo Margulis came toward me and bowed as if he were still in uniform. He had been a lieutenant colonel in the Yugoslav Royal Army.

"My two sons want to study medicine," he announced. "They were already in medical school when we lived in Belgrade. They will make outstanding doctors."

His two sons were romantic figures on the ship. Rajko, at twenty-five, worked in the ship's dispensary; Aća, or Alex, at twenty-three, spent most of his time courting Renée Reisner, as if they were on a cruise ship. They had met in Aversa, the insane asylum—their assembly point—before boarding the ship.

"You must have the answer." Dr. Margulis pressed me. "You must know whether these young people, so hungry for education, will be able to go to school."

I shook my head, about to tell him I did not know, when the loudspeaker began to crackle.

Everyone stopped talking. Adam Munz was reading the news: in German, then Yiddish, then French and Italian.

" 'Monday, July thirty-first. Thirteen hundred heavy U.S. bombers escorted by eight hundred fighter planes have attacked Berlin.' "

No one moved.

" 'Fires are blazing all over the city. Oil storage tanks are shooting their flames into the sky.' "

Someone murmured, "Dear God, I thank you."

" 'On the Soviet front, the Red Army has reached the outskirts of Warsaw.' "

Adam's voice rang out. "Warsaw is rising!"

THIRTEEN

IN THE NEXT DAYS, while we steamed through the Atlantic, a change came over the refugees and the soldiers. Some of the young women, who had come aboard pale, frightened, haggard, were beginning to blossom as the good food rounded their bodies and the sun and wind brought color to their cheeks. Soldiers found ways to circumvent the nonfraternization orders and came to the deck to talk and flirt with the girls. Some stood inside the waterproof doorway, bringing chocolate and cookies for the children.

The tension on both decks was beginning to relax. Each day Korn, Stauber, and I, meeting with the committee leaders, helped calm the handful of angry men, while I made a discovery—that even in war and danger there is humor on the high seas. The crew of the POW ship were apparently jealous that our ship was the glamorous girl of the convoy. Their captain flashed lights to the flagship that we were out of line in the convoy columns.

Commodore Blau, commanding the convoy, flashed us a gentle rebuke. "Have your men keep better watch."

Captain Shea flashed back, "Sorry. But after all we have a few distractions aboard."

"Any worthwhile?" the commodore queried.

The soldiers had indeed found several worthwhile. Romances grew as young American men made trysts with young women and found dark corners on the ship; even the lifeboats became retreats. Married couples, who could not sleep together in the open dormitory holds, made love under blankets on the deck. The sense that each day we were moving closer to the Promised Land stoked fires that years of hunger and flight had cooled but never extinguished.

On the GI deck, a group of soldiers pelted me with questions.

"When y'all gonna bring those gals back here to sing again?" a Texan with corn-yellow hair and cornflower-blue eyes asked. "Some of them got better gams than Betty Grable."

Laughter rang across the deck. "My wife loves opera," a middle-aged officer said. "She would sure love to hear that opera singer. You think they'll send him to Detroit?"

"We'll only know after we get to the camp in Oswego."

"Hell," the Texan growled, "y'all ain't set to lock those fillies up in a stockade? That's a waste of good stock."

"Maybe it's a good thing we're bringing in a thousand refugees to America," a paraplegic soldier in a wheelchair mused, as if he were talking to himself. "That show you put on—we saw real people, not some picture we got in our heads of refugees. We saw the kind of people Hitler's been trying to exterminate." He looked down at the stumps of his legs. "Maybe Hitler would like to do that to a lot of us Americans."

In the galley, the GIs who served the food adopted our three little Greek girls, Stella, six, Meropi, five, and Evangelina, four, and their mother, Athanasia Economou, a strong-faced woman dressed always in black, whose husband had been killed by a bomb. Nicknaming the children "the Dionne kids," the soldiers built a little table in the galley so that the Greek family could sit and eat while the rest stood at the counters.

Tuck, the bos'n, fixed a saltwater shower on the deck, and all day children ran in and out of the water, laughing and racing each other. Major Allen then surveyed the space. "We gotta give these people a little more room. Let's swing two of these lifeboats off the deck." Tuck was still hoisting one of the lifeboats when a group of women came behind him, hanging their clothes on his line. I recognized Mirković's pajamas.

Time on a ship is different from time on land—especially during wartime. The convoy moved cautiously, scouting the sky and the sea for the enemy; but, for the refugees and the soldiers, time had two frontiers—breakfast and supper. In between were hours to be filled, days, perhaps even weeks. Despite the urgency of reaching a safe harbor, no one could pinpoint how much longer the journey would take. We had already spent a week at sea. The Luftwaffe and *Seebooten* helped chart our course. We filled the time with more English classes, one in American history run by Montgomery of the Red Cross, another in advanced English literature and composition taught by our chief gunnery officer, Lieutenant Don C. Martin. "If my students at the U of Michigan were half as enthusiastic as you," Martin told his overcrowded class, "I'd feel the way I feel on this ship. I'm teaching you, but you're teaching me."

One morning I was at the blackboard teaching English when Major Allen, in charge of the armed escort, stepped around the class and came toward me. "You must tell them," he said, "that the name of the ship is secret. And they must not tell anyone where we came from."

I told the people what Major Allen wanted and then printed on the blackboard THE NAME OF THE SHIP IS SECRET. WE CAME FROM THE NORTH POLE. It was another joke we could share, like "How do you feel? I feel fine" when they were miserable with seasickness. Now, walking around the ship, I could hear people reciting to each other in all accents the litany of their first words of English, "How do you feel? I feel fine. The name of the ship is secret. We came from the North Pole."

The classes were made up mostly of adults and girls; the teenage boys had no time to learn English. They worked as part of the crew, the only refugees with access to the ship's giant-sized refrigerators and freezers. The boys had never seen so much food in their lives—crates of frozen chicken, turkeys, frankfurters, beef, all to feed the 2,200 people on both sides of the ship twice a day.

Each morning the boys took out the food the chief steward requisitioned and delivered it to the galleys. Food, once it left the refrigerators, could never be put back. Each evening, when the danger of Nazi boats detecting us through our garbage was lessened, the boys tossed the uneaten food and even unopened crates into the ocean. For teenagers who had been hungry for years, it was heartbreaking. They were compensated by going back to the galley, where they were given Oreo cookies, an American delicacy. Some wanted onions and lemons.

After each meal, the boys scrubbed the galley and mopped the red linoleum floor. Then, holding twenty-pound sacks in one arm, they threw salt on the floor to prevent anyone from slipping. They had not seen salt since 1941.

The young people could laugh and sing; middle-aged couples could relax under awnings the soldiers put up and hold hands; the children could race around the deck. But the horrors of what they had gone through filled their days and nights.

"I am a refugee, just a single word," Dolly Sochaczewska, a forty-four-year-old Polish woman, told me, as we found a corner on the ship where we could be alone. "The meaning of the word *refugee* can be understood only by those who have heart and are willing to understand."

She had come one morning after the English class. "I am tired now," she said, "but I must talk to you when I'm rested, when my heart stops beating so hard. You are our witness. You are our hope in the new land. Can I meet with you later?" Now in the late afternoon we were talking.

"I am alone," she said. "I belong to the displaced persons. There is no road back to my country. This is why I had to talk to you. I have to continue my life. Until now I could not talk to anyone.

"Just before we came on the ship, I learned that my whole family, parents, three sisters, three brothers, and my fiancé, were killed—tortured first, then killed. Poland, my escape, my life in prison, then in a concentration camp—these I'll never forget. But I am surprised what kind of jokes destiny makes with me. Whenever we were bombarded, I tried to help others. People told me that as a woman I was very brave. I am not brave. I wanted to help those who help life. But I could not talk about my own life without opening the wounds, without tearing off the scabs. My life is an open wound."

I searched for words of sympathy.

"No, don't talk. You have helped me—just by listening."

Each day as we moved closer to America, they brought me their stories of incredible survival.

All through the years of Hitler's occupation of the Balkans, people somehow found ingenious methods of escape. Some of them bought passage aboard unseaworthy vessels whose captains promised to sail them down the Danube and through the Black Sea to Palestine. One of these vessels was the *Pentcho*, an eighty-five-year-old paddlewheel steamer. In charge were a captain and his wife who were both drug addicts.

Hans Goldberger, forty-seven, a former textile merchant from Bratislava, Czechoslovakia, described the voyage of the *Pentcho* one evening when rain had driven us off the deck. I invited him and his wife, Jolan, a dress designer, to my cabin. Mary and Caroline were working in the sick bay, treating the seasick, as the *Henry Gibbins* rose on high waves, then fell into troughs.

But Hans and Jolan seemed unaware of the foul weather and the tossing, lurching, battered ship. They took turns telling me how the *Pentcho*, overloaded with 511 refugees, set sail down the Danube in May 1940. For four and a half months their ship lay in the Danube. No country would let them land. No country would give them food or water. They could see restaurants on the shores and hear music from cafés while they starved. They painted the word HUNGER in three languages on the ship, and still no one brought them food.

"Our equipment," Hans said, "consisted of only one anchor, and we had no lifeboats, no life preservers, no radio—in fact, nothing at all."

Romanian warships finally forced the creaking boat into the open Black Sea. The captain, his mind besotted with opium, led them on a wild journey through minefields into the Aegean Sea. An engine exploded. They were shipwrecked off the Italian Dodecanese. They spent eleven days on an uninhabited rock island and then were taken by Italian warships to an Italian concentration camp.

Of those who survived, twenty-four from the *Pentcho* were now aboard our ship.

The Goldbergers left my cabin. My notebooks and my briefcase were thick with case histories. I began to see a pattern, a refugee pattern, of flight across mountains, dangerous frontiers, mine-infested waters; of hunger and filth; of bombings; of hiding in caves; of capture, imprisonment, and obscene torture.

The path of their flight was the path of Hitler's march across Europe. He came to Germany. They fled to Austria. He came to Austria. The Germans and Austrians fled to Czechoslovakia. He came to Czechoslovakia. They fled to Poland. He came to Poland. They fled to France, Belgium, Hungary, Romania, Yugoslavia, and on to Italy.

They were a cross section of Europe's culture, Europe's occupations, Europe's nationalisms. Living with them on the ship made me aware that the most indestructible thing in the world is man. He survives the Gestapo, he survives the Vichy French, the Yugoslav Ustachi, the Poles, and the Ukrainians, who all helped in the slaughter. He survives hunger and wanderings and crippling torture. These people lived because they scratched and tore and hid and bought false identity papers and never believed in their own death.

I realized that every one of them was alive through a miracle. But I began to see something far more profound: that every Jew in the world was alive through a miracle; that since Egypt's Pharaoh, persecutors had tried to do to Jews what Hitler was now trying to do in Europe. Before Hitler, I was an innocent, convinced that someday there would be no more nationalism, no more racism, no more anti-Semitism. Hitler had taught me I was wrong. I became a "Hitler Jew" with three thousand years of history.

Now I realized that even if we were born Jews, there was a moment in our lives when we *became* Jews. On this ship, I was becoming a Jew.

Like some mythical leviathan taking us farther and farther from the furnaces and hell of Hitler's Europe, the ship had become a journey out of darkness and fear, out of despair and death, to hope and life and light. From this voyage on, I knew, my life would forever be inextricably interlocked with Jews. I felt myself trembling in the Atlantic night, trembling not from the wind but from the revelation.

We had been at sea for ten days when Captain Shea announced to the crew, "Three more days we should be there. Any of you who have wives or sweethearts in America, speed the ship one knot."

On Tuesday, August 1, knowing it was to be one of our last nights in the Atlantic, we sat in little groups on the deck floor, singing songs in Yiddish, in Italian, in French, and popular songs in English. But Eva Bass, with her baby in her lap, seemed so drained she could neither sing nor smile.

Their lives, Dolly had said, were open wounds.

The waves were swishing against our hull. The moon lit up the deck, spreading gold over the water, over their faces, and over their ragged clothes. Were they thinking, as I was, that this same moon was shining down on the trucks with quicklime, on the alpine mountains they had crossed, on the death camps?

I went below to the hospital. The only child of Maria and Morris Montiljo of Yugoslavia, six-month-old Elia, was fighting for her life. Born in a concentration camp, malnourished in the first critical months of her life, little Elia had contracted pneumonia on the ship.

I sat holding the young mother's hand. "Make them keep her alive," she pleaded, her eyes filled with tears. "Don't let her die."

The refugee doctors hovered over Elia. They shook their heads. "She's gone."

I took Maria in my arms.

"She couldn't live," Maria sobbed. "She had to die before we reached America."

A ship's officer cut a white bedsheet and made a shroud. A carpenter built a tiny wooden coffin on white wooden legs. Little Elia was placed inside on a soft white pillow. Two candles were placed at each end of the little coffin. All night we held a vigil as friends came down to sit with the heartbroken father and mother.

Elia, we decided, should not be buried at sea. She would come to America, the guest of President Franklin Roosevelt, to be buried in a graveyard in Oswego.

Part Three

—⟪ ⟩⟫—

THE OSWEGO
ADVENTURE

FOURTEEN

THURSDAY MORNING, August 3, our dark ship began to glow like a plain woman who becomes beautiful on her wedding day. Excitement built up in every corner—among the refugees, the wounded soldiers, the officers, the sailors giving the ship a spit-and-polish cleaning.

"Today," we told each other. "Today's the day. Today we reach New York."

Only the weather was not cooperating.

Except for a few days, most of the voyage had been in warm, golden sunlight. Now we had storm warnings. A hurricane was moving toward us in the Atlantic.

By midafternoon the rain stopped, but the sky remained ominously overcast, so that we saw almost no land until we moved into the bay. Suddenly she emerged, the green mythic figure. The Statue of Liberty. The thousand refugees waved at her joyously, tearfully, as if she were a granite mother welcoming them to the new homeland.

"The greatest day of my life," a bearded old man wept.

"Mine too," I said.

The people moved aside to let Rabbi Mossco Tzechoval come toward me. With his black beard framing his chalk-white face, he could have stepped out of a Rembrandt painting.

"With your permission, I would like to conduct a service now, while we are passing the Statue of Liberty."

"Of course." We made a little space for him on the crowded deck.

The people grew silent. The rabbi knelt and kissed the iron floor. Then he rose and pronounced the Shehecheyanu. We joined him in the ancient Hebrew prayer, giving thanks that we had survived to this day.

The people listened, their eyes still glued to the statue, as he spoke.

"We must never believe the things the Nazis say about us—that we brought evil upon the earth. We did not bring evil upon the earth. Wherever we wandered, we brought the blessings of the Torah and we have brought Truth. The countries that have tried to destroy us have brought evil upon themselves."

His eyes swept across the silent faces on the deck. "As we enter America, remember we are one people. We must speak with one voice, with one heart. We must not live with hatred. We must live with love."

He held his palms outstretched, the thumbs joining, as if he were touching our heads in the benediction. "May God bless you and keep you and make His countenance to shine upon you and bring you peace. And may God bless this new land."

"Amen," we sang in unison.

I felt a surge of pride and patriotism. This was my city. My country. "Do you know what it says on the base of the statue?" I wanted the people to feel toward America as I felt. "It's a poem written by Emma Lazarus, an American Jewish woman. She was a Sephardic Jew, born in New York, with her roots in Spain. She wrote this about eighty years ago, after she heard the terrible stories of the massacre of Jews in Russia."

I pulled the lines of the poem out of my memory:

> Give me your tired, your poor,
> Your huddled masses yearning to breathe free,
> The wretched refuse of your teeming shore,
> Send these, the homeless, tempest-tossed, to me:
> I lift my lamp beside the golden door.

Major Allen prepared me for our arrival. "When we tie up, army people will meet us. From here on, the refugees are under the Second Service Command—headquartered at Governor's Island. They'll be giving you your orders. The Navy is in the picture too."

The navy chaplain, Captain Joshua Goldberg, had already come aboard with the harbor pilot. "What about the press?" I asked Allen.

"Press! The Army won't allow civilians anywhere near us. It's wartime. Spies can pose as reporters. If they do allow photographers, they'll be carefully screened soldiers from the Signal Corps."

Sailors tossed our lines out at Pier 84. The sign over the green-patinaed shed read HAMBURG-AMERICA LINE. We had escaped the Germans only to come home to the pier they had once owned.

Wounded soldiers were carried down the gangplank on stretchers and lifted into the waiting ambulances. Behind the stretchers came men in wheelchairs, pushed by their buddies, then the soldiers on crutches, ambulatory men, airmen, Red Cross workers, doctors, and nurses, all hurrying to make connections and get home.

Only the refugees did not leave.

The officers of the Second Service Command, in summer uniform, came aboard with new orders. "Tell the refugees," they told me, "they are to spend the night aboard the ship. Tomorrow morning we begin disinfestation and processing."

No one complained. They stood on the deck, fascinated by the New York skyline and the frenzied activity on the dock.

I stayed for a while and then began saying goodbye.

Olga, holding International Harry, looked at me tearfully. "Ruthie, are you going to be like all the others? You'll leave us now, and we'll never see you again."

"I'm only going home for the night." I tried to reassure her. "My mother and father haven't heard from me for weeks. I've got to show them I'm really alive. I'll see you again, I promise."

"Come back soon," the people shouted, as I followed a soldier carrying my bag down the gangplank. Was it only thirteen days since I had climbed the Jacob's ladder in Naples and begun this voyage?

On the pier crowded with army jeeps and trucks, I looked for the Signal Corps photographers. There were none. I clutched my camera bag with its rolls of precious film. The only photos of the refugees on our ship were in this bag.

Dusk was falling as the yellow cab drove toward the Williamsburg Bridge and Brooklyn.

Off Bushwick Avenue, the cab turned into Harmon Street, its quiet one-family houses shaded by broad maples. We pulled up in front of the castlelike gray stone house with its stoop on which I had sat as a child reading books. I rang the bell under the stoop.

My mother came to the iron gate. "Thank God. Thank God!" she screamed toward the back of the house. "Dave, she's home!" I bent down to throw my arms around her.

She bustled ahead through the hallway to the huge kitchen. "God answered my prayers. Did you eat? You must be starved. Let me look at you. I bet you never went to sleep."

I smiled. Her questions needed no answer.

My father hurried in from the backyard with a newspaper under his arm. He took my face between his hands and kissed me.

We sat around the kitchen table, my mother bouncing up and down to bring more food. Now at last I could tell them what my mission had been. My father listened to the stories of the people, stroking his white mustache. His handsome face, framed in white hair, looked stricken; shadows of grief drew dark lines around his mouth.

"What's next for you?" he said.

"I don't know, Pop. I have to call Ickes first thing in the morning. Then I'll find out. Now I'd like to take a bath." I kissed them both good night, climbed the stairs, filled the pink bathtub, and lay back luxuriating in the hot sweet water. I could still taste the cold saltwater showers on the ship.

Relaxed and refreshed, I stretched out on the bed I had slept in as a child, wide awake, my mind churning.

How could I tell Ickes the story of this voyage? How could I compress into the ten or fifteen minutes he usually gave me the life stories of a thousand people?

From the bookcase next to my bed I pulled out the well-worn cloth-covered *A Thousand and One Nights*. A thousand. A thousand romantic tales to entertain a sultan and his harem. The stories I was bringing back to a small man in a blue-carpeted office would not entertain him. On the ship they had torn me apart. Some of the people, like Manya, were still bleeding. And I bled with them.

How could I tell this all to Ickes?

"I'm glad you're back." Ickes sounded cheerful on the telephone the next morning. "What did you find?"

"Incredible stories, Mr. Ickes. Of terror. Heroism. Survival."

"I want to hear them when you get back to Washington. But this is what I want you to do now. Dillon Myer has sent his public relations chief, a man called Morrill Tozier, to New York to meet the press."

"But the Army says no press."

"Well, there's been such an uproar from the newspapers that the Army has backed down. Since you're the only one who knows their stories, I want you to help Tozier and his men. They're waiting for you in the Empire State Building."

"I'll get right over there."

"After that I want you to escort the refugees up to the camp and stay with them for a few days until they're settled."

"Fine." I could keep my promise to Olga immediately.

"Then come back to Washington and give me a full report."

At the Empire State Building, Tozier looked harassed. "The press is on our backs screaming, 'We want to see the first real live refugees!' Late today the Army is going to move them to Hoboken by ferry and take them from there by train to Oswego. They've agreed to let the press meet the people inside the Hoboken railway terminal." He paused. "We'd like you to choose ten people and introduce them to the press. We'll meet you and the refugees early this evening in Hoboken."

I taxied back to Pier 84 and hurried up the gangplank. The threatened hurricane had given way to a balmy summer day. A Red Cross ship had come alongside the *Henry Gibbins,* and women in Red Cross uniforms were smilingly handing up to the refugees doughnuts, sandwiches, coffee, and soft drinks. A military brass band sat on the main deck, entertaining people with an unending medley of popular songs.

The ten men and women whose stories I thought would most affect the press all agreed to be interviewed. I mimeographed their case histories and returned to the deck.

Sixteen-year-old Paul Arnstein stared at the towers etched into the sky. "I've seen this skyline so many times in the movies. It was always unreal. Now it's real, and I can't believe it."

"All night I stayed up," Zlatko Hirschler told me, "and I just looked at the electric lights. Do you know what it means to see a city lit up when you've lived in blackouts for more than three years? To know that planes won't bomb you. To know you won't be arrested by Nazi patrols for walking the streets at night. It was worth staying awake all night, just to feel that."

But many were distressed. Early in the morning they had been taken along the wharf to a Quonset hut, where the men were separated from the women. They were terrified. Separation in the camps had meant death.

"We had to strip naked." Eighteen-year-old Margareta Spitzer was still pale. "We had to march in front of soldiers. Then the soldiers began to shoot us all over our bodies with DDT. They put our clothes through a gas chamber to disinfect them. Most of the clothes they put in that steam are ruined—burned or shrunk or full of holes. Anything in leather was destroyed."

"They sprayed us all over from head to toe." Rolf Kuznitzki ran his hand expressively from his head down. "But several parts of our body they sprayed especially. You know what parts I mean."

With a touch of irony he added, "They don't want lice or insects coming from Europe—like us—without passports."

The refugees all had cardboard tags hanging around their necks or twirled around a button. In bold letters the tags read U.S. ARMY CASUAL BAGGAGE. Each tag had a number. It was their identity card, their passport to the Promised Land.

The sky was giving up its light when the Army lined us up, led us down the gangplank onto the wharf, and transferred us to two huge harbor boats, each with the name of an army general.

Once again we were a swarm of humanity crowding one another in iron decks. Each crowd takes on its own character, its own meaning, its own dynamics. The throng of refugees, ferried now across the Hudson, staring at New York's skyline as we sailed away from it, was radiant with hope.

Everything in me seemed to be focusing on one goal. I wanted the press to capture in a few minutes what had taken me days and nights to question and learn. I wanted the reporters to grasp, instantaneously, years of terror and running; I wanted them to understand, so that they could tell the rest of the country about human courage and heroism and the human will to live.

But there were pitfalls. I had been on both sides of press tables—interviewing as a journalist, interviewed as a government official. Reporters tried to be objective. But who was really objective? The most widely listened-to radio commentator in America was a Detroit priest, Father Coughlin, a vituperative anti-Semite. Would some of the reporters be Coughlinites?

At Hoboken, soldiers helped the refugees down from the ferries onto the terminal dock of the old Delaware, Lackawanna and Western Railroad. One hundred MPs, in full battle uniform, with several attractive young WACs, lined up at attention. Twelve army ambulances carried off more than a score of the sick and elderly, and several pregnant women, to be put in the army hospital car. The rest of us were marched by the MPs into a blacked-out waiting room, cavernous, empty of passengers.

I stepped out of the line and waited to corral the refugees who were to meet the press. We kept together while the MPs moved the throngs of people to the tracks. Some of the soldiers lifted little children from their tired mothers' arms and carried them. Others picked up hand baggage; the grateful refugees hurried at their side, afraid to lose sight of the few things they had saved.

Zlatko Hirschler pleaded with an MP, "Please just let me telephone my sister in Tennessee. To tell her I'm alive—in America."

"Sorry. Our orders are, 'No contact.'"

"But it's my sister. What are you afraid of, Nazi spies? After what we've been through, you can't be afraid of *us*."

The MP was silent. Zlatko reluctantly stepped back into line.

"We've got to make sure," a WAC holding two children by the hands explained to me, "that the refugees meet nobody and speak to nobody until they're safely in the camp. War precautions, you know."

War precautions had also turned down the lights of the waiting room; even the Tiffany-glass ceiling had been painted black. It was a forbidding setting for a press conference.

A long table had been set up in front of an arched stairway. The conference was to begin as soon as the Army had herded most of the people onto the trains. The ten refugees who were to meet the press waited behind the table with Tozier and me. Some looked frightened and bewildered.

"I'm so scared." Mathilda Nitsch's round body was shaking. "What will they ask me?"

"Just tell them the things you told me. Reporters are human; they'll have to be moved by what you went through. They have a job to do. They want a good story."

"But I don't speak English," Mathilda worried.

"I'll translate."

"Look at my clothes. They're full of holes. I wanted to look good when I arrived in America."

I hugged her ample body. "Mathilda, you couldn't look bad if you tried. They'll love you."

As the last of the refugees straggled out of the waiting room toward the tracks, a new crowd of reporters, photographers, and radio commentators pushed and shoved one another toward the press table, their press cards protruding from their slouched hats.

Colonel Shaw of the Second Service Command gave the signal to begin. "The trains depart Hoboken at nine-thirty tonight." He looked at his watch. "You have thirty minutes."

"Thirty minutes!" a reporter with purplish jowls and a red bulbous nose spluttered. "How the hell can you get a story like this in thirty minutes?"

The colonel shrugged his shoulders and marched off toward the tracks.

Tozier opened the conference, reading a statement. He quoted the statistics Stauber had garnered on the ship, the number of refugees, the breakdown of the countries they came from. "In Oswego," he explained, "the War Relocation Authority will take over from the Army and administer the Emergency Refugee Shelter in Fort Ontario, one of the oldest military posts in America."

The reporters scribbled rapidly in their notebooks.

"The refugees," he went on, "will be housed there for the duration of the war."

"What happens to them when the war's over?" a middle-aged reporter, who kept studying the faces of the refugees, interrupted.

"They will be returned to their own countries. Every one of them signed a paper agreeing to go back."

"What if those countries are destroyed? What if they have no homes to go back to?" He held his pencil in the air, waiting. He had asked the key question.

"They signed a paper. They'll have to abide by it."

I clutched the edge of the table. I longed to give a different answer. To tell them, "The war's not over by a long shot. Let's wait until the war is over—then we can make that decision." But Tozier represented Dillon Myer and WRA. I could not undermine his statement; and the decision to send them back had been set by the War Refugee Board and the President himself.

A reporter held up a mimeographed sheet. "I have a press release. It's from John Pehle, executive director of the War Refugee Board."

"Read it," a young reporter shouted.

"I'll read this line. 'The arrival of almost one thousand refugees from Italy demonstrates this nation's willingness to participate in an international program to find havens for the survivors of Nazi persecution.' " He turned to Tozier. "Does the President plan to open any more such havens in America?"

I caught my breath. Would Tozier know?

"No plans," Tozier said, "to this date, have been made for the reception of any other such colony. And now," he said swiftly, as though eager to change the subject, "I would like to introduce the special assistant to the Secretary of the Interior who accompanied the refugees on the ship."

I had prepared a statement in my head; instead I said, "You can ask me questions later. But with the time that's left, I think you ought to meet and hear from the people themselves."

"That's right," the *Daily News* man said, leaning against the table. "Get going."

"Let me introduce Dr. Rafailo Margulis from Yugoslavia. He speaks English. You can question him directly."

Dr. Margulis, in a dapper blue beret, a necktie, and a gray suit that had somehow stayed miraculously pressed during the voyage, left the huddle of refugees. He walked upright toward the center of the table, adjusted his glasses, ceremoniously took some handwritten notes from his pocket, and began to read. His voice was formal, precise, as if he were addressing a detachment of troops.

"Allow me to introduce myself. I am a physician and a lieutenant colonel in the Yugoslav Royal Army. I wish to extend my personal gratitude to the American and British armies who came to our country and are fighting now to liberate us from the Nazi yoke."

A short peppery reporter from *The New York Times* beat his fist on the press table. "Cut the crap, Doc."

Dr. Margulis stood erect and continued to read.

"Listen, Doc." The journalist punched his words across the table. "Thank the Army some other time. We're here to get a story about what the Nazis did to you and what they did in Yugoslavia."

Dr. Margulis seemed oblivious. The press was in an uproar. Irritated, red-faced, some seemed ready to riot.

My fears had been trouble with the press, not with the refugees. "Dr. Margulis," I said in a whisper, "just answer their questions. They're not the enemy."

He stopped reading, took down his glasses and polished them carefully. Then he looked at the angry reporters.

"It is hard to tell you what the Germans did in Yugoslavia. I think, proportionately, of all the countries Hitler invaded, we are among the ones who lost the most. Of the seventy thousand Jews in Yugoslavia, so far less than four thousand have survived—most of them by fleeing the country."

A reporter, writing furiously in a stenographer's notebook, hardly looked up. "Keep going."

"In my city of Belgrade, there were twelve thousand Jews before the war. As soon as the Germans came, they rounded up all the Jews, put them in the city zoo, and then led them out, hundreds at a time, and shot them. Of the twelve thousand, less than nine hundred are left."

"What about concentration camps in Yugoslavia?" someone shouted.

He seemed not to hear. Once again he lifted his notes and began to read. His words were drowned out by the angry shouts of the reporters. An MP pulled him away from the press table and led him toward the train.

"We have a whole group here," I tried to talk over the din, "ready to answer your questions. You can see how nervous some of them are. Most of them have never met the press. They're tired not only from this long journey but from years of running and hiding. I will introduce them to you one at a time. I'll try to give you whatever information I can. Then you can question them."

I extended my hand to a thin, frightened woman holding a little boy close to her body. "This is Serafina Poljakan and her son Milan, who is nine. I will give you a copy of her story with all the others at the end of the conference."

"Just give us the gist now," a serious-faced reporter from the *New York Herald Tribune* called over the hubbub.

"Serafina," I said, "is thirty-six, a middle-class Jewish woman who lived near Zagreb. Her father, her mother, and her eighteen-year-old brother were all murdered by the Ustachi, the Yugoslav fascists. She fled to Italy with her husband and little Milan."

"How did she escape? How did she survive?" The reporters threw a barrage of questions, interrupting each other.

Now the *Times* reporter shouted, "Quiet, you guys. Why don't you let her talk? Don't you see she's trying to help us?"

The dark waiting room grew still.

"In 1943, Yugoslav partisans came to the house where Serafina was hiding, searching for Nazi sympathizers. Her husband opened the door; the partisans mistook him for another man and killed him before her eyes. They admitted their mistake and took her and Milan with them into the mountains. For months she and Milan lived among the partisans, hiding. Once she and Milan spent ten days in the woods under pouring rain, unable to get food, while German soldiers were all around them searching for fugitives."

"Ask her how her little boy reacted," the *Herald Tribune* man said.

"Milan"—I bent down toward him—"what was it like when you were hiding, with the Nazis around you?"

The reporters waited while Milan whispered, as if he were reliving the months in the mountains. "You always had to speak so low. They were always telling you, 'Shh, shh. The Germans will hear you.' "

Colonel Shaw returned to the press table. "You've got to terminate. We're already late."

"Come on, Colonel," a reporter protested. "We're just getting into the stories now."

The officer crossed his arms over his chest. "I'll give you a few more minutes."

"We'll speed things along," I promised him.

Mathilda was next. "Where do you come from?" a reporter asked her directly.

Mathilda understood his words. She had learned them in the English class on the deck.

"We come from the North Pole."

The reporters burst into laughter. I was beginning to relax. They lost their hearts to the little Greek "Dionne girls," and roared at the story of International Harry's birth.

Hans Goldberger had just begun answering their questions about the shipwrecked *Pentcho* when Colonel Shaw shoved the reporters aside, lined his MPs up in front of the press table, and shouted, "We're half an hour behind schedule. The conference is terminated."

Within minutes, I distributed the case histories. Some of the reporters and photographers, cleared by the Army, were making the night journey with us. On the dimly lit tracks, we jumped aboard the train. The doors closed instantly.

I walked through the dark coaches as the train pitched and jerked from side to side. Most of the children were curled up, sleeping on the coach seats. Adults were talking in low voices. Through the open train windows came cool night breezes as the train hurtled northward.

A hand reached out to me in the dim aisle. "It's me, Manya. Sit with me a few minutes."

Manya's friend, Ernst Breuer, stood up. "Take my seat. I'll find another one while you're talking."

"I'm scared, Ruthie," Manya said. Over the noise of the wheels I could hear her agitated breathing.

"But you're safe now—in America."

"It's the train. Trains scare me. I know it's—it's not a cattle car, but . . ."

She was silent for a few minutes. Two MPs walked down the aisle. Then the words burst from her.

"The soldiers—they aren't shoving us together. They aren't pushing us into those terrible trains, crushed up against each other. People died in them. Still—oh, God, I'm so scared."

"Manya, this is all behind you."

"I know. But I can't help the fear."

Ernst returned, hovering over her.

"Ruthie," Manya said, "go to your seat; you look so tired."

Leaning back in a coach seat, I shut my eyes. We were on our way to the first haven in America—where they were to find rest, surcease from running, time to heal pain, to obliterate nightmares. I should have been filled with joy. Instead, Manya's fear of trains and the key question one of the reporters had asked kept reeling in my head like the wheels of the train: "What happens to them when the war's over? What if they have no homes to go back to?"

FIFTEEN

LIGHT WAS GENTLY STREAKING the sky as people began to stir and wake and peer excitedly through open windows at America's villages, towns, and graceful dairy farms.

The train pounded toward Syracuse and then rolled north on a branch line to Oswego until, at exactly 7:30 A.M., the iron wheels ground to a halt at a railroad siding.

An MP waved his white gloves to the right. "We're at the camp. No one is to leave until we give the order."

The people on the far side of the train rushed across the aisle to gape through the windows for their first glimpse of Fort Ontario.

"A fence! Another fence!" a man gasped. His words, chilling, plunged through the train. For there, stretching as far as we could see, was a tall hurricane fence of chain links, topped with three rows of barbed wire.

Artur Hirt reached forward, rattling my shoulders. "How could you do this? In the free America? It's another concentration camp!"

The train grew ominously silent. "It's an old army post." I tried to dispel some of the fear. "All army camps in America have fences."

My words had no effect. The silence persisted, awkward, nervous, disbelieving.

"The fence doesn't bother me one bit." It was Kitty Kaufman, a young Austrian traveling with her Yugoslav husband and young daughter, Eva. "If you ask me, I feel safer behind a fence. Even in America."

The fence, I realized with a start, was a psychological symbol for refugees. For most of them, the fence meant a prison, a concentration camp, a locked door, an end to freedom. To Kitty, the fence meant security. Her enemy could not enter.

A burst of activity temporarily deflected the rising anger and dismay. There had been no food on the night coach. Milk and cookies were being handed up through the open windows, and the children were eagerly munching and drinking, when the Army announced we could begin leaving the train.

The people gathered their hand baggage. I held little Joachim Bass's hand and climbed down the steep steps, suddenly aware that dozens of Oswego's citizens were watching us from the roof of a factory that made tanks.

More townspeople were hurrying out of modest wooden houses lining the street along one side of the fence. Reporters from New York, Chicago, Syracuse, Rochester, and the local *Oswego Palladium-Times* swarmed around us. Photographers snapped their shutters, movie cameras rolled—catching the weary and frightened eyes of the elderly, the tentative smiles of teenagers, the lost look of children still without shoes, a violinist clutching his fiddle in a broken case, the knapsacks and torn boxes tied with rope in which many carried their most precious possessions, the flotsam and jetsam of the war, wearing their cardboard tags: CASUAL BAGGAGE.

We straggled into the camp through a side gate at the railroad spur. It was a huge encampment of eighty acres that stretched from the town to the shores of Lake Ontario. A grassy oval parade ground filled the center of the camp, framed on one side by white wooden barracks in which the refugees were to be housed and, on the other, terraced up a small hill, by red-brick Georgian houses with freshly painted white columns, the officers' quarters, where the director and part of the staff would live.

Beyond the brick houses was a gray stone rampart and a stone arch leading into the two-hundred-year-old fort itself. Sitting behind a small table just inside the fence, Military Intelligence officers began the registration and identification, checking everyone against a master list.

Multilingual translators flanked the officers; they wore armbands with the word DOLMETSCHER—translator—printed in red ink. They had been sent to the camp by private Jewish and Christian agencies to help the government through these hectic days.

I listened carefully as the army officers began the screening. Would a few, like Artur Hirt, explode again? They had been screened when they were first selected in Italy, to keep out potential fifth columnists or spies. They had been screened again in Aversa, the insane asylum. Some had dropped out during the screening (one of the reasons we had 982 instead of one thousand). Now they were being screened a third time. The questioning was sympathetic, benign. Name. Nationality. Country of origin. Name of spouse—if any. Names of children—if any. Profession—if any. Some were asked if they had firsthand information, photos, or documents that could help our Army win the war faster. The screening became a two-way street, with the people offering eagerly to answer any questions to bring victory even one day closer.

"I'm Joe Smart." A small slender man in an open-necked white shirt extended his hand to me. The director of the camp, he had wide clear eyes and a serious face with deep ridges from his nose to his chin. At forty-three he had already had a colorful career, seven years as special agent of the FBI, regional director managing New Deal resettlement projects, regional director of half of the ten Japanese-American relocation centers, and assistant national director of the WRA. He had been working in Peru with the Institute of Inter-American Affairs when Dillon Myer, his former boss, telephoned asking him to take the job in Oswego. Now he was shaking hands, telling those who seemed terrified that perhaps they had come to another concentration camp, "Whenever there is a knock on your door, it will be a friendly one."

Ravenously hungry—we had eaten little all the day before—we were led to the white barracks mess halls, where long tables were stacked with pitchers of steaming hot coffee, bottles of rich cold milk, giant boxes of cornflakes, loaves of white bread, jars of peanut butter, and bowls overflowing with hard-boiled eggs.

Manya, her mouth stuffed with one egg, reached into the bowl for another. "We never got fed like this in Gurs."

Customs inspection on the parade ground was fast and cursory. Some of the customs men were misty-eyed as they looked into torn suitcases that held nothing but newspapers, or family photos wrapped in frayed underwear or rags. A customs agent who found only one torn shirt in a battered bag copied the man's name from his tag, spent his lunch hour in a shop, and bought the man a pair of pants, a shirt, and a jacket.

By midmorning, there was an explosion of euphoria that caught me up in it. I accompanied some of the people to their homes in the two-story white wooden barracks.

"Such efficiency. Only America can do this." Olga Maurer stared at the entrance of her apartment. Her name and the names of her whole family, even International Harry's, were fixed on the door. "I feel already it's mine. My first apartment."

A tiny woman in her mid-fifties raced down the steps of her barracks near Lake Ontario. "Fräulein Ruth"—Elsa Neumann flung her arms around my waist—"this is more beautiful than anything in Europe. I have a villa by the sea." She sped off to share the news of her villa with others.

The morning sun shone down on the shady tree-lined streets and the huge grassy parade ground where once soldiers must have drilled and horses galloped. Now children were romping and rolling and tagging one another. Some of their parents strolled leisurely like tourists in a resort hotel.

"Come inside." A woman's voice called from a barracks window. It was Kitty Kaufman, who had found security in the fence. I entered her small partitioned apartment to find her stroking two cotton bedsheets. "In the caves of Italy I used to dream about bedsheets."

"And I used to dream about a mattress," her husband, Branko, a photographer, said softly. "How many years since we've seen a mattress?" He stretched out on the unmade bed. His face broadened into a smile that seemed to spread through his whole body.

The apartment had been furnished, GI style, with two metal cots, a small table, two chairs, and a metal locker. "Please sit down," Kitty insisted. "I'm so sorry I have nothing to offer you to eat or drink."

The bedsheets were still in her arms when Margareta Spitzer called from the doorway of their apartment, "Come see how excited my mother is."

Her mother had opened the bedsheets and was fixing a cot ready for sleep.

"Bedsheets," her mother whispered in awe. Moses' Jews in the desert, I thought, must have whispered the same way as they watched manna falling from heaven.

She took off her shoes, lowered herself onto the precious bedsheet, and turned her head to the wall so we would not see her cry.

In a cab, I left the camp and taxied to the Pontiac Hotel, a three-story white building set on a lawn far back from the street. It took only minutes to register and to drop my bag in a typical traveling salesman's hotel room. On a small writing table was a pile of stationery with an etching of the Pontiac Hotel on the letterhead and in the center the words *On Beautiful Lake Ontario Along the Roosevelt Highway.*

I opened the window. Fresh sweet air rushed in. The Oswego River flowed swiftly below; the rear of the hotel sat on the riverbank.

Back in the cab, the driver took me through the town that had taken a thousand strangers into its midst. The warm sun fell on the busy main streets and the quiet residential avenues that seemed miles and millennia away from the war in Europe. It threw shadows on the churches and schools and the simple one-family frame houses shaded with thick trees. Oswego was smaller than a metropolis, larger than a whistle-stop, plain and solid and peaceful and completely American.

In Washington I had read that the town's 22,000 people were a heterogeneous mix, descendants of immigrants who had come here in the late nineteenth and early twentieth centuries from Germany, Ireland, Quebec, Poland, and Italy, and the majority were Roman Catholic.

Like many provincial New Yorkers, I had never heard of Oswego, but in Europe many people had learned about this small town in central New York State lying between Syracuse and Rochester on the shores of Lake Ontario. The Office of War Information had selected it as the "typical American community" and filmed a movie as part of OWI's wartime documentary services.

Its polyglot population, I thought, as we drove through its tranquil streets, should bode well for accepting refugees from eighteen different countries; and the refugees too would find it charming, for it was part of the picturesque series of locks and canals that make up the New York State Barge Canal System.

It was a town surrounded by water. The Oswego River ran like a blood artery through its very center, dividing it into two equal halves. *Bridge* was the word I saw everywhere; of the two steel bridges flung across the river, one was even called the Bridge Street Bridge. The two main thoroughfares were East Bridge Street and West Bridge Street, and on each of them, flanking the river, were the shops and marts and emporia of American culture and commerce and trade.

The President's choice of Fort Ontario in Oswego was a stroke of timing. The Army had closed the camp in March, and townspeople had rushed to the White House and the War Department, pleading that it be reactivated; Fort Ontario was one of the mainstays of their economy. Thus, Fort Ontario was on the Army's mind when the search began for an available camp for the refugees. Only two campsites were suggested: Madison Barracks in Watertown, New York, and Fort Ontario. The War Refugee Board chose Fort Ontario, and in June the people of Oswego learned, most of them with delight, that the camp was to be reopened and officially designated the Fort Ontario Emergency Refugee Shelter.

I returned to the camp and showed my pass to the guard at the main gate. The only ones given passes were government officials, staff, representatives of private agencies, and the press. The people were to be kept in quarantine for a month, behind the fence.

"How can you have a fence in America?" Those who were angry and obsessed again confronted me. But others, born survivors, had already turned the fence into their own bridge. Peering through the chain links, the refugees inside the fence talked and gesticulated in sign language to citizens of Oswego, who were talking and gesticulating just as animatedly on the other side.

Some Oswegonians sprinted home, armed themselves with clothing, especially with children's shoes, and tossed them like baseballs over the top of the fence. Others shoved cookies and candy through the metal links. A sweet-faced nine-year-old, Susan Saunders, brought her Shirley Temple doll for a wistful little girl her own age. The reporters and photographers captured the scene.

Near the Fitzgibbons boiler plant next to the camp, Geraldine Desens, a tall, ebullient brown-haired waitress, braked her bicycle to a halt. Geri had never seen a refugee; these newcomers to her quiet town could have dropped in from outer space. Yet she felt strangely pulled to them.

She heard children shouting eagerly, words that sounded like "Beecycla. Beecycla."

She understood.

"Here, you guys, help me," she called out to three strong young men standing near her outside the fence. They raised her bike over the fence, then lowered it carefully to youngsters who caught it inside. Go ahead, ride it, she pantomimed. The youngsters took off, careening around the camp.

Geri made a decision. Prowling along the outside, she searched the ground. A mischievous grin spread across her face when she discovered a hole under the fence, an underground opening she knew well.

She raced home and changed into old clothes to look like a refugee. She knew the danger of being arrested for illegal entry. She hurried to the fence and wriggled on her backside through the hole. A woman neighbor gaping through the links shouted, "Geri, what in the name of all that's blessed and holy are you doing in there with all those Jews?"

Geri burst into laughter and walked through the camp, shrugging her shoulders. Her neighbors, she was sure, would never understand. She waved delightedly at the teenagers riding her bicycle like cowboys in the Wild West. Strolling on the grassy parade ground, she stopped Edith Semjen.

"Hello," she said.

"Hello," Edith answered.

"I live here."

"And you're inside the camp?" Edith's eyes sparkled. "How did you get in?"

Geri led Edith to the hole. "We always got in this way; it's right opposite Big Rock, our swimming area; it's a shortcut for us."

"You got chutzpah."

"What's *hutz*—?"

"Army says nobody can come in. You find a hole—and you come in. That's chutzpah."

The two young women walked around the parade ground,

Edith fascinated by Geri's bravado and warmth, Geri by Edith's wide-set brown eyes, her startlingly beautiful figure, and her thick blond hair.

"I know a few Jewish people in town, but I never saw a refugee," Geri said.

"A refugee is no different than the rest of the world." Edith waved a cigarette at the people milling on the parade ground. A few young women had settled on the grass, their faces upturned so that the warm radiant sun would tan them. "We're like everybody else, only maybe a little bit more tired."

"I guess you went through hell, though." Geri surmised. "I guess we Americans can't imagine some of the things you lived through. We only see it in the movies."

"It was hell, all right."

"Maybe you don't feel like talking."

"I'll talk. First my brother Darko disappeared. One day the Yugoslav fascists, the Ustachi, came to our house. 'We're taking Darko to a work camp for the summer. Pack a knapsack with work clothes.' We didn't think it would do him any harm. He was just two years older than me. He was a chemistry student at the University of Zagreb. They took him, along with two hundred fifty other students."

Edith lit another cigarette and began to talk rapidly. "We didn't hear from him. Then we started to hear horrible stories. That all the students were taken away and shot and never buried. My father wouldn't believe it. He had good political connections. He was a rich lumberman. He thought he could find my brother and get him out. He went to the Ustachi. They didn't know anything. He went to the Gestapo. They didn't know anything, either. Now *he* was on the list. A few days later they came for him. They took him away to the Yugoslav concentration camp in Croatia; it's a terrible place called Jasenovać. Christians who worked in the camp told us, 'The prisoners had to dig their graves and were shot.' One of them told us my father was hit on the head; he fell down, and they buried him alive."

"My God."

A young boy whizzed past on Geri's bicycle, but Geri saw only Edith's father falling into an open grave.

Edith lit a new cigarette on the butt of the old one. "It didn't happen only to my family. It happened to every family. I was a rebel; I wouldn't obey army orders, curfews, anything. To save me, my mother sent me to Split. But the Italian fascists threw me in prison."

"You—in prison!" Geri winced.

"From there they sent me to a concentration camp on one of the islands in the Adriatic. I escaped to the partisans, and I worked with them. I was a secretary, a teacher for little kids; I did whatever was needed. Then the Nazis came—in a big offensive—and I escaped again. To Vis, another island in the Adriatic, with my mother. The partisans brought us to Bari, and from there we came to America." Edith laughed. "And the first day I meet you, an American—another rebel, like me."

Geri looked at her watch. "I've got to go home and change my clothes. I wait tables in a restaurant. When I finish my shift, I'm coming back with the biggest steak I bet you ever saw in your life. And it'll still be hot."

At another part of the fence, Adam Munz drew a shiny dime from his pocket, a souvenir one of the soldiers had given him on the ship. He called out to a boy who seemed sixteen or seventeen, about his own age, "Can this buy a Ping-Pong ball?"

"I think so." The boy took the dime Adam pushed through one of the chain links. "Wait here, I'll be right back." He jumped on his bike and wheeled furiously down the street.

Adam waited. He had dreamed for years of playing Ping-Pong again. Prowling the camp, he had entered the recreation hall and discovered a new table complete with paddles and a net. But no balls.

A few minutes later, the boy, back on his bike and breathless, threw a brown bag over the fence. Adam opened the bag; inside were three gleaming-white Ping-Pong balls.

"Thank you. Oh, I thank you. I thank you. What is your name?"

"Jim. What's yours?"

"My name is Adam. Jim"—Adam smiled expansively—"you are a big ass."

Jim's face changed from a friendly grin to a puzzled scowl. Others outside the fence looked shocked.

Thinking he had been misunderstood, Adam repeated in a louder voice, "Jim, you are a big, big ass."

He saw the mood through the fence grow dark and threatening.

"What do you mean?" Jim asked.

Adam spread-eagled his arms, thrust his head forward like a plane zooming down on an enemy, and spluttered, *"Ack-ack-ack."* Then he fell to the ground, the enemy plane destroyed. Looking up at Jim through the steel chains, Adam shouted, "The pilot, he is a big ass—just like you."

The grin returned to Jim's face. "Oh, you mean big *ace.*"

Late in the afternoon, I left the fence and the barracks to explore the encampment. Crossing the parade ground, I climbed a broad winding road toward the stone ramparts of old Fort Ontario.

It was the oldest garrisoned fort in the United States, built by the British in 1755. Its cannon and fortifications had protected the British from the French, the French from the Indians, Americans from all potential enemies. The stone wall was a pentagon of five "faces," five jutting points protecting the garrison from invasion.

Slowly I walked around the old fort, overgrown with grass, then left it to wander down toward Lake Ontario, blue-green, sparkling, and seeming wide as an ocean. I stood on a cliff, looking out at the endless water, the lighthouse, the thousands of seagulls screaming, challenging the air.

A sense of solace and refuge washed over me. Here, I thought, the refugees sitting on the banks of this great magical lake may find the peace they have so long yearned for.

Sunday afternoon we gathered for the official welcome on American soil.

Dillon Myer had arrived from Washington with several government officials. We sat with city officials and clergy on the speakers'
platform, while the refugees stood on the parade ground.

"I welcome you all in English." Joe Smart, dressed formally in a
tie and jacket, opened the meeting. "And Fredi Baum will translate.
I know many of you speak other languages and may resent German.
However, we are not at war with the German language, only with the
Nazi oppressors. We will now sing 'The Star-Spangled Banner.' "
People listened in silence, the words of the anthem unknown.

Myer read a personal message from Ickes. " 'I hope that this
haven from the intolerance, suffering, and persecution that you
have undergone will in some measure ease your tragic memories.' "

He paused to let Fredi translate, while Ickes's words etched
themselves into my brain: *this haven from the intolerance, suffering,
and persecution.*

" 'I hope from my heart' "—Myer continued reading—" 'that
the time you spend in this retreat will bring you strength and faith
with which to face a future in which the dignity of the individual
man will be recognized and assured everywhere.' "

Would his words be prophetic?

Other speakers followed: Mayor Joseph T. McCaffrey, a large
burly figure, offering the hospitality of the city; Anne Laughlin of
the War Refugee Board, bringing greetings from John Pehle.

Dr. Juda Levi of Yugoslavia, speaking for the refugees, turned to
the dignitaries on the dais. "There is not one single family among us
whose members have not been deported and killed by the Nazis."

On the parade ground, the faces were a mingling of sorrow,
memories, tears.

Then the Reverend A. S. Lowrie of the West Baptist Church
brought greetings to the Christian refugees from the Oswego
Council of Churches. "You have had a great variety of experiences,
dangers, and difficulties. These are now in the past, and a new life
opens before you."

Mathilda Nitsch was gazing at him adoringly, though she understood not one word.

"As Christian ministers," he said, "it is our desire to do all we can to make your stay here, in our midst, one you will always remember because of the Christian friendship, fellowship, and goodwill extended to you by the people of the city. May God speed the day when war shall cease, when peace shall prevail in the world, and all men shall dwell together as brothers in Jesus Christ."

A warm breeze swept across the parade ground, rustling the leaves. Rabbi Sidney Bialik, the rabbi of the Adath Israel Synagogue in Oswego, rose to end the program. "The Talmud says that silence expresses more than words. Your very presence here relates thousands of tragic occurrences, your countenances express numerous horrible experiences and travail at which words are senseless."

The people nodded. He was speaking their truth.

He blessed America, President Roosevelt, and the United Nations, and then, joined by many of the refugees, intoned El Moley Rachamin, the memorial prayer for the dead.

On Monday morning I spoke with Ickes in Washington. I told him of the euphoria, the unexpected beauty of the camp, the "villa by the sea." "Everyone wants to help," I said, "even the customs men. They found a nine-year-old-boy with only torn shorts and a ragged shirt on his back. They made a pool and bought him a whole outfit of clothing and toys."

"It's good to hear." Ickes's voice suggested he was smiling. "Dillon Myer just left my office. He came back on the sleeper from Oswego. He says you did a fine job, on the ship and now in the camp."

I caught my breath. Dillon Myer—who had done his best to keep me from going over.

"He asked me to let you stay on for another couple of weeks, at least until the refugees are settled. I suggest you stay up there for a while longer."

SIXTEEN

"ERNST AND I want to get married."

It was early in the morning when Manya Hartmeyer and Ernst Breuer came to see me, speaking urgently. "We asked the captain on the ship to marry us," Manya explained. "But he refused. He said, 'Wait until you get to America.'"

Still wearing her father's shirt, she looked younger than her years, a tall green-eyed child-woman. Ernst seemed older, though he was just twenty-six. The high bones above his narrow cheeks, the pencil-thin mustache, the strong chin made him a dashing figure. In a different time and a different life, he could have been a swashbuckling buccaneer. Now, with haunted eyes, he had the long sober look of maturity.

"I want to protect Manya." He put his arm around her shoulders. "I want to take care of her for the rest of our lives. She's all alone in the world. My family's wiped out too; only my sister Lisa, who's here with us, is left. Manya needs me—and I can't live without her."

"I don't mind waiting," Manya said, "but Ernst would like us married." She hesitated, then said slowly, "Today."

"Today!"

"It's not possible?" she asked wistfully.

"It takes time."

I would have to find out first if the War Refugee Board would allow them to get married during the quarantine; then if New York State would consider them residents and issue a marriage license; and, finally, if WRB would give them permission to leave the camp to register at City Hall so they could get the license.

"How much time will it take?" Manya asked.

"I can't say."

Strips of light filtered through the vertical bars of my office. It was the old army jail; when Joe Smart offered it to me apologetically, I had laughed. "It's OK. Now I too am fenced in."

Manya was crestfallen. "Can't the rabbi marry us?"

"Certainly, but only after you get a license."

"Don't tell me," Ernst exploded, "that we can't get married in America."

"I'm not telling you that, Ernst. I'm telling you there are obstacles because of your extraordinary legal status."

"It's pretty rotten, if you ask me. Why shouldn't two people in love get married?"

"We'll have to get a policy decision from Washington." I felt bleak and helpless. "They've got the lawyers. They decide how to interpret the law."

Ernst's haunted eyes turned fierce. I imagined it was that rage that had helped him survive. He had been a resistance fighter with the French underground. His mother had been arrested with thousands of other Jewish refugees and deported to Auschwitz. Manya had told me how, with the Nazis searching for him in Paris, he had escaped to Nice. But the Nazis continued to track him down and found his hiding place. Once again he escaped.

"Ruthie," Manya said, "I don't like to see Ernst get so mad. You think it will take long?"

"I'll call Washington today."

She leaned across the desk. "Before I came on the ship, I was beaten on my body and in my soul. I felt I'm nothing, I'm nobody. I'm a dirty Jew they're trying to take away from this earth."

Her green eyes were moist. "I was like a person falling into a big dark cave, deeper, deeper; nobody cared, nobody helped. Then they took us on the ship and a door opened, a light came through. And the light—that was you. We looked up to you with so much hope and happiness. You represented America to us—the land that was taking us in and shielding us from harm. It's that America that I believe in."

I reached for her hand and pressed it.

"Please, Ruthie. Ernst is my father, my mother, my brother. Please. He wants to get married right away. Help us."

She walked around the desk, pressed her wet cheek against mine, then grabbed Ernst's hand and ran out of the office.

The legal obstacles to their getting married mounted in my brain, a pyramid of nightmares—all because they had entered America outside the immigration laws. Even now, letters were going back and forth between government agencies, trying to define the group's legal status. The War Department wanted to register them as aliens under the Alien Registration Law. Then they would have both a legal and a political entity. The Department of Justice refused. "They cannot be registered as aliens, because they are not aliens."

POWs were aliens. Enemy civilians allowed in from Latin America were aliens. But the 982 refugees, "guests of President Roosevelt," were in limbo: stateless, paperless, homeless. It was as if this camp on the banks of Lake Ontario were on another planet, isolated from the rest of America, spinning in space.

An American woman, smartly dressed with a straw hat and white gloves, entered my office.

"I am the president of the Rochester section of the National Council of Jewish Women." She introduced herself. "Our national office asked me to contact you." In her hand she held the special pass the private agencies were given.

She took the chair at the side of my desk. "I've been walking around the camp a little, talking to some of the people. God, what they look like. Some are like skeletons. All these years, we charitable organizations have been raising money to help refugees, but we never saw any—maybe one or two, but surely never a whole group like this. Wait until I tell my women. I've already heard that every voluntary agency in the country wants to help you. What can my Rochester women do?"

"Do they sew?"

Her face fell with disappointment. Perhaps she had expected

some lofty lifesaving task. She spoke dryly. "What kind of sewing do you have in mind?"

"We need curtains. Shower curtains especially. The showers are all together at the end of each floor: the men's are on the first floor, the women's on the second. Four open showers with no partitions, no doors. Some of the women have come to me, pleading, 'Can we have a little privacy?' After what they've been through, it's a high priority."

"A high priority." She leaned forward, her spirits lifted. "What about curtains for the windows? And perhaps bedspreads and tablecloths? They might make the camp a little more homelike."

"They certainly would."

"My members will have those showers and windows curtained by next week—the other things a little later."

"Can you get enough fabric, with the war shortage?"

"We'll get it if we have to beg, borrow, or steal. I'm going right back to Rochester and call a meeting."

The telephone rang as she started to leave.

"Don't go yet. It's Flora Rothenberg in your national office in New York." Flora, an old friend, was the executive director of the organization. "Your Rochester president is here right now," I told her.

"That's good. You'll also be hearing from our Syracuse section soon. I want to know how we in National can help too."

"We have twelve babies, Flora. We need twelve cribs, twelve baby carriages, and twelve high chairs."

"My brother is with Gimbels in Pittsburgh. Between him and my organization, we'll rush them up to you. Talk to you again soon." The Rochester president said good-bye.

Two rabbis entered next, one middle-aged, heavily bearded, and paunchy, the other young, pale-faced, with a Vandyke beard framing his chin. They wore black slouch hats and heavy black suits crumpled from the hot train ride from New York City. The young rabbi spoke English flawlessly in a singsong rhythm, as though he were rocking his body in morning prayers. They had come from Agudath Israel, an organization of ultra-orthodox religious Jews.

I extended my hand to the younger rabbi, expecting a hearty handshake. He pulled back as if my hand were foul-smelling, evil dirt.

Seeing my embarrassment, he explained. "We are not allowed to shake the hand of any woman except our wives."

He drew a white handkerchief from his pocket and held it before me. I touched the corner and flailed it awkwardly.

"Forgive me. I should have known. Gentlemen, please sit down."

Growing up in a modern orthodox home, I had never encountered the ultra-orthodox. Silently I vowed to fill the gaps in my education.

"We have come about the children." The middle-aged rabbi stroked his graying beard. "Some have probably never been to school. It is a sin to allow children to go uneducated. We would like to take them to our yeshivas in New York. We have families who would be happy to board them. If you agree, we could take them back with us tonight."

"I appreciate your concern. But we are under quarantine. No one, not even a child, can leave the camp until September first."

"Even to be educated?" he asked in disbelief.

"Education is one of the problems we're grappling with right now. We don't know yet whether schools will be opened in the camp or whether children will be allowed to go outside to local schools. But there is something you can do—right away."

"What is that?"

"One hundred sixty people have signed up to eat kosher. We've set aside a kosher kitchen and mess hall. But Rabbi Tzechoval tells me no one can eat in it because the dishes have been used before and therefore are not kosher. Can you get us new dishes right away?"

The two rabbis rose in unison. "You'll see." They hurried out, their black coattails flying.

The next morning a truck rolled up in front of the kosher kitchen and out flowed two hundred sets of dairy dishes, two hundred sets of meat dishes, and assorted pots and pans and flatwear.

Rabbi Tzechoval and the orthodox refugees rushed to the mess hall as the word spread: "Now we can eat."

Each morning, Manya appeared at the office. "Any word yet from Washington?"

I shook my head. "Not yet, a little more patience. We're pushing it."

Each day telephone calls came into Building 104, the administration building. The telephone, the lifeline to the outside world, outflanked the fence and the quarantine.

Joseph Flink, an army sergeant, called from New York. "I've just read the newspaper. My parents' names are on the list. Can I talk to them?"

His father and mother were victims of Kristallnacht, the Night of Broken Glass in Berlin, when the Nazis had smashed Jewish shops and beaten hundreds of Jews. Now his parents hurried to the phone, quivering with emotion.

"Miracles, miracles are happening," sixty-six-year-old Naftaly wept into the phone. "That I should hear your voice again, after six years!"

Joseph had left Berlin with a visa in 1938; he had become an American citizen and was now home on leave from the war.

"Maybe there will be another miracle," Naftaly breathed into the phone. "Maybe your sister is alive."

"Papa, because I hear your voice, for the first time I believe it can happen. When can I come to see you?"

Naftaly put down the receiver and asked someone on the staff, "When can my son come to see us?"

He returned to the phone. "You can't come. Not till the quarantine is over. Imagine! A sergeant in the U.S. Army and you can't come through the fence!"

In a small apartment in New York's borough of Queens, a woman sipping her breakfast coffee read the list of 982 refugees in a newspaper. One named jumped at her. "Dr. Hugo Graner."

She shook her children. "Wake up—wake up! Daddy's in America!"

She and their two children had sailed to America on the last ship in 1939. Born in Vienna, they had visas; there were still quotas for Austrians. But Dr. Graner, born in Hungary, had been denied a visa. The Hungarian quota was full.

She reached him by telephone. "Hugo," she cried. She had planned all the things she would tell him, how proud he would be of fourteen-year-old Otto and of Hildegarde, now eleven, how bright they were in school, how she had gone to work as a domestic to support them. There were a hundred questions she wanted to ask him. Instead she kept crying, "Hugo. Hugo. Hugo." She heard her husband crying.

Finally she said, "When can we come up to see you?"

"I'll go ask. Call me again in an hour."

He turned to me, hoping I could help.

"When can they come?"

I shook my head sadly. "On September first. It's the first day visitors will be allowed."

"I don't know if Hildegarde even remembers what I look like."

"It's the quarantine."

"But that's three weeks away!"

I didn't trust my voice to answer. His shoulders sagged; he walked slowly out the door.

Screams of joy made me jump from my desk to the barred window.

"She's alive!" seventeen-year-old Miriam Weinstein called to her younger sisters and brothers. "Come quick. Mama's alive!"

I hurried outside, where a crowd was beginning to surround the Weinstein children. Tears streaked down Miriam's cheeks.

"My mother is in Switzerland looking for us!" She held up a copy of *Aufbau*, a German-language newspaper published in New York.

Some had called the six Weinstein children "the Weinstein orphans." On the ship, Miriam, shy, soft-spoken, had told me how they and their parents had escaped from Belgium to southern France, where they hid for a few years. Then the rumors spread: "The Americans are in Naples, soon they will liberate all of Italy." A committee of Jewish leaders told the refugees, "Mothers with small children should try to get to Italy by bus; all others should go by train." The Weinstein family separated. Mrs. Weinstein took her three youngest children on the bus; the father and the six older children went by train. The mother and the three babies disappeared.

"We were sure," Miriam had told me, "they were caught by the Nazis and were dead. Then, just before Rome was liberated, the Nazis swept up every Jew they could find in Italy, like a last gasp of hatred. They caught Papa and deported him to the death camps. And now Mama is alive."

While Rabbi Tzechoval blessed this latest miracle, assuring us, "God has arranged it," I went back inside my office and put my head on my desk. I was now working twelve and fifteen hours a day, waking at dawn, leaving late at night for my room at the Pontiac Hotel, spending hours with the refugees, acting as liaison with the Jewish and Christian agencies, sitting on committees, speaking with Washington.

The joyous scene outside my window left me elated and depressed. The Weinstein orphans were orphans no more. Their mother was alive. We would send her a cable in Switzerland that her children were safe.

But they could not be reunited. The children would not be allowed to leave the town even after the quarantine was lifted—because they had come outside the quota. And, with the war, there was no way of sending them to Switzerland or bringing their mother to America.

They were in limbo.

The next days sped swiftly.

International Harry was circumcised. According to Jewish law, he should have been circumcised eight days after he was born. But on the ship Olga had insisted, "No doctor will butcher my baby. Only a *mohel* will circumcise him." A *mohel* was neither a doctor nor a rabbi but a technician with a special knife for circumcisions.

The *mohel* was imported from New York City, and a mob of people squeezed into Olga and Leon's little one-room apartment. "We have to see how it's done in America."

Red-bearded, dressed in a white ceremonial caftan, the *mohel* carefully placed Harry on a pillow, intoned a prayer, and, while Harry screamed and Olga turned white, cut the foreskin.

"That *mohel* is as good as anybody in Warsaw or Vienna or Zagreb," the Brith Milah mavens approved. Leon poured wine for the guests, who toasted the proud parents. "He should bring you *naches*. You should have a long life with him together."

Remembering the prophecy of the GIs who had helped deliver Harry, I asked Olga, "How does the brigadier general feel now, after his Brith Milah?"

"What brigadier general?" Olga, rapidly becoming Americanized, exclaimed. "He's going to be a doctor!"

As the days passed, people began to adjust to the life of eating, sleeping, walking, gaping through the fence, and building friendships with visitors from Oswego and Syracuse who talked through the chain links. The young people had discovered an American delicacy, Eskimo Pies, and each afternoon those who had five cents bought Eskimo Pies from a vendor, marveling at a country that could put ice cream on a stick.

Most were still euphoric, but none more than the orthodox, who had been given a barracks near the lake for a synagogue. Jack Cohen, a short, dynamic businessman from Rochester representing B'nai B'rith, brought a Sefer Torah, the Holy Scroll, so that services could be held the first Friday night.

Meanwhile the need for clothing was critical. WRA decided that the refugees should be allowed to buy their clothing in town, to create good relations with local shopkeepers. The refugees would be given a monthly clothing allowance of $4.50 for children under eleven, $7.00 for young people from twelve to seventeen, and $8.50 for those over eighteen. But until the quarantine was lifted no one could go downtown, and many still had no shoes.

A few volunteers went into town and bought hundreds of shoes for children, teenagers, and adults and distributed them from a warehouse. Manya found a pair of white kid pumps with low heels. "They fit," she shrieked. "I haven't had shoes that were fitted just for me for years. They're going to be my good-luck shoes."

But some people's feet had grown swollen and calloused; they could find no shoes that fit. And thus many were barefoot for the first Friday-night service in the orthodox synagogue.

All week men and women had scrubbed the barracks building until the floor, the windows, and the walls glistened and smelled of scouring powder and soap. Carpenters had built an altar and an ark for the Holy Scroll.

The spirit of Shabbat settled on the camp at sundown. Men and women walked with their children down the tree-lined streets, past the post cemetery, its soldiers' markers casting long shadows on the ground, toward the synagogue barracks overlooking the lake.

Rabbi Tzechoval stood behind the altar, bearded like an Oriental prince, a white prayer shawl encircling his shoulders and arms. The fortunate men who had little sons led them, like precious possessions, to the front of the synagogue as we joined together, reciting the prayers, singing the songs written hundreds of years ago, songs from the halcyon days of their childhood.

The men in their ragged jackets, women in their patched and shapeless housedresses, children in torn sandals, joyously greeted the Sabbath:

> "O come, my friend, to meet the bride,
> O come and welcome the Sabbath queen."

The voices carried through the open windows down to the lake. The next day, Shabbat morning, Joseph Langnas, having come of age at thirteen, born in Vienna, hiding and running for six years, celebrated his bar mitzvah. In a white silk prayer shawl, reading the Holy Scroll in the ancient tradition, he became a man.

Sunday morning, the Catholics celebrated mass in the post chapel, followed by services for the Greek Orthodox and the Protestants. In the quiet afternoon, a long limousine drove through the gate. Tall, white-haired Rabbi Stephen S. Wise stepped out of the back of his car and entered my office. I remembered his impassioned speech at the Stop Hitler Now rally, and the terrible letdown when no action was taken by the government and millions more died.

"I would like to visit the camp. Will you show me around?" Rabbi Wise asked, his mellifluous voice rolling through the little office.

We drove around in the limousine. His wife, Louise Waterman Wise, famous for her work in finding families to adopt orphan children, sat up front with the chauffeur, while the rabbi and I sat in the back. Word spread that the Grand Rabbi of America, *der Grossrabbiner Amerikas,* had come to visit. People crowded the streets to wave at him. Sitting like a monarch, he waved back.

That evening, in his honor, Leo Mirković, Otto Presser, Anny Pick, Manya—the whole retinue of artists who had entertained the soldiers on the ship—performed in the post theater. At the piano Charles Abeles played three songs he had composed: "The Captain Korn March," "Miss Gruber's Slow Foxtrot," and "I Have a Girl in Springfield, Mass."

During the intermission, Manya came to the front row where I sat with Rabbi Wise and his wife.

"Any news about us?"

"Come to my office in the morning; I expect a decision tomorrow."

Early the next morning, Manya and Ernst pushed open the door. "Well?"

"Washington has told us, 'Follow all regulatory procedures.' "

Manya looked bewildered. "What does that mean? Is it good or bad?"

"It's good, Manya."

We wasted no time. Within the hour, Manya and Ernst were given blood tests in our camp hospital. The forms were sent to the Syracuse Department of Health. Then, with an escort, the two were driven past the army guard at the main gate. They entered the office of the city clerk in Oswego, answered more questions, signed more papers, and received the legal document—their marriage license.

"Can we get married tomorrow?" Manya pressed me.

"I don't see why not."

She looked down at her father's shirt. "But, Ruthie, I have no dress!"

I telephoned my mother in Brooklyn. "We're having a wedding tomorrow, Mom. Can you come up and bring the cocktail dress I left in your house, and a veil for the bride?"

"Would she . . ." Manya hesitated. "Would your mother give me away?"

I nodded swiftly.

Thursday, August 17, was a perfect wedding day. A gentle wind sighed off Lake Ontario. Manya and a few of us raced around the camp picking flowers and leaves for her bridal bouquet.

In the barracks room, my mother and I helped Manya slip into the gown; ankle-length for me, it came to Manya's calf, swirling gracefully over her long shapely legs and her white "good-luck" shoes. We angled a mirror so she could see how the necklace framed her slender throat. The pearls my mother had thoughtfully packed made her white skin glow.

She turned and twisted to see the dress curving around her breasts and her slender hips. Her hair, brushed up into a French twist, lay in a soft wave on her forehead. My mother stood on tiptoes and, unfolding the gossamer white silk shawl she had crocheted, draped it over Manya's hair and shoulders.

Manya bent down and kissed her. "Maybe my mother is alive. Maybe God is keeping her alive. But today you are like my mother. I will always love you for this."

My mother's eyes filled with tears.

A little after ten o'clock Adam Munz's mother, Fradl, small, soft-spoken, entered the barracks; Manya had asked her if she would also accompany her to the *chupa*, the bridal canopy. Fradl took one arm, my mother the other, replacing the father and mother Manya prayed were alive.

The three women moved slowly past the crowd of refugees on the parade ground, then past the staff, most of whom had never seen a Jewish wedding under the sky, and finally past the corps of journalists and photographers recording the first bridal ceremony in the first government haven for Holocaust survivors on American soil. Ernst, waiting solemnly under the *chupa*, stared at the beautiful young woman being led toward him. Their eyes met and held.

Fradl and my mother handed Manya to Ernst and stepped behind her under the canopy, and the ceremony began.

An American rabbi was needed to make the marriage legal. Rabbi Bialik of Oswego intoned, "May He Who is Supreme Power, blessed and glory, bless this bridegroom and bride." Holding a prayer book in his left hand and a wineglass in his right, he proclaimed, "The sanctification of all great moments in Jewish life is symbolized by the drinking of the wine."

He handed the goblet to Ernst, who sipped a few drops and then held the cup to Manya's lips.

"As you share the wine of this cup," the rabbi pronounced, "may you share all things, from this day on, with love and understanding."

Ernst slipped a gold ring on Manya's finger and in a strong voice repeated after the rabbi. "By this ring you are consecrated to me as my wife in accordance with the law of Moses and Israel."

Manya looked at the ring for long moments, then, turning her face up to Ernst, recited the biblical "I am to my beloved and my beloved is to me."

"Be thou, Marjam"—Ernst spoke her given name—"my wife according to the law of Moses, I faithfully promise that I will be a true husband to thee and I will honor and cherish thee."

"And I," Manya answered, just above a whisper, "plight my troth unto thee in affection and in sincerity."

Again the rabbi gave them wine to sip. "I pronounce you husband and wife. May the Lord bless you and keep you and cause His countenance to shine upon you and bring you peace."

Rabbi Tzechoval, partaking of the service, blessed them; then Rabbi Bialik placed a wineglass on the ground at Ernst's feet. "We break the glass, to remind us, even on this day of joy, of the destruction of the Temple in Jerusalem."

Ernst stamped on the glass, shattering it.

"*Mazel tov! Mazel tov!* Good luck! Good luck!"

Ernst reached for Manya and held her in a long passionate kiss. Manya clung to him. He finally released her so that we could all kiss her—my mother, Fradl, the refugees, the staff.

As if it were a garden wedding, we walked in small happy groups toward one of the mess halls, where the chefs, forgetting the budget, had prepared a sumptuous feast complete with a wedding cake. The reporters rushed to their typewriters. Late in the afternoon, a newsboy brought us copies of the *Oswego Palladium-Times,* the town's one daily.

"What does it say?" my mother asked. We had been walking the grounds, talking to people. "Read it to me."

A small group assembled as I opened the paper. I read so that everyone could hear. "The bride wore a gown of steel gray, fashioned street length, and a headdress of Spanish lace."

"Spanish lace!" My mother burst into laughter. "I finished crocheting it on the train coming up."

I read on, translating for those who spoke no English, "Her flowers were roses of Sharon intermingled with ferns, in a hand bouquet."

The reporter had written it up as if it were a Junior League wedding.

SEVENTEEN

LIFE CAME TO OSWEGO.

"Refugees Arrive from Europe," *Life* headlined its August 21, 1944, lead article. In a myriad of faces, Alfred Eisenstaedt, *Life*'s ace photographer, captured the emotions of the first days, the bewilderment, the lines queuing up for two towels and a bar of soap, the people peering through the fence.

The photos were so moving, the article so sympathetic, that hundreds of readers wrote letters to the camp, especially to Edith Semjen, whose sultry beauty, set off by her partisan uniform, made her look as if she had stepped out of a Yugoslav version of *For Whom the Bell Tolls*. From New York to California, men asked her to marry them. Soldiers wrote that they were pinning her *Life* photo on their lockers. "Let me get you away from that fence and free you."

Edith carried a bagful of mail to my office. "What do you do in America? Do you answer every letter you get?"

"For a lonesome soldier, a letter from you could be a shot in the arm."

Edith lit a cigarette. "I'll get my girlfriends to help me answer them." She inhaled, then flicked an ash. "Maybe it'll help speed up the war." For the war was never more than inches away.

On the parade ground, Mirković rushed toward me. "Have you heard? Churchill is meeting with Tito. Maybe they'll be liberating Yugoslavia soon."

Waves of joy spread through the camp with the news that a thousand bombers had dropped their fire on German strongholds from Paris to the sea, and that the Seventh Army was landing in the very area from which so many had begun their trek across the Alps.

But fears for their relatives, especially in Hungary, hung heavy on the camp. Until a few months before, Hungary had been able to stave off Hitler's plans for total *Vernichtung*, annihilation. Admiral Miklós Horthy, Regent of Hungary, had insisted on his country's right to handle Hungarian Jews in its own way; Hungary was a co-belligerent, not an occupied or conquered land. Hitler, angry and irritated, attributed Horthy's actions to an unnatural sympathy for Jews. Horthy had a Jewish wife.

Then, on March 19, 1944, Hitler decided to wait no longer. German troops occupied Hungary. The mass extermination of Jews began. The Prime Minister of Hungary, Miklós Kállay, understood the Nazi action only too well. "The greatest enemies of the Nazis," he wrote, "the targets of their deepest hatred, were living unmolested in the very heart of the German sphere of power—a million strong. Was one little country, one man, to hinder the execution of their totalitarian plans?"

In the camp, we tried to bolster each other; there were ways now to save the Jews of Hungary. The War Refugee Board, which had created our shelter, was sending emissaries to rescue them. Perhaps more neutral countries would help. Perhaps the Vatican. Perhaps even the International Red Cross, never distinguished for its compassion for Jews. In moments of despair, we suspected that help would be too little and come too late. Eichmann, the great overseer of *Vernichtung*, engineer of the death trains, made sure the trains ran on time, rushing five and six thousand Jews each day to feed the ovens of Auschwitz. The guards in Auschwitz, with incredible callousness, were calling their newest victims "Hungarian salami."

Meanwhile, the day-to-day living problems, even the smallest ones, had to be coped with. "Those two slices of white bread they give us"—Abe Furmanski, short, rotund, sat in my office, gently complaining—"they're on one tooth. We want bread you can cut yourself with a big knife." He circled his left arm as if he were embracing a round loaf; then, with his right hand clutching an imaginary knife, he sawed through the bread, his eyes shut as if he could still smell the delicious aromas of the bakeshops of his childhood.

White bread versus black bread became a cause célèbre, picked up by the press. A columnist charged that we were starving the people "with uneatable white bread and undrinkable bitter tea."

"Would you look into this crisis," Joe Smart asked me, "before the papers make it sound as if we're having a riot?"

The budget for food was forty-five cents per day per person. The chefs, largely recruited from WRA, were serving the same menus, with the same two slices of white bread, that they had set before the Japanese Americans in their relocation centers.

After a few days I reported to Joe, "We've got a thousand people with a thousand different reactions. Some tell me they never ate so well and so much; one of them [it was Manya] still hides the bread under her pillow. But others say they're hungry all the time and whatever they eat is tasteless."

"Sounds like soldiers bellyaching in every camp."

"But, Joe, the yearning for black bread is different. Black bread is their oxygen, their culture. Why don't we establish a bakery on the grounds and bake black bread right here?"

"No problem."

The crisis was over.

"Washington wants us to set up an advisory council," Joe told me in his office. "I'd like you to help."

Flyers were sent around the camp in all languages, announcing the elections.

The leaders who had emerged on the ship now converged on Joe's office.

"The only way to elect these representatives is by nationality groups," Dr. Juda Levi of Yugoslavia insisted.

I expected a replay of the fiery confrontations on the ship, with Artur Hirt, the Polish judge, opposing him. To my surprise, Hirt agreed. "The nationality groups can be a bridge, helping the American staff understand us."

"Your arguments are well taken," Joe also agreed. "We will hold the election by nationality groups. The council will be made up of ten men. Two each will be elected from the four largest groups: Yugoslavs, Austrians, Poles, and Germans. The final two will represent all the other smaller national groups."

Now it was Dr. Levi who protested. "That's not fair. We Yugoslavs are the largest group in the camp. We should have more representatives than all the others."

Hirt's face reddened. "There you go, you Yugoslavs. Always wanting more than anyone else. You suffered less than most of us. Some of you could even bring clothes with you. We have only the shirts on our back." He turned to me. "You didn't follow our advice about housing."

It was true. The staff, unaware of the confrontation on the ship, had assigned the barracks even before we arrived. Not nationality or intellect but the size of each family had been the criterion. The dire predictions had evaporated. In housing, at least, the frontiers of Europe had been washed away.

"I have to admit to you, Fräulein Ruth," Hirt said, smiling, "that we were wrong about the housing. But on this council, if you give the Yugoslavs more representatives than you give the rest of us, we will fight even if it starts a riot."

"The discussion is academic," Smart said. "Washington has approved a ten-man council."

The Yugoslavs held the first election. By six-thirty in the evening more than half of the 368 Yugoslavs in the camp crowded into the social hall. Arguments rose and fell, people yelled at one another, women carried out their sleeping children and returned to the fray. At midnight, the debate was suddenly halted. Ten men were elected, and they in turn chose two to represent them on the council. They were Dr. Levi and Filip Baum, Fredi's father.

In the next few days the other nationality groups met, until at last the ten representatives were chosen. Joe asked me to address the first meeting of the new Temporary Advisory Council.

Building 3, an old headquarters near the lake, was to become the parliament house, the mecca of democracy in the camp. The ten council members sat on hard chairs facing a wooden table at which Joe sat, flanked by Dr. Levi (the elected president), Fredi (the secretary and interpreter), and me.

Smart opened the meeting, greeting the council with the solemn dignity of a man cloaked in history.

"We meet," Smart said, "as a council on common grounds for a common cause, for the general good of the people in the camp." He waited while Fredi translated the words into German.

The basic policies of the camp, Smart explained, would come from Washington. "Over these policies I have no discretion. But other policies I can make, and these are the ones we shall be discussing in the days to come, changing them if they need to be changed, working together to implement them.

"The government's function"—Smart outlined the spheres of influence—"is to provide food, shelter, and clothing. Yours is to maintain spirit and morale."

He suggested that the councilors set up committees for such needs as housing, education, and food, appoint a "house leader" for each barracks and meet with him every morning at eleven. The men then talked quietly among themselves. "We know this is a temporary advisory council," Dr. Levi said. "We would therefore like to suggest that after thirty days we have a general election for the whole camp. We would like to elect a council"—he spoke slowly, emphasizing each word—"not on the basis of nationalities but on the basis of barracks."

They were de-Balkanizing themselves!

"Mrs. Reid would like you to come to dinner this Sunday evening. Some of the guests may be helpful to you with the refugees."

For anyone connected with the *New York Herald Tribune*, an invitation to dinner at Mrs. Ogden Reid's was a kind of command performance. "Queen Helen," a national magazine had labeled her. Scarcely five feet tall, with delicate features and chinalike skin,

Helen Reid was a publishing giant, owner of the most powerful Republican newspaper in the country. "Queen Helen" was herself a kingmaker, who tried and failed to make Wendell Willkie president in 1940 and would later succeed in helping to make Dwight Eisenhower president in 1952.

It was a warm August evening when I rang the bell of the Reid town house off Fifth Avenue on East Eighty-fourth Street in Manhattan. After the barracks of Oswego the house seemed more palatial than ever, with its marble foyer, gracefully curved stairs, Persian rugs, and crystal chandeliers.

Mrs. Reid, in a long silk gown, introduced me as the guests entered: politicians, foreign correspondents, industrialists, and John Cowles, the senior member of the Cowles publishing empire, owner of the *Des Moines Register,* the *Minneapolis Tribune,* and *Look.* After cocktails and hors d'oeuvres, we entered the dining room, lit with tall candles, festooned with fresh flowers. Seated at the head of the table, Helen led the conversation. The war. The Allied armies sweeping across Europe. The battles in the Pacific.

The talk swirled past me. I kept thinking, How can they help? Cowles's papers and the *Herald Tribune* were the liberal vanguard of the Republican Party. They could create a climate of sympathy throughout the country. More refugees could be saved. More havens could be opened. Moreover, they could influence the townspeople of Oswego, for it too was a Republican stronghold.

After dinner we adjourned to the drawing room for demitasse. As the guests lit cigarettes and cigars, and sipped coffee, Mrs. Reid announced, "You all know, of course, about the thousand refugees who've come to this country at the President's invitation."

John Cowles and his wife, Betty, looked up from their coffee.

"Ruth brought them." Helen put her cup down on an end table and turned to me. "I wish you would tell us some of your experiences."

I told them of the three-day trek over the Alps, of International Harry, of Mirković and the beautiful young women entertaining the soldiers on the ship.

"Now we were on the train to Oswego—" I was saying, when Betty Cowles interrupted.

"What! You brought the refugees to Oswego?"

She leaped from her chair, her eyes dancing. "Oswego is my hometown! I was born up there. My mother's still there; they call her the Dowager Queen. When are you going back?"

"I'll be there tomorrow morning."

"The minute you get back, go see her. I'll phone her to expect you. She can open every door you need opened."

The next morning I presented myself at Florence Bates's three-story white mansion.

"Of course I read about the refugees in our *Palladium-Times.*" She waved me to a sofa. "I even read about the wedding. Betty repeated some of the stories you told them last night. I've already decided I'm going to help you." She was smiling. "Our town has needed something like this to wake it up."

However Florence Bates worked, she helped create the climate of goodwill we needed and opened innumerable doors, as did many others, merchants, educators, lawyers, and religious leaders. Even before we arrived in the camp, Joe Smart had met with some of the town's leading citizens. Now they formed the Oswego Advisory Committee.

Charlie Goldstein, the owner of Oswego's department store, addressed one of the first meetings in Joe's office. "On the whole," he reported, "the town reaction to the refugees has been nearly one hundred percent favorable. We've even started a 'fence club,' where people make friends talking through the fence. People on the outside are getting a bigger thrill than the people on the inside. But, unfortunately, yes, we do have anti-Semitism, and rumors are starting up against the camp."

"What kind of rumors?" I asked.

"That the refugees all have private bathtubs."

"Bathtubs! They don't even have privacy in the showers." The shower curtains from Rochester had not yet arrived.

"They're spreading other rumors—that every apartment has a

refrigerator and they're lavishly furnished, all at the taxpayers' expense."

"I'm not worried about rumors," said Ralph Mizen, a thin, tight-lipped attorney, who spoke with authority. He had just been elected chairman. "I remember the furor that broke out in this town when the Associated Press notified us sometime around 1941 that Negro troops were being shipped here after they had shot up the town of Brownsville, Texas. Rumors were flying. 'Our women will be raped. They're going to rob us. Drunken soldiers will burn the town down.' But after they came, we found they were as good as any soldiers we had here.

"We felt the same way when the 'morons' were sent here," he went on. "They were illiterate soldiers sent here for remedial work. Each group turned out much better than we suspected. Now it's our job to make sure that the town takes the same attitude toward the refugees."

Turning to me, he said, "Help us to understand the refugees better. What is their most urgent need?"

"Each day," I said, "young people come to my office with one request: 'When can we go to school?' There are two brothers, Rajko and Alex Margulis. They were medical students in Belgrade. Most of their fellow students who were anti-Nazis or Jews were murdered. Their only dream now is to continue their studies. They're brilliant young men."

I paused.

"I hope soon you will meet them. You will admire them, as I do. Young people, filled with a passion for learning."

"What is the War Relocation Authority's position on schools?" Mizen asked Joe Smart.

"The head of our agency in Washington, Dillon Myer, feels that government shouldn't have too much responsibility in education. There should be some schooling, to be sure. But the government doesn't want to make Americans out of them, because they aren't going to be Americans. They're going back to Europe when the war's over. We have two options. We can keep them in the camp and bring in teachers; the private agencies have already agreed to pay for them. The other alternative is to throw the Oswego schools open to them. The invitation must come from you."

"I would think," Mizen said, "we will have to discuss among ourselves some of the problems this raises. The smart thing to do—to use your name, Mr. Smart—is for the group to organize itself into an education committee and study this question."

In the Pontiac Hotel, lying in bed, I listened to the rush of the Oswego River below my window. I had been in the camp for nearly two weeks. It's time, I thought, to go back to Washington. To report to Ickes.

Even in these weeks of quarantine, people had begun settling into a rhythm of life. Some of the adults and teenagers had started giving informal classes in English; the entertainers were putting their acts and skits together. Yet anxiety hovered over the camp.

"What will happen to us when the quarantine is lifted on the first of September? Can we leave the camp? What about jobs? Schools? Freedom to travel? Freedom in the land of America?" I had no answers.

Whatever power I had lay in Ickes's confidence. In the totem pole of Washington bureaucracy, the top man made decisions. But below him, his staff formulated recommendations, gave him options, fought, if necessary, for their convictions and, once the decision was made, carried them through.

Ickes had to know some of the problems before they escalated.

Friday morning I telephoned him. "Mr. Secretary, I feel I must come back to Washington."

"But I've just had a letter from Rabbi Stephen Wise, asking me to let you stay on for some weeks longer. He writes you've been so useful—"

"I must see you. There are urgent problems."

"Very well. I'll see you at ten on Monday morning."

Friday evening the beauty of the Sabbath once again spread across the barracks and the parade ground. The knowledge that this would be my last weekend in the camp, for a while at least, gave this Sabbath evening special poignancy.

Some still in their rags, others in the clothes that had been thrown over the fence, the people walked across the camp. A second house of worship was to be inaugurated this evening for the conservative and reform Jews, in the former army chapel. The chapel was used on other days for the Christian refugees.

In the late-afternoon sun, the army barracks where the orthodox were worshiping and the white wooden army chapel with its tall spire seemed like sanctuaries of peace. Inside the chapel, the altar had been covered with a white silk cloth, and people sat on wooden benches in the glow of the Holy Torah and the Eternal Light.

Dressed in a black robe and a white prayer shawl, Rabbi Hajim Hazan led the services in Hebrew, Serbo-Croatian, and Ladino, the language spoken by many Jews of the Balkans. Expelled from Spain in 1492, the Jews had created this Judeo-Spanish language; its base was Spanish, with a mixture of words from lands in which the Sephardic Jews had settled. Rabbi Hazan, who spoke almost no German, began his sermon in Serbo-Croatian. A young Yugoslav sitting beside me whispered, "He's talking about the ones we lost— sons, brothers, husbands, wives, children. . . ."

Behind me, two women began complaining in German. I turned and put my finger on my lip, hoping they would be silent. Instead one of them leaned toward me. "*Schrecklich. Ich verstehe nichts.*" (It's terrible. I don't understand a thing.)

A few men stalked out of the chapel. Joe Smart, a devout Mormon, believing that the service was over, followed them.

When the Friday-evening prayers ended, I left the chapel, only to find a small cluster of men waiting for me.

"How dare he?" they shouted.

"Who?"

"Hazan! That he would give a sermon in a language not one of us understands."

An argument on Shabbat! When would these rivalries end?

Seeing my dismay, an Austrian Jew explained, "Most people in the camp, even the Yugoslavs, understand German. But only the Yugoslavs understand the Yugoslav language."

A Yugoslav waved his fist at some of the Germans. "You are Germans first, then Jews. You want to inflict the German language on everyone. Remember, out of seventy thousand, the Germans have wiped out sixty-six thousand Yugoslav Jews. We want to kill the German language in our minds, in our hearts, in our souls. We have a right to our language. But in this camp the hated German language is constantly thrown at us."

Bitterness and resentment, stored up for generations, erupted. The Sabbath peace was broken.

Mr. Campbell, in charge of the camp guards, was called to the fray. He frisked the men and discovered a knife in an Austrian's pocket. He took the Austrian, and a Yugoslav with whom he had been arguing, to Joe's office. Joe was called from his home to determine whether the town police should be involved.

Joe decided to wait. He asked both Campbell and the leaders of the Advisory Council to investigate and report to his office the next afternoon.

In the evening, a few of the older men sought me out.

"Look what's happening to us," Ernst Wolff said. "That we can have a fight over such a little thing. There's a war against us in the world, and we fight among ourselves. It's a disgrace."

Fewer than ten people had been involved, but it needed only a few to poison the air. The men were soul-searching now, trying to understand the outburst and put it into perspective. The German and Austrian Jews had lost more than their homelands. They felt they were being reviled by the others in the camp because they were a constant reminder of the German madness that had darkened the earth. Victims themselves, they felt betrayed, rejected, hated. The sermon in Serbo-Croatian was the final straw.

Saturday morning, Dr. Margulis, a leader of the Yugoslavs, met me on the parade ground. "You must attend this meeting. We lay much weight upon it."

I had no intention of not attending.

Joe sat behind his desk, holding a typescript in his hand. "I've had the report from Mr. Campbell. There were loud arguments, but there was no violence. One man had a knife in his pocket, not in his hand, and there was no evidence that he tried to use it."

"What about the Oswego police, will they arrest anyone?" Dr. Margulis asked.

"I would like to explain something to you about our country. The police in America are given considerable discretion; they decide whether to make arrests or not. Mr. Campbell has recommended that no one be arrested or tried."

Dr. Milorad Novović, a Serbian Orthodox lawyer, looked worried. "We hope this ugly incident will not be published in the newspapers."

"This is a free country, and not even the government can censure the press," Joe said. "I hope you members of the council agree with our decision to arrest no one."

The men nodded.

"I realize," he went on, "that I made a mistake by walking out. I have therefore written an apology, which I should now like to read to you:

> I went to the service happy to worship in reverence, happy to worship a common God who knows no difference of language and nationality, and proud to worship with people I thought shared a common bond of humility and devotion. Racial or national and religious differences have no place in Fort Ontario or anywhere else in America. I, of a faith different from yours, came to worship with you a common God; and I hope you will respect that difference, as surely as you must the differences amongst yourselves which result from the many cultures represented.

The council members sat openmouthed; they had obviously never heard a man in a position like Joe's offer an apology.

"We are so impressed by your wisdom in handling this crisis,"

Dr. Novović said, "that we would like to translate your apology into all our languages for the whole camp to know."

Saturday night I took the midnight sleeper to New York. My mother and father were wide awake as my taxi pulled up to the stoop early Sunday morning. Neighbors in their Sunday best were walking to church.

"I'm learning a lot about your work," my father said mysteriously. We were eating breakfast in the huge kitchen-dining room. My mother was in the alcove, toasting bagels.

"I guess Mom's been telling you about the camp—and the wedding."

"She told me. But I get a lot from the newspapers." He walked toward a stack of papers on the buffet. He was obviously saving every scrap of information about the refugees.

"Listen to this from Friday's *Forward*."

My mother called from the alcove. "Dave, don't you dare start reading until I bring in the coffee."

"You want to hear it again? You've only heard it twelve times."

"So I'll hear it thirteen times. All right, now begin."

He adjusted his glasses, stroked his mustache, and began to read. " 'Darling and mother of the shelter is a young woman named Ruth Gruber—' "

My mother broke in. "You should have heard them. *'Unser Mutter Ruchel iss offgeshtanden.'* " (Our Mother Ruth has risen.)

"Come on, Mom," I protested, "you didn't hear them say that."

"Would I make up such a lie? Would I know that women older than me are calling my daughter their mother?"

"You two can argue later," my father said impatiently. "Let me go on. 'She is an official of the Department of the Interior who was sent to Italy to accompany the refugees on their journey across the sea.' "

"Pop, we know all that."

He seemed not to hear. " 'During the thirteen-day trip across the ocean, Miss Gruber taught the refugees English, listened to their life histories, and tried to help them with their personal problems. In camp, also, the refugees come to Miss Gruber with many of their problems and complaints—' "

"You should have seen how they came to her." My mother interrupted again. "Like she was a *rebbe*."

My father continued. " 'Frequently heard at the shelter is the phrase "She is our guardian angel. Miss Gruber will intercede on our behalf; she will help us." And the smallish young Miss Gruber must listen to all the complaints, appeals, and requests of the refugees.' "

"I don't know what kind of guardian angel I am, but anyway I'm taking some of those complaints and appeals to Ickes."

On the four-thirty express to Washington, I sat thinking of my mother, small, sharp-witted, acerbic, and my father, tall, wise, the patriarch to whom all our relatives and friends came for advice. Theirs was the immigration experience of the first generation, sweating their way up the ladder from poverty to the middle class so their children would get the education they never had. Perhaps their passion for education was why I felt so much empathy for our young people in the camp who were determined to go to school. My parents had given me the chance for education, but they had never come to terms with how I used it. Their highest ideal for me was to be a secretary or a schoolteacher. For them I was the maverick who caused them both pride and apprehension. A teenager in Germany, a young woman in her twenties flying across the Arctic—they were in constant fear that I might be killed and they would lose me forever. They were warm and loving; they had molded me but found it hard to understand me. In their Old World yearnings, I was a stranger who had invented myself.

Now, for the first time, I was doing something they could understand. I was helping Jews. Maybe somehow I could even help rescue the relatives in Wolyn—if they were still alive.

·   ·   ·

Ickes studied the photographs I had taken on the ship. He kept shaking his head. "Look at those children! What those people must have gone through! Let me read one of these case histories."

He picked the first one in the pile. It was marked SCHLEUME FRISCHWASSER.

The horrors of the concentration camp at Dachau are briefly described here. This story must be kept confidential. Mr. Frischwasser begged me not to reveal it, for fear that the Nazis would harm his wife and daughter, who are still in an Austrian concentration camp.

Statement of Schleume Frischwasser:

"I am 55 years old. I was a textile merchant in Vienna. On May 27, 1938, I was captured in my business and taken prisoner. I had to close my business; they took the key and sent me to Dachau. The trip was terrible. My wife and daughter are in the concentration camp in Theresienstadt under Hitler. I am afraid that they will be harmed.

"I was in Dachau, then in Buchenwald, about 11 months in both. As I left the camp, they said, 'If you say anything about what happened to you here, we will harm your wife and daughter.' So please, please don't say that I was there.

"They beat us with sticks as soon as they threw us in the trucks. In the concentration camps they made us stand for hours looking into light. They then made us stand and keep twisting our heads in both directions. They made us beat each other on the toes and kick each other. Men and women were hanged constantly. The worst thing came when one of them escaped. Then all of us had to stand out in the open until he was caught. About 20 percent of the camp died during one such period. Others contracted pneumonia and TB.

"The Nazis had their jokes; they put all the doctors to work cleaning out latrines. They called them Division 4711, the name of a German eau de cologne. Other times they would ask for all the chemists and then would put them to work in latrines.

"Please don't tell this; my wife and daughter will be harmed."

Ickes wiped his glasses.

"Of course we won't publish this," he finally said. "That man has suffered enough without endangering his wife and his daughter—if they're still alive. Is this one the most dramatic?" He placed his hand on the stack of case histories.

"They're all dramatic, Mr. Secretary. They're all people still in pain."

"I can almost hear them talking to you." He drew another history from the pile, shaking his head as he read, occasionally muttering, "My God."

I sat silently, remembering our talks on the ship: *You are living witnesses. You are the ones Hitler tried to kill. . . . You have a mission: to tell America and the world what's happening right now.* Now, I thought, Ickes will have documentary evidence when he speaks to the President and the Cabinet.

The phone rang; Ickes pressed a button. "I want no interruptions," he told his operator. He hunched his shoulders over his desk and continued reading.

He's a fighter, I thought. He's been fighting all along. Maybe now he'll fight harder—against the isolationists in Congress, against the State Department, against men like Breckinridge Long. But not only the isolationists are guilty. We are all guilty. Why didn't we scream? Why didn't we march on the White House?

Ickes lifted his massive head. Once again he wiped his glasses. Then he put the case histories into a bulging briefcase. "I'm going to finish reading the rest at home tonight. I want Jane to read them too."

He snapped the briefcase closed.

"Now, what are the problems you want to discuss with me?"

EIGHTEEN

AT LAST, on a day when the sun turned the camp into a haven of warm light filtering through the trees, and diffident cool winds presaged autumn, the quarantine was lifted.

It was September 1, 1944. Ickes had asked me to go back to the camp to help with the open house.

The whole town of Oswego, 22,000 strong, was invited. People who had stood outside the fence for nearly a month making new friends now swarmed inside. Zlatko Hirschler's sister Vera came up from Crossville, Tennessee, and threw her arms around her brother and his wife, laughing and weeping. Zlatko still wore his only pants from the ship; they had a hole in each knee.

Joseph Flink, dressed in his U.S. Army uniform, searched for his parents. He found them standing in front of their barracks, unable to move toward him, so great was their joy.

Ralph Faust, the principal of the high school, came toward me, clearing his throat. "I'm a little shaken. I just saw an elderly woman kneel down and kiss the ground."

All morning and through the afternoon, thousands of visitors, surrounded by the press, milled through the camp. Florence Bates and the members of the town's Advisory Committee led throngs of friendly (and a few unfriendly) townspeople into the barracks. The sparse GI furnishings, the communal toilets and showers (now neatly curtained) scotched the stories of lavish living at taxpayers' expense. The bathtub rumor died with the open house.

And Oswego opened its schools.

Ralph Faust interrupted his vacation to meet with the camp's young people.

"I'm twenty," Steffi Steinberg said worriedly. Steffi spoke English well, with a German inflection. "Can I still go to high school? I'm afraid I'm too old. It's six years since—"

"Of course you can come."

Steffi registered with nearly forty others, whose ages ranged from sixteen to twenty. Faust himself selected the classes they would enter, depending on how much schooling and how much English they had had. A day before school opened, he took a group on a tour of his high school, proud of the handsome four-story brick building that spanned a whole block on Mohawk and West First. In the basement carpentry shops, he kept hearing *"Magnifique! Magnifique!"* In all his years as an educator, he had never known such enthusiasm.

So important was this next day, when the school doors swung open, that most of the camp—parents, single men and women, mothers with babies—stood at the fence waving goodbye to 193 children and teenagers.

For the children themselves, it was a day never to be seen again, for some a day of joyous anticipation, for others of painful loneliness and even fear.

Tamar Hendel and her cousin Giselle, both nine, squeezed each other's hands tightly as they walked two short blocks to P.S. 2, a little American schoolhouse on Mitchell Street. The principal, Susan Donovan, greeted them solemnly and asked a little girl to escort them to the third-grade classroom. Tamar looked around the classroom, observing everything, the curious chairs attached to wooden desks, the big blackboard, the American children staring at her, the lady teacher behind a big desk calling names from a book. She was elated; there were so many things she would tell her parents back in the camp. Giselle sat beside her, lonely and miserable. The language was mysterious, the classroom was strange, the children seemed cold. She had no parents to confide in.

Branko Hochwald sat toward the back of the room. In the month of quarantine he had acquired a few words of English, but none of the words helped him or his good friend Ivo Hirschler as the teacher began the morning lesson.

Ickes Family Archives

*Secretary of the Interior Harold L.
Ickes, who sent me on the journey
that was to change the course
of my life.*

Courtesy author's collection

*Here I am shepherding
the refugees through
Nazi-infested waters.*

A typical day aboard the Henry Gibbins. *We crowd together with little space, but no one complains: We are on our way to America.*

Ruth Gruber

Day and night we pace the deck as the people tell me their stories. Often I have to stop writing because tears are blurring the words in my notebook.

We begin each day wrapping ourselves in life vests, practicing what to do if we are attacked by Nazi planes or submarines.

Some of the refugees are still in their tattered concentration camp clothes.

The U.S. Army gives the refugees new IDs: tags marked CASUAL BAGGAGE. *The irony is not lost on them.*

Some spend the day getting to know one another. Others sit silent and alone with their grief.

Our ship carries not only one thousand refugees in its bow, but a thousand wounded soldiers from the bloody battles of Anzio and Cassino in its stern.

Among us are Army and Navy officers, pilots, navigators, bombardiers, doctors, and nurses who have finished their tours of duty and are on their way home.

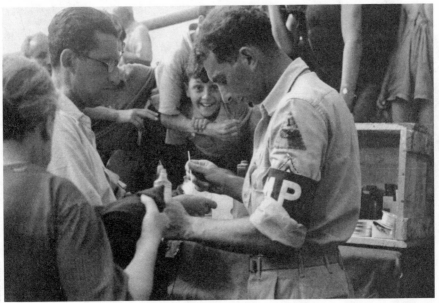

The much-loved medic dispenses pills to the seasick and liquids for those whose stomachs reject the American food after years of starvation. Best of all, he dispenses hope and cheer.

The soldiers bring candies and cookies for the children, and make trysts with some of the beautiful young women. Even the lifeboats come to life.

The children play games they learned in their home-lands, though the curly-haired boy on the left seems lonely and sad.

Ruth Gruber

Children make fast friends, entertaining one another.

Ruth Gruber

Ruth Gruber

The children ask, "When do we reach America?"

Two-year-old André Waksman wears a ribbon in his hair because his mother, Jenny, wanted a little girl.

Ruth Gruber

The children blossom as the good food and fresh air bring color to their cheeks.

Ruth Gruber

We distribute books in English.

Ruth Gruber

The bosun, who looks like Popeye the sailor, becomes a popular figure.

Popeye arranges a tarpaulin in a corner of the deck for shelter.

Abe Tauber, a teacher of English and speech at the Bronx High School of Science, arranges entertainment for the soldiers. Next to me is a volunteer army worker.

Edith Semjen, the Blond Bombshell, brings cheers from the soldiers when she sings "You Are My Sunshine."

I begin teaching the refugees English.

Army officials take turns teaching in our improvised school.

The refugees wave excitedly at the Statue of Liberty.

Our first day in Fort Ontario.

Jack Cohen, a businessman in Rochester, shaking hands with Rabbi Tzechoval, brings two holy scrolls. I stand at the right.

Ruth Gruber

Eva Bass, with Edith Piaf–like wistfulness, finds solace in singing.

Leo Mirković, singing on the camp street in front of the wooden barracks.

The children parade around the campgrounds dressed in their new clothes.

Eleanor Roosevelt and Elinor Morgenthau, at her left, the wife of Henry Morgenthau, Jr., secretary of the Treasury, visit the camp.

Eleanor writes in her newspaper column, "My visit to this shelter has been one of the most wonderful days I have ever spent."

Mathilda Nitsch, a Yugoslav Roman Catholic, is one of our heroines.

Seven-year-old Rachel Frajerman and her little brother Harry, whose head is turned, show their brand-new shoes.

The refugee women become the teachers for the pre-kindergarten children.

Manya and Ernst Breuer's wedding. Manya wears the veil my mother crocheted. The women, my mother at her right, and Fradl Munz at her left, lead her under the chupa.

Miriam Sommerburg, a sculptress from Berlin, writes a play called The Golden Cage, *with music by Charles Abeles. It is the story of the thousand refugees saved from the Nazis but kept behind a fence in America's "golden cage."*

Farther downtown, twenty-four youngsters lined up on a vast green lawn and marched into the Fitzhugh Park School, a brand new three-story junior high school on East Tenth Street.

Henny Notowicz, fourteen, witty, with the gallows humor of a survivor, entered her class humming an English song under her breath. She had learned it in one of the camp classes in the accent of the volunteer refugee teacher:

> I valk to de vindow
> Und I valk to de door,
> Behind me is de vindow
> Und before me is de door.
>
> Above is de ceiling
> Und below is de floor,
> I valk to de vindow,
> Fon de vindow to de door.

Irene Danon, in the row behind Henny, felt that her world was being turned upside down. With ink-black eyes, she was bright, bubbly, effusive in camp, but now she was frightened. Schools had bad memories. She had been expelled from her first school in Belgrade when all the Jews were expelled. Her parents had innocently enrolled her in a private school, not aware it was a school for juvenile delinquents, but soon even that school was barred to Jews. With her parents and her little brother, she began to run, hiding in sewers, living furtively on a false passport as a Russian Orthodox Serbian. Her picturesque Serbian name, Ljiljana, so fit her joy and effervescence that even in the camp she was Ljiljana. But there was no joy this first day. She had dressed in her best clothes, a pair of slacks. The teacher motioned to her angrily. "You go right back to the camp and change to a skirt." She thought she heard the teacher mutter, "Damn refugees."

"I don't believe this," Sonia Sommerburg whispered to herself. "A classroom! The eighth grade. I never thought I would ever in my life sit in a school. I never thought I would even be alive at fifteen."

She had told me much about herself. Her first memory, as a child of four in Hamburg, was of the day Hitler came to power. Her father, Rudolf, who was not Jewish, was an anti-Nazi political writer who had been jailed several times trying to prevent the rise of Nazism. Her mother, Miriam, who was Jewish, was already becoming well known as an artist. With four small children, the family fled to the Italian Riviera. Sitting in the classroom now, watching the teacher draw rounded vowels, *e* and *a,* on the blackboard, Sonia thought of her father. He had been unhappy in Italy. German was his language, not Italian. He decided to return to Germany and granted Miriam the divorce she wanted. The family never heard from him again. Miriam hid their Jewishness from her children until they discovered it themselves when they were arrested by the Italian fascists. They were sent to a small mountain village, where they had to report to the police every day. Miriam later explained that she had hoped she could save their lives by denying their heritage.

For Sylvan Boni, it was a day of sheer adventure. How proud Papa would have been, he thought, if he knew I was now in junior high. Papa had saved the family's life and the lives of one hundred other Jews fleeing Bulgaria. He had bought a boat with his last money and hired a captain for the four-hour voyage from Albania to Italy. They took no food and little water. Nazis came aboard while they were still in harbor; they hid below the deck, silencing the children. As soon as the Nazis left, the captain, the only seaman aboard, weighed anchor, got drunk, and was never seen again. No one knew how to sail the vessel. They drifted for days; the ship sprang a leak; they were half in the water when British soldiers sighted them and towed them to Brindisi. Papa died of a heart attack soon after the rescue.

In the high school, Ralph Faust waited at the entrance to greet the young people who had crossed the bridge over the Oswego River.

"We're going to have an assembly this morning," Faust explained as he led them into the building. "Wait here, we'll be calling you in a little while."

In his office, he sent for the president of the student council. "This is a unique experiment in American history. I would like you to give the welcoming address."

"I won't do it."

"Why not?"

"I don't think they should be in our school or even in our town. The whole community should have been asked if we wanted refugees in Oswego."

"You may leave now. I'll welcome them myself."

The assembly began. The American students, already seated, stared at the unprecedented spectacle of foreigners walking down their aisle in strange clothes, tall and short, fat and scrawny, acne-faced and clear-skinned, plain-looking and handsome, some shy, some apprehensive, some filled with hope.

Among them was Paul Arnstein, slender, medium height, bright-eyed, as curious about the Americans as they were about him. Paul could hardly wait for classes to begin. In Zagreb, his mother, a real-ist, had forced them to flee with the clothes on their backs. "Nobody will harm us," his father had insisted naïvely, even after most of the town's 25,000 Jews had already been murdered or had disappeared. "Everybody knows us; they come to buy their clothes in my shop."

The two Levitch brothers, Eddie and Leon, were already distin-guished in the camp. During the quarantine, their father, a phar-macist who wrote poetry, had pushed his last five dollars through the fence and asked a stranger to buy him a clipper, a straight razor, and a shaving brush. He practiced his new art on Eddie, who then gave haircuts to the teenagers in the shower rooms, which now doubled as "Levitch's Local Barber Shop." Leon, a talented pi-anist at seventeen, accompanied most of the singers in the camp and formed the youth choir, arranging the music for children and young people. They gave several concerts. In Yugoslavia, their fa-ther had taught his two sons, his little daughter, Manon, and his lovely wife, Fortunée, how to hang themselves if the Nazis caught them.

Rosa Moschev, portly and soft-spoken, came next. Her mother

too had saved their lives. Daughter of a Yugoslav banker and married to a Bulgarian, Bella had sewn cloth over her gold napoleons and worn them as buttons on her dress. From Bulgaria, Rosa and her parents fled in a covered wagon driven by oxen to Albania, where, with her gold napoleons, Bella bought a sailboat and crowded seventy people on the deck. It took them six hazardous days in the Adriatic to reach Italy.

Adam Munz, searching the auditorium for his Ping-Pong friend, Jim, the big ace, followed with some thirty others, among them Lilly and Edith Bronner, two handsome girls who had danced the czardas in the camp's first festivities. They had been expelled from their native Hungary when Hitler invaded Poland. Their father, born in Poland, had never been allowed to become a Hungarian citizen, and their mother had lost her Hungarian citizenship when she married him; as stateless Poles, they were thrown into jail in Hungary, then transferred to a concentration camp; after a year, they were told they would be released only if they left Hungary immediately. The family fled to Yugoslavia, already crowded with refugees from Poland. Soon the Germans invaded Yugoslavia; they were forced almost overnight to wear yellow armbands with the word JUDE and work as slave laborers for the Nazi army, cleaning latrines, washing soldiers' laundry, mopping the floors of the barracks. They decided to make their way to the Italian-occupied Dalmatians, but just as their train neared Split, Yugoslav fascists examined their papers and found they were false. The Bronners were pulled off the train and handed to the stationmaster, who promised to have them jailed. It was Christmas Eve. The stationmaster, an Italian, brought them a tray of cookies. Their mother, strong until now, fainted. The stationmaster, who hated the fascists, helped them escape.

Three young women walking together saw Ralph Faust smiling at them. In the weeks before school began, Steffi Steinberg, Lea Hanf, and Edith Weiss, inseparable friends who spoke English, had become Faust's indispensable aides. Behind them came Rolf Manfred Kuznitzki. An only child from a small town in East Prussia, Rolf had learned to speak and even write English with style. But Ivo Lederer, who followed him, boasted that the first English word he had learned on the ship was "fuckin.' " "I kept hearing the sailors up on the bridge shouting, 'Those fuckin' refugees,' " he had told me. "I thought it was a wonderful word."

Then it seemed that the whole auditorium turned to gape. Edith Semjen was strolling down the aisle nonchalantly, her blond hair gleaming. In two days Faust would catch her smoking a cigarette in the corridor and, calling her "the blond bombshell," would ask her to leave. This would not trouble Edith. She had signed up for high school only to get out of the camp. She would find other ways to get out; she had not been with the partisans for nothing. In fact, she had already found a way out. Joe Smart's son, Stanley, had fallen in love with her and even proposed marriage. She told him she would think about it. Meanwhile, like many others, they had broken the quarantine: Stanley hid her under a blanket in the back of his father's car, drove easily past the guard at the gate, and took her out jitterbugging and to the movies.

Last in line was Kostia Zabotin, tall, round-faced, with awesome green eyes. Kostia's father, a gifted painter and a nobleman, had caught Eisenstaedt's eye for his *Life* portraits. Baron Vladimir von Zabotin was Russian Orthodox; Kostia's mother, a landscape painter, was Jewish from Germany; Kostia himself had been born in Karlsruhe. In Italy they had been imprisoned in three different jails until they were reunited in the Ferramonte concentration camp.

Faust watched them all solemnly as they took their seats. Then he asked everyone to rise. The refugee students stood at attention while the Americans pledged allegiance to the flag and sang "The Star-Spangled Banner."

Thus, in all the schools of Oswego, the first day began. Of them all, the high school was to be the most pivotal in the lives of these young people, who brought with them a commitment and an eagerness for knowledge that was to penetrate the town.

Within weeks, Frieda Schuelke, the American-history teacher, came into the camp with members of her honor society to describe the clubs the refugee students could join. In the recreation hall, she realized that not only her students but hundreds of adults were crowding in to hear her. She spoke to the parents in German. "Your young people have shown us they are thrilled to go back to school. They read voraciously, with a dictionary always beside them. I find them delightful, and their hunger for education is heartwarming. We are all benefiting from their presence in our classes. I think the whole community will benefit from your presence in Oswego."

The shop teacher, Thomas Crabtree, piled a group of young men in his car and drove them to Syracuse. It was illegal; no one was supposed to travel outside Oswego, but Crabtree wanted his students to see American industry at work. He took them into industrial plants and showed them such mind-boggling mechanical equipment that several decided that very day they would become engineers.

In Fitzhugh Park Junior High, thirteen-year-old Joseph Langnas was elected president of Class 7B1. "In Austria," his beaming mother boasted, "Joseph could not even go to school, and here he's president of his class."

The students joined the after-school clubs, played baseball and football, basketball and softball, and spent their nights doing homework. And when one of Ernest Spitzer's high school classmates complained that Ernest studied too hard and played too little, he told him, "In prison camp, I was too hungry to study."

Standing outside the high school, an American senior watched the refugee students head for the Gothic-style public library. "At first a lot of us laughed at them for being grinds," he told me. "It made you feel small. But then you felt, If they can do it, when they came here knowing so little English, we can do it too. I guess I'll be taking myself over to the library."

.   .   .

Lord, what is man that Thou art mindful of him?

The voices of the congregants reading the ancient words filled the synagogues.

It was Yom Kippur, the Day of Atonement, the holiest of all the Jewish holidays.

> *Man is like a breath,*
> *His days are as a passing shadow.*
> *In the morning he flourishes and springs up afresh,*
> *By evening he is cut down and he withers.*

Outside, the sun shone on the camp and the barges and ships sailing on Lake Ontario, while in the barracks synagogue near the lake we sat singing, fasting, reading the prayers, soul-searching, asking forgiveness for sins we had committed "publicly or in private, through haughtiness of heart, by word of mouth, by the violence of hand, for showing disrespect to parents and teachers. . . . For all of these, O God of forgiveness, forgive us, spare us, let us atone."

This was their first Yom Kippur in a free land. In Hitler's Europe, Yom Kippur was a day of heightened terror. It was a favorite Nazi technique to choose Jewish holidays for their worst sweeping "actions," when the SS rounded up scores of Jews, herded them onto fields and cemeteries and riverbanks, made them strip naked, and shot them.

The Ark of the Torah was opened. Rabbi Tzechoval and the other men drew their prayer shawls over their heads like ancient Jews praying in the desert. We stood facing the Ark, singing the solemn words:

> *On Rosh Hashanah it is written*
> *and on Yom Kippur it is sealed,*
> *who shall live and who shall die. . . .*
> *Who shall perish by water and who by fire,*

who by the sword and who by hunger,
who by earthquake and who by plague. . . .

Some sobbed as they sang:

Who shall be cast down and who shall be exalted.

The weeping ended. We found refuge in the affirmation that

Repentance, prayer, and charity avert the evil decree.

The day was long, but almost no one left the synagogue. In the afternoon we read the stories of the martyrs in the Middle Ages, taunted by kings to convert. They had been tortured and burned, yet they had kept their faith, dying with the songs we were singing now on their lips.

All through the day we repeated the words:

Remember us to life, O King, who delightest in life,
Seal our fate in the Book of Life for Thy sake, O living God.

Now, through the windows, we could see the sun setting over Lake Ontario. The first stars appeared in the sky as we recited the welcome Ne'ilah, the closing at eventide.

The ram's horn was sounded.

The eerie desert notes filled the night air. The congregation rose, smiling; men shook hands; women kissed their children.

Joyously, we walked to the mess halls and broke our fast.

Two days later, Eleanor Roosevelt arrived with her good friend Elinor, the wife of Henry Morgenthau, Jr.

"The First Lady of America!" Dr. Otto Lederer stared unbelievingly. "The First Lady of America, and she comes without police guards, soldiers, or ladies-in-waiting. Who would believe this in Europe?"

Shaking hands, smiling, Mrs. Roosevelt walked among the people, acknowledging their love. They presented flowers, embroidery, drawings, pieces of sculpture, encircling her as if she were someone they had always known. And as she walked she asked questions—about life in the camp, about self-government, about the schools, about the reactions of the townsfolk.

Joe Smart was prepared. He led her toward number 154 and, still on the street, introduced Dušanka Grin, the twenty-six-year-old wife of a Yugoslav physician. "It would be an honor," Dušanka said, "to have you visit my apartment."

With artful simplicity Mrs. Roosevelt said, "I wonder if I might first visit that building across the street."

"I hope the bed is made," one of the council members muttered in German.

Mrs. Roosevelt knocked. A young woman, nursing her baby, opened the door. The room was bare but spotless. The army cot with its khaki blanket was neatly made. A sprig of flowers on the wooden table was the only decoration.

The President's wife apologized for coming unannounced, admired the baby in his mother's arms, and then asked the young woman how she felt coming now to America.

"Happy. Very happy. Just to stop running. To rest. And now— to meet you. I—I don't know what to say."

The President's wife put her arm around the young woman's shoulders. No words were spoken, but a bond seemed to form between the tall, graying, motherly American and the no-longer-frightened refugee.

In her syndicated column "My Day," on September 20, Mrs. Roosevelt described Dušanka Grin's apartment.

Although clothes have to be hung on hooks in the wall, she had covered them with a piece of unbleached muslin, and up above had painted and cut out figures of animals, stars, and angels, which were placed all over the plain surface to become a decorative wall covering. The effort put into it speaks volumes for what these people have undergone, and for the character that has brought them through.

Walking again through the camp, she asked Dr. Juda Levi, head of the camp council, what the most serious problem was.

He pointed. "The fence."

"All camps—" she started to say, then stopped.

"We see Nazi prisoners of war outside our fence," Dr. Levi said. "True, they have soldiers guarding them. But they are outside, and we are inside." He continued. "Even our children have a card and a number, and they must show it or shout their number to the guard when they go to school and when they come back."

"Dear Mrs. Roosevelt," said Magrita Ehrenstamm, a motherly fifty-eight-year-old woman from Frankfurt, "what will happen to us when the war is over? Will we be sent back to Europe? I have no home to go back to. The Gestapo took everything. My daughter is here, and she wants me to live with her in New York. My son Hans is a sergeant in the U.S. Army in Europe. I want to be here when he comes home."

Mrs. Roosevelt shook her head. "I don't know," she said, with an honesty no one could doubt. She walked for a while in silence. Then, learning that a large white wooden building was the hospital, she climbed the steps to visit the sick. Five refugee doctors and the Oswego chief of staff halted their work to introduce her to their patients.

She stopped at David Levy's bedside. Dark-haired David, twenty-two, was truly a survivor. His entire family had been killed in Yugoslavia. He had one goal now—to get a university education. When Mrs. Roosevelt asked him how he liked America, he wasted no time. "I love America, and I love the camp. But I want to go to college."

Mrs. Roosevelt turned to Joe Smart. "I believe I was told all the young people are in school?"

Joe explained that the State Teachers College was prepared to take them in. "But unfortunately the semester started before we could finish the arrangements. Rules, regulations, the problem of who would pay for the buses—all the other schools are within walking distance—we were stymied."

"For the sake of these young people," she said pointedly, "I hope you will find a way. If you need my help, please write me."

Joe tried to reassure her. "We're doing our best to get them into the spring semester."

David put his hand out to Mrs. Roosevelt. "I have the feeling your coming here today was *beshert*—destiny—like the hand of God."

While the two visitors joined the refugees for a lunch of soup, salad, pie, and coffee, the camp's actors and singers rehearsed for a special afternoon performance in their honor.

Hundreds followed the women into the auditorium. The house lights dimmed. The spotlight lit up the stage. Everyone's eyes were fixed on the tall woman listening intently to the chorus, the skits, the soloists. "An opera singer from Yugoslavia sang for us"—she described Mirković in her column—"and I have rarely enjoyed anything more."

The lights went on. She climbed the stairs to the stage and looked at the audience, whose applause sent ripples of love toward her. Somehow they seemed to know she had been fighting for them for years, fighting against the restrictionists and the quotas, fighting to open the doors.

"My visit to this shelter has been one of the most wonderful days I have ever spent." She paused for a moment. "I know how the fence troubles you. I know the restrictions are plentiful. But at least the menace of death is no longer everpresent."

People murmured, "Yes, yes." She seemed so truly to understand them.

Gracious as always, she thanked the staff and the citizens of Oswego. "Oswego is a community that is cooperating with the government and is doing a wonderful job. Both the shelter and the city, I believe, can profit by their contacts. This haven has shown me that if the *human side*"—she stressed the words—"of a government undertaking is understood, complete cooperation is possible."

The human side was what she personified, and even those who did not understand her words understood her meaning.

In a few weeks her husband would be running for his fourth term as President. But while his strong image filled the hall—he was the Great Father who had gathered up these men and women and children—her presence spoke not of politics but of understanding and love.

She ended her column that night:

> Somehow you feel that if there is any compensation for suffering, it must someday bring them something beautiful in return for all the horrors they have lived through.

The crowd thronged around her as she entered her limousine. She seemed to them to represent all that was idealistic, unselfish, and compassionate in America.

NINETEEN

AFTER A MONTH back in Washington, I was asked by Ickes to return to the camp. He wanted a progress report, and I welcomed the assignment.

Minutes after I entered the camp gate, I was simultaneously hugged and kissed and assaulted with complaints.

Rabbi Tzechoval's wife, Mindla, pulled me to the side as we walked toward my office in the jail. "Dear, beloved Miss Ruth," she said in Yiddish, "it is terrible for the women."

"What is terrible?" I asked the thirty-year-old *rebbetzin*, a peppery little woman who wore a flowered scarf over her head. As an orthodox wife, she had shaved her head on her wedding day to make her unattractive to any man except her husband. On holidays and Shabbat she wore a brunette wig.

"What is terrible?" She repeated my question indignantly. "The women can't sleep with their husbands."

"Why can't they?"

She stared at me with consternation. "Because we have no *mikvah*." This was the ritual pool in which wives cleansed and purified themselves before they had sex with their husbands.

"What did you do for a *mikvah* when you were running?" I asked.

"We used the rivers. The lakes."

I waved my hand toward Lake Ontario. "You have a lake right here."

"This lake"—her voice was shrill—"this lake is freezing. We would freeze to death."

I tried to be sympathetic. I knew how important the *mikvah* was to orthodox Jewish women. But the *rebbetzin* would have to understand. "I can go to the government of the United States," I told her, "and explain why we should have black bread, and why we need additional funds for winter clothes. But how can I go to the government and ask for a *mikvah*?"

She looked at me slyly. "Because we'll get sick if we don't sleep with our husbands. And they'll get sick too. I won't give up. I'll get my *mikvah*."

At lunchtime, Joe brought me up to date.

Lydia Franco from Libya had given birth to a girl, and Washington was in another legal hassle. No one could decide whether little Miriam Mary was an American citizen. The lawyers in Interior argued that any child born on American soil was a citizen. The lawyers in WRB argued that Fort Ontario was different. They asked Justice to determine the issue, but so far no decision had been made. Little Miriam Mary, I thought ruefully, is probably the first child in history born in America but still in limbo.

"Army Intelligence," Joe continued, "came back to recheck some thirty of our people. The Army wants more detailed information about their homelands, countries we have to liberate. One of our refugees, they told me, is the legal heir presumptive to the throne of Lithuania. So among us"—his light eyes crinkled—"we may have a king. Imagine a king living in this emergency shelter!"

The next days raced by as people invited me into their homes to sip tea, to chat, to show me their children's report cards, to let me see how they had turned their barracks apartments, with a few handmade doilies and tablecloths, into little replicas of their homes in Europe.

David Levy, recovered from his bout of illness in the hospital, burst into my office. "Tell Mrs. Roosevelt she did it. She did it! We're going to college in the spring semester!" Once again the government had bent its rules for education.

Meanwhile several small private and religious agencies had begun to help individuals in the camp. Their intentions were good, but chaos threatened until three national agencies agreed to form the Coordinating Committee of Fort Ontario. The three—HIAS (the Hebrew Immigrant Aid Society), the National Council of Jewish Women, and the National Refugee Service (NRS), which was funded by the United Jewish Appeal—were soon joined by a host of other Jewish, Christian, and secular agencies: representatives of the three communities close to Oswego (Rochester, Buffalo, and Syracuse), ORT (Organization for Rehabilitation through Training), Hadassah, the National Jewish Welfare Board, the Jewish Labor Committee, Agudath Israel, the American Friends Service Committee, the Catholic Welfare Committee, the Unitarian Service Committee, and the American Committee for Christian Refugees.

The agencies were genuinely eager to make life in the camp bearable and to prepare the refugees for life after Oswego. They agreed to fill their educational, recreational, rehabilitation, and religious needs, thus lifting the burden from the government and the taxpayers; the government supplied the basics—food, shelter, clothing, and medical care. The government took the position that its responsibility was to maintain people in the state in which they had arrived—like freight in transit.

Joe Smart informed the Coordinating Committee that many

people complained of foot trouble. Bernie Dubin of the NRS sent Dr. Harold Lefkoe of Philadelphia to the camp with Louis Yellin, a Philadelphia dealer in orthopedic appliances. Some two hundred people turned up to be examined by Dr. Lefkoe. At the end of the day, he told Dubin, he was "bleary-eyed," while Yellin dreamed all night he was casting arch supports.

Malnutrition in Europe, running, climbing mountains with torn shoes or no shoes at all, had weakened the refugees' feet. Hundreds now wore arch supports and orthopedic shoes, courtesy of the NRS. Many whose teeth had deteriorated in the years of flight were also outfitted with false teeth.

The Coordinating Committee assigned each agency the kind of service it performed on the American scene. The NRS assumed major responsibility for most of the programs. ORT and the NRS furnished the educational and vocational services. B'nai B'rith provided furniture and equipment for the synagogues, the Service Club, and several smaller clubrooms. The clubs were a defense against loneliness; one even called itself the Club of the Lonesomes. It was a kind of Harvard Club for people over fifty, organized by Magrita Ehrenstamm and run by a corps of volunteer "welfare workers."

I attended one of the Wednesday-afternoon meetings in the Service Club. Outside the door hung a sign: CLUB OF THE LONE- SOMES. *Ladies of an uncertain age have the use of a reduction of 50 percent.* There was nothing to reduce; everything was free. Middle-aged and elderly men and women sat in deep soft chairs donated by B'nai B'rith, drank coffee, ate cake, and listened to songs composed by one of their members and sung by another. Some shut their eyes during the lilting music, as if they were dreaming of a romantic past lost to them forever.

"But we must learn English," the adults clamored. A few classes in English were still given by refugee volunteers, but the classes were sporadic, and people talked in a circus of languages.

They surrounded me. "Remember how you taught us English on the ship? Why can't we have regular classes here?"

The Coordinating Committee in Oswego delayed a decision; professional teachers, books, and supplies would require a budget of thousands of dollars. Joe Smart asked me to call Ickes to intervene.

I decided to tackle the problem myself.

I made a quick trip to New York to meet with Ephraim Gomberg and Bernard Dubin of the National Refugee Service, and with the chairman of its board, Joseph Chamberlain, professor of law at Columbia University, whose long white hair and fine-boned face made him look like a minister ready to do battle for his flock. I knew they were friends the moment I entered their office, in a nondescript building at the foot of Manhattan. It took only minutes to convince them.

"I'm one hundred percent behind you," Chamberlain said.

Dubin telephoned the National Council of Jewish Women. It was agreed that both organizations would underwrite all the cost.

I returned immediately to tell Joe and the jubilant would-be students. Within days teachers were hired, and soon there were twenty-nine classes with five hundred adults enthusiastically "breaking their teeth," mixing their *v*'s and *w*'s, bravely trying to fathom the mystery of why they should not pronounce words like *though, thought, through,* and *tough* the same way.

From nine in the morning to nine at night, the camp seemed like a giant school for adults. ORT set up classes where people worked in mechanics and in carpentry, learned jewelry making, painted, sculpted, sewed, and learned the art of beauty culture. Edith Semjen sauntered into the beauty-culture class one morning and, at twenty-one, found herself. "She has golden hands," the women told each other as they made appointments weeks in advance for her to style their hair.

The agencies would help solve some of the smaller problems. The big policy decisions still had to be made in Washington.

"But it's so cruel," Magrita Ehrenstamm protested at my desk. From the first days on the ship, she had asked if she could leave to live with her daughter in New York. The answer came now. It was no.

"They've examined us up and down." She was desolate. "Can't you do anything to help us?"

I shook my head sadly. Even Ickes could do nothing. The decision had been made by the War Refugee Board. No visits outside the camp. No one could leave even overnight; they could, however, go into Oswego for six hours with a pass.

But they were survivors. And the humor that had sustained Jews through centuries of persecution became part of the business of surviving in the camp.

"Let's sing our national anthem for Ruth," Otto Presser announced at the opening of the evening's entertainment in my honor. I stood up, expecting "The Star-Spangled Banner," but sat down swiftly. They were singing "Don't Fence Me In."

Survivors, they even breached the fence. You needed a pass to go out, but if you crawled underneath no one knew if you hitchhiked down to New York, as Adam Munz and David Hendel did frequently, exploring the wonders of New York and sleeping in Central Park. Only their friends knew of their escapades. There were no bed checks, no sergeants counting heads.

Ickes will be pleased, I thought, when I report to him that the refugee terror in people's eyes had almost disappeared and nearly everyone had gained weight. "Look at me," Mirković said, strutting a little. "I've put on nearly sixty pounds. A singer needs weight for his breath."

Whether it was the food after long starvation, the suddenly cold nights, or the sense of having found refuge at last, the life juices that had begun to return on the ship now flowed so freely that a dozen women walked around the parade ground with burgeoning bellies. Manya came to tell me that she was expecting a baby, and like most pregnant women, she looked radiant.

Each day the hole under the fence grew larger, until it became a two-way street. Boys slithered through to make dates with Oswego girls. Bobby-soxers from junior and senior high, in short skirts and saddle shoes, crawled through the hole, struck up friendships with the boys, walked with them down near the lake, and found empty barracks near the little post cemetery, where they shared Dixie Cups and Eskimo Pies and, the boys assured me later, kissed harmlessly.

The girls in the camp were caught between the old morality of Europe and the free ways of this brave new American world. Zealous adults and ingrained mores inhibited them. Still, they had their own romances. Fredi Baum had eyes only for Jennie Baruch; Elfie Strauber was in love with David Hendel; Renée Reisner and Alex Margulis were inseparable, as were Vesna Culić and Rajko Margulis. Kostia Zabotin fell in love with an American girl; Henny Notowicz had a crush on Rolf Kuznitzki, who was infatuated with Edith Bronner; several girls pined for Adam Munz's affection, and Edith Semjen had become temporarily engaged to Stanley Smart.

On a brilliant autumn morning, Joe drove me out of the camp. The countryside was ablaze with golden birch and flaming scarlet maple and oak trees. New York State had never looked more beautiful.

We were on our way to visit some of the apple and pear orchards being harvested, and to see some of our men at work.

The work policy had been fixed. The refugees would maintain the camp themselves, with as few outside employees as possible. They would all earn the same wage, $18 a month, whether they were doctors, chefs, house leaders, or maintenance men. Anyone unable to work would receive $8.50 a month, $7 if they were between the ages of twelve and seventeen, $4.50 if they were under twelve.

No one was to work outside the camp. But the farmers in the area were desperate. "We have to have manpower to harvest our crops," they pleaded with Washington. "The Army has taken most of our workers."

Pehle at the War Refugee Board relented "for this harvest only." Fifty men immediately signed up.

Joe and I visited a large orchard where a taciturn farmer led us to a sorry sight. "See that," he said, as though his anger was burned out. Most of his pear crop lay rotting on the ground. For him, the decision from Washington had come too late.

Toward the end of the day we drove to the Birds Eye cold-storage plant. I stopped in dismay at the entrance. A handful of our refugees were stacking crates of apples, heavily outnumbered by a contingent of Nazi POWs. Suddenly I was back on our ship looking out at the shipload of POWs. The cold-storage plant seemed transformed into a warehouse theater of hunters and hunted, of Nazis and refugees.

The foreman was explaining to Joe Smart. "We pay the government fifty cents an hour for the POWs. The government gives them eighty cents a day, and the Treasury Department pockets the rest."

Eighty cents a day. "And the refugees?" I asked the foreman.

"We pay them the regular wage—fifty cents an hour."

Joe interrupted. "The men decided to put twenty percent into a fund to be used by the whole camp. Besides, in a few weeks they'll be back in the camp, getting eighteen dollars a month."

I did some swift arithmetic on a pad. Eighteen dollars a month for five and a half days a week came to just about eighty cents a day. Apparently that was the government wage for refugees *and* POWs.

They were two sides of the same coin, and the coin was war. A hundred thousand POWs . . . one thousand refugees.

On the whole, Ickes was pleased with the progress report.

"I had a call from Dillon Myer," he said. "He asked me if I'd release you. He says Joe Smart would like you to stay up there all the time."

"And?"

"I told him I thought you could do them more good going back and forth. He also tells me the refugees all love you."

"Maybe," I said slowly, "maybe people love you when they know how you feel about them."

"You never said it in your report, but I caught it between the lines—you really do love them."

"They're part of my life."

The news from Europe was bad. On Saturday, December 16, Hitler launched the Battle of the Bulge and threw back the 8th Corps of the U.S. First Army.

Depressed, anxious, the camp people read newspaper stories of appalling weather that grounded the Allied air forces. The Germans pushed forward on the ground, their panzers unaffected by the blinding snowstorms. Eight thousand Americans were dead, 47,000 wounded, and 21,000 missing.

Just before Christmas, Joe Smart telephoned me in Washington.

"We're going to be on national radio! The National Broadcasting Company is going to do a Christmas broadcast right from here. We're still big news, I guess."

December 23, I turned down an invitation to a pre-Christmas party in town. I wanted to be alone in my apartment listening to the broadcast.

Dorothy Thompson, who had decried Nazism long before most of her fellow journalists took Hitler seriously, opened the broadcast. "In Oswego, New York, tonight," she began quietly, "around a thousand people are singing Christmas carols and rejoicing over the greatest boon that could possibly have befallen them. That boon is that they are in the United States, and that to save their lives the United States has actually waived the usual visas. Legally, it is dubious whether they are here at all."

Her voice darkened. "A thousand people are very few in a world in which millions are dying and concentration camps are teeming with the politically and racially persecuted. . . . What is one, or what are a thousand, amongst the millions? . . . The whole fate of mankind is contained in a single person, and in a single person is the whole fate of mankind. . . . Therefore . . . it is to the credit of the

United States that it tried to save some human beings, and that it has saved a thousand of them."

She was paraphrasing the Talmudic phrase my father had taught me as a little girl: *He who saves a single life, it is as if he had saved the world.*

The broadcast switched to Oswego. The camp choir sang "Silent Night," and then Joe introduced several of the Christian refugees. Fifteen-year-old Visko Marinković talked of the terror on the island of Vis, where his father was a farmer and a fisherman, and where he had seen twenty of their neighbors killed. "Now we go to school in Oswego, and fear has passed."

The program ended as Margaret Weinstein told the audience, "I am a Christian married to a Jew, and in Vienna we were both thrown into prison. Now we want only freedom and security and the right to live as human beings, not as hunted animals. I wish for you in America, and for all of us in the camp, peace."

Then, on December 28, tragedy struck.

Karoline Bleier, a frail thirty-two-year-old Yugoslav woman, was tormented by guilt. As a married woman with two children, she had fallen passionately in love with Geza Bleier some years earlier. She had divorced her husband and was forced to give up custody of her children in order to marry Geza. She had given birth to two more children, Ronald, now an apple-cheeked two-year-old, and, nine months ago, little George. But she grieved for the two children she had left behind. "Why did I abandon them?" she kept flagellating herself. "If they are dead, I am to blame. I killed them."

During the winter, first Ronnie and then Georgie contracted whooping cough. Karoline spent sleepless nights, exhausted and despondent. Geza tried to comfort her. "There's a movie in camp tonight. You go. I'll watch the children."

Karoline protested—she was in no mood for a movie—but Geza prevailed and Karoline left the barracks. The camp, engulfed in snow, was once again whipped by a blizzard. Neighbors began returning from the movie; Geza heard their steps. "Where's Karoline?" he asked them. No one had seen her.

Hours passed and Karoline did not appear. Geza alerted the camp police. They set out to search, digging through snowdrifts ten feet high.

"Maybe she went walking and lost her way." People who had joined the search spurred each other on. The wind howled off the lake. The waves broke in huge whitecaps, angry as an ocean. The holiday spirit only exacerbated the anxiety for Karoline.

The searchers bent their bodies against the wind, which was blowing now at fifty miles an hour. Karoline could easily have been blinded by the snow, a victim not of her own demons but of the vicious winter that had turned the camp, so idyllic in the summer, into a bleak prison.

Through the night Geza begged them not to give up. "If we don't find her soon, she'll die of exposure." They continued searching until they too felt stiff and frozen.

Early the next morning they found Karoline on the banks of the barge canal. An autopsy revealed she had swallowed one hundred tablets of aspirin.

TWENTY

Karoline's death shattered the holiday spirit.

Geza was numb with pain. A band of sorrowing women led by Magrita Ehrenstamm brought him food, bathed and fed little Ronald and George, and, in the end, seeing Geza incoherent with grief, scarcely able to rise from his stool of mourning, placed the two little boys with a family who could care for them.

Men, sorely needed to maintain the camp, complained of

strange pains in the chest, headaches, backaches, swollen legs. The doctors were the arbiters of the work force. Each day they filled out a batch of slips "Unable to work." The deterioration threatened to tear the camp apart.

Dr. Ernst Wolff brought me a manuscript that he had titled "Storm in the Shelter." Suave, crinkly-eyed, with a light mustache, Dr. Wolff was the author of sixty novels that had sold three million copies. He had even worked in Hollywood in the twenties as a screenwriter before returning to his native Vienna.

"I've been up all night writing this for you. Please read it now." He settled himself into a chair, watching me through large troubled eyes while I read.

Night. I am lying in bed, and outside the storm is howling—no, it isn't howling; it's racing—at forty-three miles an hour. It pipes in a hellish concert through all the seams in my lightly built quarters. I thank the Lord for the noble American nation and its wonderful President. Yes, I thank them with all my being—*but*. It is a "but" even after I am offered humanity, radio, underwear, clothes, shoes, food, quarters for living and recreation, and so forth. Despite all this, "but"? Yes, *but*. Because none offers me that for which my heart is languishing and to the sanctuary of which every last creature on God's earth is entitled: FREEDOM! . . .

I am told we refugees are prisoners (we were told we would be guests—what irony!) because we have no status under the law: So we exist in a legal vacuum, under a sentence more cruel than that of a common criminal—the sentence of uncertainty. . . . For what have we cried blood from our eyes and mankind beaten its breast in lamentation over us? That we should be prisoners in the Land of Promise? For what freedom is America fighting a war abroad only to lose it in shame in Fort Ontario?

I will not be supported any further: I will be a free man again.

January continued bleak and cold. Fifty inches of snow fell in less than a month, freezing so high that the elderly could not leave their barracks even for food, and the sick were marooned.

Fewer visitors came. One or two newspapers occasionally carried stories of the haven on Lake Ontario.

On January 17, news came that Russia's Marshal Georgi Zhukov had entered Warsaw. The Allies were advancing on all fronts in Europe. Hope grew that the war would be over soon, that the killing would end, and that they would know whether their families had survived.

But the misery in the camp fed upon itself. "I fear," Joe Smart wrote, "it is becoming impossible to maintain the people in health and safety without actual peril to life."

A psychologist, Dr. Curt Bondy, sent to the camp as a consultant by WRA, recommended "giving the residents permission to make visits of, say, up to thirty days' duration with their relatives and friends." Such "sponsored leave," he hoped, would "diminish some of the stress in the shelter."

On January 31, 1945, a number of private agencies, led by Professor Chamberlain, issued a statement strongly urging sponsored leave. They would assume all financial responsibility, promising that "none of these individuals would become a public charge."

Ickes approved the idea and wrote to General William O'Dwyer, who had just been appointed executive director of the War Refugee Board (John Pehle had returned to Treasury), urging that the refugees be granted sponsored leave until the United States decided what it wanted to do with them.

A copy of the letter went to Attorney General Francis Biddle; Justice would have to approve any change in the status of the people.

"On a number of occasions," Biddle answered, he had "assured members of Congress that the admission of these refugees did not give them any right to be at liberty here or to remain permanently in the United States, and that they would be detained in a refugee settlement until they could be safely returned to their homelands."

Biddle was not to be moved by Ickes's arguments, nor was President Roosevelt, who had informed Biddle earlier that he "wholly agreed that the people should *not* be permitted even to apply for immigration to the United States. They should in fact be returned to Europe as soon as a favorable opportunity arose."

Ickes showed me the correspondence. I read it, appalled. Roosevelt, in his original cable, had announced that the people would go back; I had been sure it was largely to placate Congress. But this confirmation to Biddle was even sharper than his message to Congress. Anyone, anywhere outside America, could apply for immigration, but not the Oswego refugees. It was as if they were being punished for having been invited to the United States.

In February, as David Levy had hoped, the daytime gates were flung open for a handful of fortunate young people to enter the Oswego State Teachers College.

Traveling in a bus provided by the Coordinating Committee, they drove to the outskirts of town and pulled up in front of a handsome brick structure with white steps, white columns, and a covered walkway. On the lawn was a bronze statue of a bearded educator, Edward Austin Sheldon, who had founded the college as the Oswego Normal and Training School in 1861. Sitting in a bronze chair, he smiled at a young lad looking up at him. The pedestal said simply THE CHILDREN'S FRIEND.

Among those winding their way around the statue into the portico were Mira Lederer, who wanted to be a writer; Jetta Hendel, who dreamed of becoming an architect; David Levy, who had evoked Mrs. Roosevelt's aid; Vadim Mikhailoff, who, with his parents, was one of the leading actors of the Russian Orthodox group; Samuilo Romano; Tina Koerner; Walter Maurer, the brother of International Harry; and Rajko and Alex Margulis.

Some twenty younger children also descended from the bus. They had been transferred from P.S. 2, the little schoolhouse near the camp, to the far-better-equipped Model School of the Teachers College, where skilled teachers and young teachers-in-training would soon be teaching them to speak English almost without accent.

For these young people, Oswego meant the opening of doors to a new life. But for too many of the adults it had become a galling and demoralizing experience.

A temporary thaw began to melt the snow. All winter, ledges of ice had built up around the piles of coal stacked in the open, near the main entrance of the camp. Now the ice began to soften. On the morning of February 19 the coal crew arrived to shovel the coal, fling it onto a truck, and deliver it to the camp's furnaces.

"I'll start shoveling today," Arpad Buchler offered. A quiet man in his early forties, Arpad worked cheerfully at any task he was given. On Shabbat, people noticed the joy with which he shepherded his young wife, Renée, their four little children, all under ten, and his widowed mother, Emilia, to the orthodox synagogue.

"Arpad, it's not your turn today," his friend Silvio Finci protested, not too vehemently.

"That's all right. I'll shovel today and you can wait at the truck."

Arpad dug into the coal closest to the ground, humming happily. Suddenly the top ledge of ice, melting in the sun, broke loose with a barrage of coal and crashed over him. The work crew rushed to pull him loose, pushing the coal with their shovels, their hands, their bodies. When they reached Arpad, he was dead.

First Karoline's suicide, now Arpad's death.

The demoralization grew worse. The doctors diagnosed 110 people as victims of neurosis.

Searching for some way to stem the disintegration, the War Relocation Authority and the Coordinating Committee asked Dr. Rudolf Dreikurs, a Chicago psychiatrist, to visit the camp.

It was late March when Ickes called me to his office. "This Dr. Dreikurs will probably need your help. I'd like you to go up there immediately."

The next night was the beginning of Passover, the most joyous family celebration of all the Jewish festivals.

At the gate Abe Furmanski greeted me. "I know you've come with a proclamation from the President—that we're all free."

I stopped in my tracks. "Where did you hear this?" Was it possible that Roosevelt had changed his mind while I was on the night train?

"Everybody has been talking about it. For weeks people have been rushing around Oswego buying suitcases. They bought every trunk in the stores. When the trunks ran out they bought foot-lockers. Some even dropped their subscriptions to newspapers."

I checked the rumor with Joe Smart. "I'm not sure how it started," he said. "Apparently somebody in New York saw some-body else who knew that Professor Chamberlain had gone down to Washington to talk with O'Dwyer. They figured that was the only thing Chamberlain could have talked about."

I spent the day trying to quench the rumor. It had seemed so logical that they would be released on the very holiday celebrating the Exodus from Egypt to the Promised Land. Of course a loving President and a caring government would set them free for the Passover.

The snow had melted, the barren trees were sprouting buds, and the wind off the lake seemed gentle. But even the end of the long winter failed to raise their spirits as they forced themselves to accept the depressing truth. The Yugoslavs were especially agi-tated. The Yugoslav consul in New York must also have heard the rumor; he had sent a notice warning the Yugoslavs that if they did not go back as soon as the camp was dissolved they would lose their citizenship.

But in the orthodox mess hall, known as Kitchen 93, there was only joy.

For weeks before the holiday, Kitchen 93 had been in a turmoil of excitement. Every corner of the mess hall was swept to make certain there was no "leaven" left; crumbs were packed together and burned. The old dishes were now all stored away; the Coordi-nating Committee had purchased brand-new dishes for the Passover week.

As evening fell in the camp, I entered the dining hall. It had been transformed into a living tableau. Rabbi Tzechoval, in a long white robe and a white skullcap, reclined on white pillows and a couch at the head of the table. Thus "freemen" had reclined in ancient times, no longer slaves unto Pharaoh. Joe Smart sat in a seat of honor next to the rabbi.

The rabbi beckoned to me. "How do your children look to you?"

I looked around at the people, the holiday lights casting a warm glow on their rounded faces. "You're all grown," I said. Even the rabbi's face, once pale and painfully thin, was now pink and plump.

The seder began, as it had for millennia, with the rabbi explaining it once again to all of us and especially to Joe. "Everything tonight," he said, while Joe listened, entranced, "is about freedom. Even the matzoh means freedom, because it means that the Jews escaping from the tyranny of Egypt had no time to bake bread."

"Look around you," Abe Furmanski said, sitting next to me. "For some of us, it's the first Passover in six or seven years. We didn't dare have seders in concentration camps, or when we hid out as Catholics in Italy. Last year I made my first seder—I couldn't wait anymore. We were in Rome under false papers. We put the children to sleep so there would be no sounds. We waited until one in the morning, locked the doors, and held the seder in whispers."

Now, instead of whispers, there was a commotion. The rabbi rose from his couch and nodded to the men, who surrounded Joe, lifted him out of his chair, and carried him to the center of the floor. Then, locking hands, they formed a circle around him, dancing, singing in ecstasy, leaping faster and faster until they could no longer catch their breath.

At last the rabbi returned to his couch; Joe, beaming, took his seat, and the story of the Exodus continued far into the night.

"I want to talk to you later at great length," Dr. Dreikurs told me the next morning. "I will want whatever insights you can give me."

He was of medium height, with a friendly unthreatening smile and a German accent. He had made a reputation as a leading

Adlerian psychiatrist who believed in solving problems through group activities.

"I see this whole camp as a Greek tragedy with all the dynamic forces interacting. I see all the players, the government in Washington, the staff here, the outside groups, and the refugees; and I see the intentions of each group colliding with the intentions of the others."

We were in a hospital room where he was to interview and diagnose some of the 110 people with neurotic symptoms and some of the staff. I promised to spend more time with him and left him to begin his work.

Saturday afternoon he invited the entire American staff to meet him in Joe's office.

"I can't imagine anybody living here as a refugee, or working here on the staff, remaining sane," he began.

We looked at each other uneasily. Was he telling us that even the staff was neurotic, that working here made "normal" people abnormal and mentally healthy people insane?

"The antagonisms," he went on, "the mutual distrust, the human relations of people living close together, create a vicious cycle in which all of you are caught. The malaise in this camp is paranoia. The closer people live to each other, the more paranoiac their attitudes become." He looked at the staff. "Do you have questions?"

One of the staff members raised his hand. "It's the work problem. Especially in sanitation and feeding. We have some who are willing to work, and they're good. In fact, they overwork. But then we have nonworkers, and the workers complain we do nothing against them. They say we should bring sanctions."

Dreikurs nodded. "Even among the nonworkers, you have two kinds of people: those who say, 'How can you ask us to work? We are guests of the United States,' and those who get sick with stomach ailments and so forth. The doctors don't find any stomach ailments, but the people really feel pain. It's a psychiatric pain, and it must definitely be treated. In fact, we have to do education with both kinds of nonworkers. And we have to treat the malaise among you, the staff, and the refugees."

In the evening, notices were sent to all the barracks. Everyone was invited to a Sunday-morning lecture by Dr. Dreikurs in the post theater entitled "Common Solution of Common Problems."

On the stage, talking to a packed house the next morning, Dr. Dreikurs established his connection with the audience. "I too am a refugee from Vienna. We all have problems of insecurity. We all feel ourselves uprooted; but I tell you, the average American feels just as insecure as you. Your problems, whether you are having difficulties in your marriage or problems with your children, are typically human problems. But in camps, there is one problem—may I say it very strongly without insulting you—a great number of people feel morally responsible to be unhappy. I confess I would feel the same in your position."

A few heads nodded in agreement.

"You believe you are unhappy because of the terror you lived through, because you are forced to live here, because you have no future. All of you have the same troubles, yet some of you are courageous while others break down and suffer more. Yes?"

The word "Yes" rose and fell in different corners of the theater.

"The cause of this, for those who suffer, is the feeling of insecurity. Whether we are big or small, fat or thin, we are all here because we have no social status. Yet it is the petty things that disturb us, not the big ones."

"Yes, yes!" people shouted again.

"We have to work for a solution. If you think of yourself alone, you can't work for a solution. The camp is full of pain and suffering. But as long as you must be here, do you want to make it better or worse? Do you want to be more wretched, so that more people will break down, or, when the camp finally closes, do you want to go out healthy? I am looking for peace workers who will help me to help you. Who will be a peace worker? Raise your hand."

Hands went up across the theater.

"Will I find more peace workers among the men or the women?"

The men shouted, "Men!"

The women shouted, "Women!"

Dr. Dreikurs smiled. People smiled too, as they walked out of the theater.

After eleven days of interviews, Dr. Dreikurs returned to Chicago and wrote a report recommending more group activities. He singled out Magrita Ehrenstamm and her fellow workers in the Club of the Lonesomes and suggested that similar clubs be organized not only for the refugees but also for the staff. His hope, he wrote, was to help the staff help the refugees and "make their good intentions, courage, determination, and perseverance more effective."

Dreikurs's visit had helped.

But the fear that time was running out filled the camp with bitterness. Everyone knew there were jobs in America; there was desperate need for their skills right in Oswego. Even the townspeople were angry. "It's an outrage," Edmund Waterbury, the publisher of the *Oswego Palladium-Times*, told me, "that they aren't permitted to help solve the difficult work problems created by the manpower shortage and that they are treated worse than German or Italian prisoners of war. We pamper the Nazi prisoners while these innocent people whom the Nazis tried to kill are treated as though they were Nazis. I just don't get it."

"Work and freedom" became the dream and the obsession. To work outside the camp. To be free.

Artur Hirt, the Polish judge, said ironically, "I am a judge, so I shovel coal in America."

Israel Willner, the cook in the kosher kitchen, read the advertisements offering chefs five hundred dollars a month.

"The years are flowing by. I am losing my youth. I want to go out and work and make something of myself. I have a visa to the United States in my pocket, and now I am wasting my life."

In the hospital, Dr. Eugene Svecenski talked bitterly as he took me on his rounds. "I'm forty-seven. When I signed up to come to

America, I said, 'If I'm lucky, Europe will never see me again.' Who knows now? Will I ever be able to resume my work and make a living?"

Back in Washington, I wrote up the report of my visit for Ickes, calling it "Eight Months Later."

For most of the refugees, I wrote,

> the camp has meant new life. The little Europe which we had on the ship and the Balkanization of the camp in the first months are disappearing. The melting pot is boiling again, and democratization has set in. But a camp is a camp is a camp, and even with the best will in the world, people deteriorate in camp life.

Only a major decision could halt the spread of hysteria and depression. I recommended that we try to close the camp as soon as possible. It was true the refugees had signed a release in Italy that they would go back at the end of the war. But at that time no one really knew these people; there were even fears there might be spies among them. We knew them well enough now to be sure they were not spies.

I ended the report:

> We should permit those who are eligible for entry to the United States to cross the border into Canada and re-enter the United States under regular quotas on an individual basis. It is time we showed that this administration has a policy of decency, humanity, and conscience and the guts to carry that policy through.

"Quite a picture you drew," Ickes said solemnly. "I agree with you. I would like to see the camp closed as soon as possible. But my hands are tied. We've got to get the War Refugee Board and the rest of the government to see it. Meanwhile, until we do close the camp, we have to try to get sponsored leave."

He put his hand over his chin as if he were mulling over the words.

"It would be a crime to send them back. A crime if a country of one hundred thirty-seven million could not absorb one thousand refugees."

On April 12 the camp went into mourning.

A full-page obituary in the *Ontario Chronicle*, the weekly newspaper the refugees wrote themselves, mourned the death of the President.

In the synagogue, the congregants stood reciting the Kaddish, the prayer for the dead. Then, led by the rabbis, they walked across the camp and entered the old fort. They raised the American flag; the orchestra played "The Star-Spangled Banner," and Mirković, his face stricken with grief, sang Sibelius's "Prayer of Peace."

In the mournful silence, everyone listened as Fredi Baum delivered the eulogy.

"He was a great fearless leader of warm qualities, upon whom the whole world focused its attention, to lead it out of barbarism to the light of liberty, freedom, and happiness. Though we are not citizens of this country, though most of us have become stateless, we understand perhaps better than any others what this death means to the entire world."

Sobs shook many of the people. They were in America because of this American President. They were banded together in sorrow. Their father, their savior, their protector was dead.

What now lay ahead?

Twenty-one

Victories in Europe pulled the camp temporarily out of its depression. People followed each campaign as if they were on the battlefield; many knew every inch of territory regained.

Saturday, April 21, Marshal Zhukov, "the general who never lost a battle," entered the outskirts of Berlin. Manya, carrying Diane, the baby she had just given birth to, called me in Washington. "Ruthie, do you believe it? It's the city where I was born."

In Italy, the Allied armies captured Bologna. General Mark Clark issued his order of the day: "We now stand inside the gateway to the Po plain, poised to destroy the Germans who continue to enslave and exploit northern Italy."

In the camp, people rejoiced for the peasants and the villagers who had risked their lives for them, given them shelter, shared their food.

A week later they rejoiced even more. Italian partisans captured Mussolini and his mistress, Clara Petacci, in their hideout near Lake Como. They met a dreadful death. They were shot and their bodies thrown into a van and taken to Milan, where they were exhibited to the world hanging by their heels from the girders of a filling station.

And two days after that, on April 30, word came that Hitler and Eva Braun committed suicide in the Führerbunker in Berlin.

The cry that went up carried over the fence into the streets of Oswego.

In camp, three of Joe Smart's advisers knocked on his door at night. "We must speak to you in strictest confidence."

Dr. Otto Lederer, Dr. Arthur Ernst, editor in chief of the camp *Ontario Chronicle,* and Dr. Edmund Landau, associate editor, entered his living room. Dr. Lederer spoke first. "We have just received reliable information. We are all to be sent back to Europe. The date has been set: June thirtieth—it's less than two months away. The War Department has already committed a ship."

"I've heard nothing of this," Joe said. "But your information is often much better than mine. What is your source?"

"It's a man with good connections in Washington," Dr. Ernst said. Joe sat back, stunned.

"You have been working very hard for us, Mr. Smart." Dr. Landau spoke next. "But we think this problem is so big, and the crisis is so urgent, only an outside organization can influence the Administration. Especially President Truman."

Joe mulled over the idea. "An outside organization with big names like Mrs. Roosevelt."

"That's right, Mr. Smart," said Dr. Lederer. "We need powerful voices to reach the new President."

"Let me sleep on this," Joe said.

The next morning Joe called his three advisers to his office. "I've made my decision. I want to promote your idea, but I cannot do it as shelter director. I am going to resign."

"You would give up your job?" Dr. Lederer asked. "We didn't expect that. Your livelihood—your family—"

"I am prepared. In my opinion, I am the logical person to take on this job."

Joe released the announcement to the press. A few days later he walked into my office in Washington. "Go ahead, Ruth. Let me have it." He looked like a little boy expecting a whipping.

I had no intention of tongue-lashing him. "What really lay behind your resignation?"

"The conviction that this was the only way to get things done. I'm going to New York, open an office, and set up a new committee to try to mobilize public opinion."

Joe had hardly walked out the door when my secretary brought in copies of the *New York Daily News* and the *Jewish Morning Journal.* The story that the camp was to be closed June 30 was front page. The source was General O'Dwyer himself, the new executive director of the War Refugee Board.

I telephoned O'Dwyer's office, only to be told he was in California making a speech. His assistant, Florence Hodel, came to the phone. I could hear her gasp as I told her of the newspaper accounts that O'Dwyer planned to shut down the camp.

"How did that rumor get started?" she asked.

"Is it a rumor?"

"It may become fact."

"When was it decided? We were never told."

"We're planning to wind up our work June thirtieth. That's when WRB will be dissolved. The board may therefore take the position to send them back on the thirtieth."

If the rumor was indeed fact, I was prepared to fight. "I would like to know what General O'Dwyer is really planning."

She answered swiftly. "I'm in no position, and General O'Dwyer is not either, to make a disposition of these people. We can only make recommendations to the board. General O'Dwyer feels the refugees are in jail here. But it is something he inherited. He was not director when this whole thing started."

At four-thirty she telephoned again. "I've just spoken to General O'Dwyer in California. He is furious. He wants you to know that he never said he was shutting down the camp."

But in the camp, people talked of little else.

In the *Ontario Chronicle*, Dr. Landau described their bewilderment:

Could it be really the intention to send a resident, who unfortunately was born in Germany or Austria, back to the countries of Buchenwald, Auschwitz, and Dachau? Could the salvation action of a people who have suffered so much have sense when the saved people will be sent back to Poland, where, as everyone knows, the political situation is more than confused? General D. Eisenhower has recently given the order that no Polish citizen who is now liberated from German camps can be forced to return to Poland against his own free will. For many of us a return to "their homelands in Europe" signifies no more or less than a death warrant.

On May 7, 1945, Germany surrendered unconditionally. The shooting and the dying in Europe was over. The death camps would be opened—Dachau, Buchenwald, Theresienstadt, Auschwitz, and scores of others whose names we were yet to learn.

The people congregated on the parade ground, hugging one another, laughing, weeping, repeating the unbelievable words, "The war in Europe is over." Some joined hands and danced in circles; some sat in the synagogues and churches praying; some stayed in their barracks alone with their hopes and their grief.

A week later I was called back to New York. My father lay in bed, stricken, his arms and legs paralyzed by a stroke, but fully aware. His eyes misted as he saw me. "It's good you came."

Early in the evening, the whole family sat at his bedside. His face seemed to brighten like a candle before it flickers out. Then my brother Harry, a physician, rose, looked at his face, and wept.

"Papa is dead."

TWENTY-TWO

I WAS AT MY DESK on a quiet Saturday morning in Washington, catching up with mail from the refugees and from would-be homesteaders in Alaska, when the phone rang.

"I want to raise an issue with you." Florence Hodel, O'Dwyer's assistant, spoke diffidently. "Would Interior like to take full responsibility for the camp when the War Refugee Board goes out of existence next month?"

I said nothing. It was almost too good to believe—Ickes and WRA in full charge, making the decisions, their hands untied.

"What are the other possibilities?" I asked.

"The State Department."

"State!" I tried to keep my voice calm. To put the fate of the refugees back in the hands of Breckinridge Long was unthinkable.

"We've also considered the Bureau of Immigration—"

"In the Justice Department." It was just as unthinkable.

"We would rather have you take it over in Interior. What do you think?"

"I would welcome it. I'll talk to some of our people and call you back."

"We can do a good job," Abe Fortas, our undersecretary, agreed, "but don't forget, State and Justice must still make the final decision on the legal status of the refugees."

Ickes had no hesitation. "We'll take it. Just let them make a formal offer."

Meanwhile, word raced through the camp that they were soon to be deported.

Caught in the growing panic, twenty-seven of Oswego's leading citizens, headed by the mayor, sent a memorial to President Harry S Truman and to Congress on May 21, pleading that the refugees be allowed to stay. The memorial cheered the people, but in the White House and in Congress it was just one more piece of paper in the burgeoning file folders marked OSWEGO.

The panic spread. The private agencies were charged by angry columnists with timidity and inaction.

Professor Joseph Chamberlain, the widely respected chairman of the National Refugee Service, came to Washington. His face was drawn; he seemed years older than at our first meeting. "I'm terribly worried. What was started in this country last August when you brought the people to America was the beginning of a much bigger refugee movement. Oswego has become the center, the world showpiece of refugees. Thousands of refugees, here and abroad, are looking to see what's happening at the camp in Oswego. I tell you, the United States cannot afford to take the lead in sending displaced persons back to countries where they would starve."

"We've got Ickes on our side, fighting it everywhere, in the Cabinet, up on the Hill—"

"If Ickes can get State and Justice to postpone decisions about the final disposition for six months," he said, "we can work on 'sponsored leave.' We can resettle these families quietly all over the country and place the orphaned children in foster homes."

But with the war in Europe over, State and Justice were in no mood to postpone a decision for six months, and now we were faced with a new dilemma.

From Miriam Wydra, whose family came from Germany, I learned that her boss, Congressman Samuel Dickstein of New York, was planning to investigate the camp. Dickstein was chairman of the House Committee on Immigration and Naturalization. "You better come up on the Hill," she said, "and see the Congressman."

"This whole matter is getting out of hand," Dickstein, short, nattily dressed, told me. "Congress has got to look into it. After all, we're responsible for immigration. We write the law. I've decided to take my subcommittee up to the camp and determine what should be done."

The next day Dickstein announced his decision to the press, promising "open hearings" in Oswego and New York.

Bernie Dubin, the financial officer at the NRS, called me in alarm. "Can't you stop Dickstein? Congressional committees are dangerous. What recourse will we have if they vote to shut the camp down and send the people back?"

"You can't stop a congressman from holding hearings. The only thing we can do is present our case so forcefully and so humanly that the committee will vote in our favor."

Ickes agreed there was reason for alarm. "You never know what these congressional committees will come up with. You could get a subcommittee of isolationists who would like to see America shut its doors altogether. The best way to handle them is public opinion. Go up to New York right away," Ickes ordered. "See if you can get some of your friends on the newspapers and the weeklies to write editorials. Then get the private agencies to send a group of their top people down here to see Morgenthau and O'Dwyer. Tell them I'll be glad to see them too."

At three o'clock on a warm June day we trooped like a little army into the office of the Secretary of the Treasury. I introduced everyone to Morgenthau: the three representatives of the National Refugee Service, Professor Chamberlain, Mr. Dubin, and Mr. Zatkin; Miss Jones of the American Friends Service Committee; Mr. Bisgeyer of B'nai B'rith; Mr. Goldman of the Jewish Labor Committee; and Mr. Cohen of the American Jewish Committee. I knew how carefully the agencies had selected them for this critical day.

Morgenthau sat behind a huge desk, a tall intellectual-looking figure with a balding head, a strong prominent nose, and pince-nez. The office was austere, the desk bare save for a silver ashtray with the engraved letters FDR TO HM JR. XMAS 1939. Behind him on a table were photographs of his family. John Pehle, former director of the War Refugee Board, sat on the windowsill.

Chamberlain presented the argument for allowing the Oswego refugees to stay. His voice was strong, his language precise; he spoke like a lawyer committed to the law but with a deep sense of justice and humanitarianism.

Morgenthau pulled the pince-nez off his nose, held it for a few moments between his thumb and forefinger, replaced it, and finally spoke. "You're asking that we change the instructions issued by the President. We wrote those instructions here. We can't go back on them now. We've got to keep faith with Roosevelt." He readjusted his glasses. "I can't go back on my promise to the dead President; I couldn't sleep with my conscience."

The air was heavy. I was prepared for such words from State and Justice. But Morgenthau was the man who had brought the cables to the President. He had exposed the State Department's machinations. He and his men, Pehle, DuBois, and others, had created the War Refugee Board. They had done a magnificent job; they had saved thousands of lives in Hungary alone. They had circumvented the State Department's rigid stranglehold on immigration and created this haven at Oswego.

I heard his words with despair. *I couldn't sleep with my conscience.*

"Mr. Secretary," I said, "I have the feeling that if the President were alive, he would be the first to change his own memos. He would see how inhumane it is to keep people—" I stopped. I saw him glance briefly at Pehle, who nodded but remained silent.

"The only way to do it," Morgenthau said with finality, "is through Congress."

"But we're worried about Congress," Chamberlain countered. "A number of people—Ickes for instance, whom we saw this morning—say the Hill is hostile to more immigration, particularly of Jews."

Morgenthau hardly heard him. "I wouldn't take any second-hand opinion. I'd go right to see the Speaker of the House, Sam Rayburn, and the President of the Senate, Ken McKellar. We are very lucky in having two such men. I would ask them how many votes they could promise on this issue."

Chamberlain looked stricken. "We feel, Mr. Secretary, we mustn't let Congress touch this issue. They might upset the whole immigration applecart. This problem has worldwide refugee implications. We don't want to do anything that will undermine the possibility of getting a new law through Congress. We're trying to legitimize the status of some ten or twenty thousand people who are now in the country illegally or on temporary visas."

"Well, that's an entirely different problem." Morgenthau bit his lower lip. "You come to me on one problem, Oswego; my heart goes out to it. When Mrs. Morgenthau came back from the camp after a visit with Mrs. Roosevelt, she kept me awake prodding me about the camp. I couldn't sleep. Now you come to me on this problem. I give you a solution; I tell you what to do; then you bring in all these other things. That's not what you came to me for; that's another whole story entirely."

I could not help feel we had placed him in an embarrassing position. Disappointed and discouraged, we left.

In the outer office we found General O'Dwyer. Still working in Washington, O'Dwyer was already campaigning for the office of mayor of New York City. He shook our hands, smiled broadly, and told us eagerly, "I've seen people in the White House, I've seen people in Justice, I'm going to see the Secretary now, and if necessary I'll go to see Truman. I'm carrying in my hand, right here, recommendations to get the people out of the camp immediately. All of you go to my office. I'll be there soon and tell you the whole story."

His office in the basement of Treasury was filled with visitors and aides. His desk, like Morgenthau's, was bare, save for an assortment of cigars and a large ashtray. He could have closed shop in minutes and left Washington for good, I thought.

We sat waiting impatiently. Half an hour. An hour. At last he strode in, puffing a long cigar. He sat behind his desk talking about Oswego.

"Those poor sons-of-guns up there, they've been through hell and high water, they've been driven all around the world, and we keep them up there in a prison. I'm against picking them up from one incarceration and dumping them over in Europe into another incarceration. Those poor people should be allowed to look out of the bars at the blue sky and smell the good fresh air."

Goldman of the Jewish Labor Committee, sitting at my right, whispered, "Have you decided whom you're going to vote for yet? He's running for mayor right here."

"It tears my heart," O'Dwyer went on, "when I think of those poor sons-of-guns who suffered so much already, and the whole government of the great United States, the President, and all the people can't do a thing for them. How can I sleep with my conscience if we don't act now?

"Gentlemen," he said, "I am glad you came to Washington today. I am going to do something for you. I am going to read you this report with the recommendations I'll be making to the War Refugee Board. It's strictly confidential; you must make no notes; it mustn't go outside this room. But I want you to know what my thinking is."

The recommendations were the very ones we wanted to hear— freedom, sponsored leave, the right to stay in America.

"I'm getting out of the picture soon," he said. "But this thing lies close to my heart. Even as a defeated candidate for mayor of New York I'll come back and fight."

I was prepared to give him my vote right there.

In the power plays of Washington, good news and bad, life-and-death decisions, arrive on intergovernmental memos.

The memo arrived at Ickes's desk. The War Refugee Board was pleased to transfer its powers and responsibility to the War Relocation Authority on the thirtieth of June.

Ickes asked me to draft a letter immediately to President Truman requesting permission to close the camp in thirty days and grant the refugees sponsored leave.

He sent the letter. But before the President could act, Congressman Dickstein announced that on Monday, June 25, Subcommittee VI of the House Committee on Immigration and Naturalization would begin its investigation at the camp itself.

Ickes was a past master at congressional investigations. He gave me new orders. "Check into the backgrounds of the six congressmen on the committee. Then escort them to the train going up to the camp. That way you'll get a chance to know them personally. And, of course, I want you up in Oswego during the investigation. My instincts tell me they'll be calling you to testify."

His instincts, as usual, were sound. A few days before the hearings were to start, Miriam Wydra, the first woman appointed chief clerk to the House Committee on Immigration and Naturalization, asked me to come to her home, where she told me, "Dickstein wants you as a witness. But you can be much more. If you see that the hearings are taking a wrong turn, feel free to tell him what you think. Don't misunderstand. If Dickstein doesn't agree with you, he'll say so. I just want you to know he has a lot of confidence in you, and he's a decent man who listens to reason."

TWENTY-THREE

GRAND CENTRAL STATION seemed empty and cavernous as I waited for the six congressmen on a quiet Sunday morning. In Washington, Ed Marks and I had tried to anticipate the pitfalls. Ed was chief of the War Refugee Division of WRA and one of Dillon Myer's ablest assistants.

We had spent hours choosing the refugees we hoped would most impress the six men of Subcommittee VI. Of the six congressmen, the two most likely to be hostile were Lowell Stockman of Oregon and Clark Fisher of Texas. Their records on immigration were little different from the State Department's; the quotas, for them, were chiseled in stone.

The six men sauntered into the huge terminal. Dickstein greeted me jovially and introduced me. Stockman was a giant out of Grimm's fairy tales. Everything about him seemed larger than life—his huge hand that engulfed mine, his enormous feet, his body that seemed to grow as I looked up at it, his strong rugged chin, his long eyes. He was like a tree out of his own Northwest. He had been a rancher in Oregon. Dwarfed by him, Fisher was medium-sized, with regular features and a slow Texas drawl. He had been a district attorney before coming to Washington, and he too owned a cattle ranch.

We headed straight for the dining car for breakfast. "Come join us." Stockman pulled a chair for me next to the window. "Fisher and I can use some female companionship."

The landscape rushed beside us. It seemed to me the wheels were grinding out the words: *Stockman-and-Fisher, Stockman-and-Fisher.* The names were synonymous with danger. I tried to get some inkling of how they felt, but they were in no mood to discuss the inquiry. They were two ranchers vying with each other to tell me cowboy stories.

They were still trading yarns when the train pulled into Syracuse. Limousines were lined up to drive us directly to Oswego.

Summer had restored the beauty of the camp. The people crowded around us. "Our liberators have come!" someone shouted as we climbed out of the cars.

Manya rushed forward to show me little Diane. International Harry, a precocious one-year-old, raced near the cars, followed by Olga, out of breath from chasing him. Ed Marks, who had gone up earlier, came forward with Malcolm Pitts, the acting director, to welcome the congressmen.

"We'd like to see some of the camp," Dickstein said. There had been processions before, but never one like this, with Dickstein commanding his troops, followed by hundreds of refugees, who had never seemed more full of hope. Apparently no one had told them of the dangers of a congressional hearing.

It was a carefully calculated tour to show them the Americanization of Fort Ontario: the classrooms where people had studied English and learned the Bill of Rights; the exhibition hall with works of art that had recently won prizes in a museum in Syracuse—oil paintings by Vladimir von Zabotin, terra-cotta sculpture and watercolors by Miriam Sommerburg. The artists' works had gone to Syracuse, but not the artists. Syracuse was out of bounds.

Early Monday morning, the huge gymnasium filled up with Washington brass, members of the staff, refugees who were to testify, and rows of journalists and photographers. Once again, Oswego was front-page news.

At the stroke of ten-thirty, the congressmen took their seats at a long table. Dickstein, sitting in the center with the committee counsel, Thomas M. Cooley II, at his side, opened the hearings formally: "By a mandate of the Congress of the United States, the Committee on Immigration and Naturalization is authorized to make an overall study . . . to determine just what should be done with regard to the number of people in this camp, from the standpoint of some humane justice for them."

Ed Marks, as the first witness, gave the history of the project, the activities in the camp, and the restrictions on freedom which gave the people an "indeterminate kind of sentence."

General O'Dwyer was next. He had promised us he would fight, and he fought with passion. "To send stateless people who have no homelands back to a destroyed Europe," he said, would "in my opinion not be in accordance with the late President's commitment and our government's political and humanitarian policies."

Whatever his political motives were, whether or not he had his eye fixed on the Jewish, Catholic, Greek Orthodox, Polish, Yugoslav, or any other ethnic vote in New York City, not only failed to trouble me, I was delighted. The reporters were scribbling furiously in their notebooks.

Now, subtly, Congressman Fisher began his attack.

MR. FISHER: General, just to get the record straight, do you understand these people, who were brought here under the conditions that have been described, understood when they came here that they were going to be taken back as soon as the war was over?

GENERAL O'DWYER: I would say they were told that. I would agree they were told that, but I do say that this committee should keep in mind the mental condition of the people at the time they were told that, running through trouble, from pillar to post, harried, and coming to America was something to them at that time, and they took their chances on what would happen to them after that.

MR. FISHER (in disbelief): You understand that these people feel they were brought here under false pretenses, do you?

GENERAL O'DWYER: No, not at all. I don't believe it was anything like that, but I do say that we won't run into people like this again in our lifetime. You have them in a very confused mental state, and they were going to America. I think any of them would have signed any piece of paper you handed to them at that time. They were going to America, that was the only place in the world, having been harassed the way they had, everyone wanted to go. The same thing happened to me thirty-five years ago, and I know how it is.

Fisher now pressed O'Dwyer. "Wasn't the Department of Justice under obligation to keep faith with the President's directive?"

O'Dwyer agreed; that had been his position earlier. But this committee, appointed by Congress, could end that obligation.

Fisher turned belligerent. "We certainly aren't called upon to amend the immigration laws, to make any special exceptions."

"All that is needed," O'Dwyer said calmly, "is just a matter of interpretation."

But as Fisher prodded him O'Dwyer became more impassioned. "I am afraid I don't make my point to you, Mr. Fisher. You at the present time have millions over in Europe, millions of displaced persons where a resettlement program for each one of them will have to be made by the United Nations. . . . What are you going to do with the handful we took? Are you going to say to them, 'The war is over; go back'? If you do, you are going to tell every neutral, 'This is the way to handle it.'"

He recommended two actions. First, that the refugees leave the camp now; private agencies were prepared to assume complete financial and personal responsibility for them. Second, that Congress make no decision about their final status until the United Nations Relief and Rehabilitation Administration (UNRRA) had worked out a policy for the millions of displaced persons left homeless by the war. His ploy was brilliant: to show that the camp at Oswego was a displaced-persons camp on American soil and that the thousand refugees were part of the whole displaced-persons tragedy.

But Fisher seemed unmoved. And it was hard to tell how Stockman reacted; he had been silent, allowing Fisher to carry the ball for the isolationists.

The morning session ended.

We lunched in the camp hospital and then strolled through the grounds. The congressmen chatted informally with the people who thronged around us, asking me to interpret for those whose English was still limited. Unaware of the morning debate, the refugees continued to beam at their "liberators."

The session reconvened at two. Bugles sounded. The Fort Ontario Boy Scouts and Cub Scouts, in full khaki uniform, marched down the gymnasium, with standard-bearers carrying huge American flags. Like soldiers parading before a chief of state, their young faces were solemn.

Photographers rushed forward and flashbulbs popped, capturing the excitement in the hall. Together the Scouts recited the Boy Scout oath in English: "I will do my best to do my duty to God and my country." Our strategy was to make the congressmen see how in less than one year the children had become one hundred percent American.

Dickstein questioned several of the boys like a grandfather showing off his progeny. "You have no home at all? Would you like to stay in this country? Do you believe in our form of government? Would you be ready to defend it if the country wanted you? With a gun?"

Sylvan Boni, though a little frightened, responded to Dickstein's questions with a resounding "*Yes!*"

I was the last witness for the afternoon session. Determined to win over Fisher and Stockman, I told them of my days and nights on the ship hearing these people's stories; of the scene at the Statue of Liberty with the refugees waving excitedly in their terrible rags; and some of the case histories. Tom Cooley, the committee's counsel, informed the subcommittee that the case histories would become Exhibit 19.

Fisher and Stockman listened but said nothing, while George P. Miller of California and Cooley asked questions about the Army's screening in Europe and health examinations.

"They had very careful medical screening by army doctors," I assured them, and related how the GIs had even helped deliver International Harry.

"Thank you very much," Dickstein said. "You have done a splendid job. We will adjourn until ten-thirty tomorrow morning."

Back in my hotel room, I opened the window to look down at the Oswego River sparkling in the late-afternoon sun. It was nearly a year since I had first seen this river. It seemed to me I was generations older, sadder and, I hoped, wiser. I had tried my best at the hearings. But had I really reached Fisher and Stockman? Had I helped these two ranchers from the West, with vast lands around them, understand what it meant for a refugee to be in America, fenced in; what it meant to children who had been hungry and frightened to wear Boy Scout uniforms, go to school, and bring the Bill of Rights home to their parents?

History had come to this small American town on a river and a lake; from its schools and movies, from its library and shops and corner drugstores, the refugees had absorbed the spirit of democracy.

The congressmen would have to see it.

I knocked on Naomi Jolles's door in the Pontiac Hotel. She was typing her first story for the *New York Post*. Ted Thackrey, editor of the *Post*, had sent Naomi, a bright, sophisticated reporter, to cover the hearings at my request. Naomi had written an article about the refugee children attending Oswego's schools, called "The Fourth R," for *Woman's Home Companion;* the fourth R stood for refugees. I told her of my fears that Fisher and Stockman were still hostile. "We've got to work on these two congressmen," I said. "Will you help?"

Naomi shut her portable typewriter. "I'll take Fisher; you get Stockman."

In the hotel dining room, Naomi took a seat beside Fisher; I sat next to Stockman. The two men seemed delighted to have companions. We ate well but hurriedly; we were due back at the camp for a cabaret show.

In the post theater, the six congressmen joined in the national anthem, applauded the dances and skits, and rose with Dickstein as Mirković sang, "Eli, Eli, my God, my God, why hast Thou forsaken me?"

As we filed out of the theater, Stockman took my arm. "It was really impressive. But after all that, Fisher and I need a drink. How about you and Naomi joining us?"

We drove to a popular watering place called the White Horse Inn, dark and deserted except for the four of us. Stockman dropped some nickels into the jukebox, and we began to dance. Naomi and Fisher made a handsome couple, but I scarcely came up to Stockman's solar plexus. Like many large men, he was surprisingly graceful and light, while I felt awkward and clumsy. In a mottled wall mirror I caught a glimpse of us and giggled. Fortunately, Stockman was telling me a joke.

It was almost midnight when we returned to the hotel, shook hands with the two congressmen in the lobby, and thanked them for a lovely evening. Naomi and I agreed that dancing in the White Horse Inn might turn out to be as helpful as the testimony in reaching Fisher and Stockman.

The hearings resumed the next morning as Dr. Ralph Waldo Swetman, the tall bespectacled president of the State Teachers College, talked enthusiastically of the students' eagerness and their determination to do good work. He singled out Alex Margulis. "We had a special assembly at the time of the VE-Day celebration, and Alexander Margulis gave a talk. There were four hundred students in the assembly, and you could have heard a pin drop, he spoke with such force and fire."

I could hear Alex's voice. "It is a rainy day, cold and miserable," Alex had begun his speech. "For four years from 1941 to 1945, I kept thinking how glorious it would be on this day; we would dance in the streets. Yet now this day has come and there is no elation. There is just profound regret that so many of the people we loved are not sharing this day. We feel almost guilty that we have survived while so many who are more worthy have not. To them, we can make only one pledge: We will try to prevent this from ever happening again."

The whole gym, even the congressmen, applauded when Ralph Faust announced that in his high school, "just today, I notified eight Fort Ontario students that they are eligible to join the National Honor Society."

Edmund Waterbury, the publisher of the *Oswego Palladium-Times*, risked the wrath of his townspeople. "There is more talent in this group than there is in all of Oswego together, and I am not discrediting my own hometown, but when you get painting, sculpture, music, acting, dancing, and playwrighting, they would do credit to a city of five hundred thousand population."

Next, some of the refugees themselves testified with stories of murder and their own escapes.

Young Alex Margulis presented a letter to the committee from the dean of the Harvard Medical School; he had been accepted in the first-year class, and his brother Rajko, because of his outstanding grades in Yugoslavia, was admitted as a junior, an unprecedented event in Harvard's history, he was told. They would both be on full scholarships. Would they be allowed to leave the camp in the fall to go to Harvard? It seemed inconceivable that two brilliant young medical students might be barred from Harvard because they had entered America outside the quota.

"Would you be willing to protect our country in case of war?" Dickstein asked Alex.

"Yes."

"Would you be ready to join the Army now?"

"Yes."

"Any other questions, gentlemen?" Dickstein asked. Since there were no other questions, Dickstein thanked the witnesses and the citizens of Oswego, "so kind and humane," who had "displayed real Americanism, and I surely want to thank the press."

The congressmen departed.

Back at the hotel, the reporters told me they had polled the congressmen; five were now prepared to vote to keep the refugees in America. Stockman had been converted. Only Fisher remained unconvinced. He told them he wanted to put the problem into the hands of the Attorney General.

Monday morning in Washington, I went up the Hill to see Dickstein. He was triumphant. "The subcommittee has just voted unanimously to allow the refugees to remain."

So Fisher too had been converted!

"Tomorrow morning," Dickstein said, "I'm reporting to the entire Committee on Immigration and Naturalization. I want you there."

The full House committee assembled around a large table, and Dickstein, its chairman, summarized the testimony in the camp. Many of the full committee, we knew, were isolationists, who were aided now by Robert Alexander, one of Breckinridge Long's men in the Visa Division of the State Department. Alexander kept moving around the table, whispering, handing out notes, as the isolationists began probing, jabbing, questioning Dickstein.

Dickstein became a boxer. He danced around their thrusts, protecting his face with his gloves, never allowing a fatal punch.

When the restrictionists realized they could not knock him out—get him at least to postpone the vote he sought—they tried a familiar technique. "Why don't you have the subcommittee take a few more days and write us a resolution?"

"OK." Dickstein was affable. "But if you do that, you spoil a perfectly good speech for me tomorrow in New York."

That was language the congressmen understood. It was a gentleman's agreement: you didn't spoil a colleague's chance to make a speech.

The subcommittee left the meeting room for privacy to draw up a resolution based on the hearings. I remained in the large room as the full committee waited. Alexander moved around the table until he reached Ed Gossett of Texas, a strong isolationist, and showed him a slip of paper. Gossett looked pleased.

"I'd like to suggest to the subcommittee," Gossett said, "that they put this phrase into their resolution: 'No groups should be brought into the United States under these conditions in the future.' " It was as if Roosevelt had done something sly and unclean in inviting the refugees to America.

A messenger took the noxious phrase to the subcommittee, who felt they had no recourse but to accept it. They returned to the committee room.

Dickstein read the resolution urging the government of the United States to allow the refugees at Fort Ontario to leave the camp. A motion was made to accept the resolution as read.

I felt a wave of gratitude. Fisher himself seconded the motion.

The resolution was passed unanimously.

Exhilaration filled the camp. The "liberators" had voted to liberate the people.

The fence would come down. The people would enter America.

The exhilaration lasted just three days.

The isolationists on the full committee lobbied hard. The resolution they had passed was easily tabled. Sponsored leave was not even to be considered! Immigration laws were not to be tampered with!

On Friday, July 6, 1945, the House Immigration and Naturalization Committee voted that not Congress but the Departments of State and Justice "should ascertain the practicability of returning the refugees to their homelands." If that were found to be not practicable, the Attorney General should declare them "illegally present in the country" and "undertake deportation proceedings."

The refugees were in even graver danger of being shipped back to Europe.

Twenty-four

Edith Semjen and Mirković were pacing the parade ground.

"When we first came," Edith said, puffing her cigarette nervously, "I was sure I would go back the minute the war was over. But now I've learned that everything we had was destroyed; everybody—our relatives, our friends—everybody is dead. There's nothing to go back to."

They were discussing the notice that had just come from UNRRA; the *Gripsholm* was sailing to Europe in August, and there was space for a number of Yugoslavs who might want to be repatriated.

Mirković put his arm through Edith's. "After that whole business with the congressmen, with our hopes going up and down like an escalator, it looks to me as if they really intend to send us back. But it's still a gamble whether we stay or not. I'm taking the gamble. Europe to me is a nightmare."

Dr. Rafailo Margulis had learned he was dying of cancer; he wanted to die in Yugoslavia, and he wanted his wife and his two sons with him. He told Rajko and Alex, "You must leave with me. They'll never let you out of this camp to go to Harvard. The camp will never be closed by September, and you'll be stuck here behind the fence."

The two young men tried to reason with him. He knew what Harvard meant to them. Maybe they would all be released before the fall term started; if not, surely some provision would be found so they could attend the most prestigious medical school in America.

Dr. Margulis insisted they sign on to the *Gripsholm* and go with him. They obeyed.

Of the 368 Yugoslavs now in the camp, fifty-three registered for the voyage. Parties and tearful farewells were given to the much-loved Mathilda Nitsch, to Dušanka Grin, who had shown her apartment to Eleanor Roosevelt, and to relatives and friends who were to sail on August 28 from New York. Thirteen Yugoslavs had sailed on the first voyage of the *Gripsholm* in May; two others had left, one for Uruguay, one for Czechoslovakia; and Elsa Neumann, who had taken such delight in her "villa by the sea," had rejoined her children in South Africa. Of the original 982, only sixty-nine in all had opted to leave the camp.

The rest waited, in anguish and despair and hope.

Letters went back and forth from Interior to State and Justice. Conferences were held. And, maddeningly, nothing was done.

But inside the camp, all was not bleak.

The little *rebbetzin*, Mindla Tzechoval, greeted me slyly on one of my visits. "I have a big surprise for you." She led me to one of the barracks.

There was the *mikvah*, the ceremonial pool.

"How did you get it built?" I asked.

She put her hands together as in prayer, lifted her face to the sky, and said, "Riboyne Shel Olem, O Master of the World, You heard our plea, and we thank You." She had persuaded one of the ultra-orthodox agencies to pay for building it.

Maria Montiljo, whose little daughter Elia had died on the ship, gave birth to another daughter on the sixth of May. She named her baby Rosica.

Kostia Zabotin entered the American Legion public-speaking contest in the high school, spoke on the American Constitution, and won first prize. The American Legion was not about to give him the award; he was not a citizen. But Ralph Faust "raised hell," he told me, in describing the incident, and Kostia walked away with the award.

And on graduation day, families and friends applauded loudly as Anita Baruch, Alfons Finci, Lea Hanf, Gordana Milinović, Steffi Steinberg, and Edith Weiss, dressed in long white robes and mortarboards, marched down the auditorium. Smiling and grateful, they shook hands with Ralph Faust, who had made all this possible, and walked off the platform with diplomas, full-fledged graduates of Oswego High School.

On July Fourth—Dillon Myer chose Independence Day to make the welcome announcement—the hated "leave policy" was relaxed. The town of Oswego would no longer be the outermost frontier. People could travel twenty miles in any direction, provided they returned at night. But Syracuse, thirty-five miles away, was still forbidden territory.

And the cruel separation of wives and husbands who had rediscovered each other when we arrived was ended. Conjugal visits were allowed. American wives or husbands could spend a night at the camp or a night in the Pontiac Hotel. Even visiting children were allowed to sleep over.

Then, early in the summer, Esther Morrison and eleven other members of a Quaker-sponsored team arrived and turned Fort Ontario, for the children at least, into an American summer camp.

The Quakers taught the young people Indian crafts; they led them on hikes and arranged picnics and scavenger hunts; they built puppets and presented "Snow White and the Seven Dwarfs"; and in the cool of the evenings they sat in the bleachers and taught children from eighteen lands folk songs about the home where the buffalo roam and the deer and the antelope play.

Thursday nights, Esther taught the adults American square dancing, and bachelors and married men fell in love with her. She was tall, with brown eyes and a lilting Mississippi accent; she could have been a southern belle with nothing but beaux on her mind. Instead, she had a master's degree in social work and had spent four of the war years in group work at a YWCA in Beaumont, Texas. She had applied to the Philadelphia Quakers for summer work, though she was no Quaker herself, and had been recruited for the summer work camp in Fort Ontario.

It was what she did for the pre-teenage girls that was to endear her to them forever. She had only to enter a room, and seven- and eight- and nine-year-old girls felt safe and happy. She led children whose earliest memories were of flight and hunger and fear into the security of American life.

In an era of accepted sex discrimination, she was told, when she helped organize the first Girl Scout troop, that there was no money for uniforms. The Boy Scouts, early in the camp's life, had all been given uniforms. Esther was solution-oriented. She brought the girls into her apartment and taught them how to bake cookies. She took small groups into the camp kitchens, where they collected fat. They sold the cookies in town, and sold the fat to rendering plants for soap. With the money they earned, she bought them Girl Scout scarves and pins, which they wore as proudly as if they had khaki uniforms.

One day she asked them, "Who has family in Europe?"

Hands flew up around the room. "I have straws here," she said. "Every one draw a straw. Whoever gets the winning straw will get a package we will send to her family abroad."

Nine-year-old Esther Danon screamed with delight. She had won. Esther Morrison and the girls bought a silk blouse in town, packed it, and sent it to Esther Danon's sister, who was with the partisans in Yugoslavia. Little Esther had learned that her seventeen-year-old sister had been wounded in the fighting and was destitute. The blouse became a symbol among the partisans; whoever had a birthday wore the blouse from Fort Ontario, America.

The Quakers, who lived together in one of the officers' red brick buildings overlooking the parade ground, asked me to spend several evenings describing the experiences on the ship and the backgrounds of the people. For they, like almost all of us whose lives had touched the refugees, had become part of the extended family. As they wrote in their "Oswego Log,"

We are not deceived into thinking that our contribution can make any appreciable lessening of the camp's total heartbreak, but we like to think that we are here as a symbol of many Americans who carry in their hearts a concern for all displaced persons.

Oswego had a thousand displaced persons. But now there were half a million displaced persons in Europe, aftermath of the war. President Truman sent Earl G. Harrison to investigate the DP camps in Germany.

Harrison, a recognized expert on refugees and dean of law at the University of Pennsylvania, had already expressed his views on Oswego in a letter to the Attorney General: "The worst thing that could happen right now would be to require that all of the people at Oswego be moved immediately, somewhere—anywhere just so long as it is outside of the United States."

In Germany, Harrison was devastated. He saw survivors of the Inferno living in a new inferno of chaos and suffering, squeezed into tents or horse stalls or former Nazi death camps, twenty and thirty in a room. "We appear to be treating Jews as the Nazis treated them except we do not exterminate them," Harrison wrote.

Men and women who needed each other, who needed to prove themselves alive, strung blankets around their beds to make love.

Harrison saw few children, none between the ages of one and five. Hitler had murdered more than one million children.

He saw few elderly people; they too had been exterminated. Only the strongest had survived, most of them young people in their late teens, twenties, and thirties.

He had gone to Germany expecting to recommend that the refugees be repatriated to their former homes. He discovered that at first many of the Jews had believed as he did: They wanted to be repatriated. They had gone back to their homelands, only to find their families dead, their homes plundered, and the smell of blood in the streets. Their neighbors, staring at them as if they were ghosts, found time-honored ways of driving them out.

Anti-Semitism, Harrison discovered, had not died with Hitler's suicide in the Berlin bunker. Polish Jews, especially, were fleeing in terror to Germany—the deathland—into the DP camps, because the Americans were there, and the Americans, they were sure, would help them.

Harrison returned to the United States and reported to Truman. The solution, he told the President, was not repatriation but resettlement. Some people wanted resettlement in America; some in Canada, Australia, South Africa; but most wanted Palestine, the homeland that had been promised them by the League of Nations in 1922.

Truman, shocked by Harrison's report, turned to Britain's newly elected Prime Minister, Clement Attlee, and asked him to allow 100,000 Jewish refugees to enter Palestine. Attlee dared not refuse point-blank. England, financially and physically battered, was too dependent upon the United States to anger Truman. Instead, Attlee suggested the appointment of a new commission; it was the eighteenth commission to study the problem of Palestine.

In Oswego, the refugees read the newspaper accounts of this new "Anglo-American Committee of Inquiry on Palestine" with excitement and hope. Oswego was a DP camp in America. Harrison had recommended resettlement in Palestine. They too sought resettlement—in America.

The President was asking Britain to open Palestine to 100,000 DPs. But for the one thousand in Oswego, the door to America was still not open.

Weeks were passing, then months, while State, Justice, and Interior fought over them. Joe Smart's committee had one hundred prominent leaders, including Eleanor Roosevelt and Robert A. Taft, the powerful Senator from Ohio, all trying to win support to keep the refugees in America.

The dread of spending another fierce winter imprisoned by mountains of snow threw the camp into gloom. Late in November, Ickes sent me back to try to bolster morale.

Just past midnight my train pulled into Syracuse. Clyde H. Powers, who had become the camp director during the summer, drove me to Oswego.

"You'll find a lot of changes," he warned me.

His warning hardly prepared me for what I found the next morning. Some of the men had aged badly; their eyes were watery, their faces sagged, and even their skin looked weary. Some of the women, heavier than ever, looked nervous and confused.

The wind howled off Lake Ontario, whistling through the naked branches of trees. The parade ground was frozen and deserted.

At lunch, Artur Hirt sank into a chair beside me. "The first days when we came, America worried about us. But now nobody worries. We're forgotten."

"Not true," I protested. "You don't know how hard we're fighting for you."

"That's you. And your department. But what about the other government agencies?"

"The fight isn't over. We have the American press with us almost one hundred percent. Only one or two columnists like Westbrook Pegler are trying to stir up sentiment to send you back." I showed him some of the articles and editorials I had brought with me.

"Then *you* must do something," he insisted. "You know I was a judge. Juridically, the paper we signed in Italy, that we would go back at the end of the war, doesn't hold. The Poland I would have to go back to is no longer Poland. My part of it is Russia. I don't want to go to Russia. I hate the Communists. I hate Stalin. Where should I go? I warn you, we can't hold out much longer."

Hirt was cocky and fighting mad, but others walked with their heads stooped, as if their lives were anchored by memories of terror and flight.

In the evening, the artists gave a special performance to welcome me back—and hear if I had any news to report.

The performance began patriotically as always with the national anthem, followed by the camp's own anthem, "Don't Fence Me In."

Then Otto Presser, a saddened Eddie Cantor, made a little speech. "Our Mother Ruth is really like Moses. He led the Jews through the wilderness for forty years. But he couldn't see the Promised Land. Our Mother Ruth led us to Oswego—and sometimes it seems we have been here thirty if not forty years. But that's where her role changes. She goes back and forth, but her *children* can't see the Promised Land."

It's true, I thought dismally, but not funny.

Charles Abeles played a tuneful song he had composed for me. Leon Levitch arranged a haunting piano solo. There were new comic skits. The Russians put on an amusing circus act. But I was too distressed by the changes in their faces to laugh, and the laughter around me seemed bitter.

Presser now called on me to speak.

I walked slowly to the stage and looked out. They were all there—Fredi and Jennie, Adam Munz and David Hendel, Edith Bronner and Edith Semjen, Olga Maurer, Abe Furmanski, Hans Goldberger of the *Pentcho,* Ernst Wolff, Steffi, Jetta, Zdenka. I saw them in the bright theater lights, row upon row.

Some smiled up at me encouragingly. Others sat cold. I too was the enemy.

I began in a low voice. "I wished I might have good news for you. We had all expected that there would be a final decision by now. But unfortunately the wheels of government move slowly."

Silence.

"This is how a democracy works. With checks and balances, so that decisions take longer. If this were a dictatorship, we would have had an answer right away. I say, 'Thank God it is not a dictatorship!' If it were, none of us would be here tonight. There would never have been a haven in Oswego."

Applause started slowly, then faded.

"Some of you tell me you think you are forgotten. That is not true! Every day conferences are taking place, government officials are meeting, letters are being written from one branch of government to another. Your cause is being defended with all the eloquence and passion your friends can command."

Magrita Ehrenstamm smiled up at me encouragingly.

"You have an important mission," I said. "You are the first DPs who were brought to this country. You are the vanguard. What the government decides should be done for you may influence what the world will do for hundreds of thousands of DPs. Your struggle is their struggle, your agony their agony. Like you, they want the right to live in a land they dream of, with decency and dignity, without hunger and without fear."

Ernst Wolff in the second row threw me a kiss.

"We must not give up hope."

The applause began.

I went on. "My philosophy is that wherever there is a door, it can be opened. There are still a few doors."

"Bravo!" someone shouted.

"Let me assure you that every one of us who loves you and has faith in you is working tirelessly, day and night, to do two things: to shut the camp down so you can work, move around, and live as free human beings again; and to get you into the country legally under the quota."

Applause burst through the hall. Swelling. In waves.

I put my hand up for silence. I felt tears in my eyes. "That first day, at the Statue of Liberty, you told me the air of America smells like free air. Believe me, we want you to breathe it."

I walked off the stage.

TWENTY-FIVE

THE WAR IN EUROPE was over, the war in the Far East was over, but the war in Washington between the bureaucracies was at fever pitch.

On December 5, 1945, Justice and State, fighting to send the camp people back to Europe, prepared a letter to be signed by Ickes, Attorney General Tom C. Clark, and Secretary of State James

F. Byrnes. The letter was to be sent to the chairmen of both House and Senate committees on Immigration and Naturalization, and it recommended that the refugees leave the United States.

Ickes objected to the draft letter and refused to sign it. Instead, he asked me to draft a letter to Undersecretary of State Dean Acheson, explaining our position. Secretary of State James Byrnes was out of town.

On Wednesday, December 12, Acheson took action. He dictated a telegram to New York inviting the private agencies to send a delegation to his office on Friday at 2:30 P.M. I was to accompany them.

Every hour counted now; I was certain this would be the decisive meeting. I prepared documents to show Acheson who the people at Fort Ontario were. I talked with Chamberlain in New York; the agencies were working ceaselessly, collecting letters of support. William Green, president of the American Federation of Labor, wrote a strong plea that the refugees be allowed to stay. Other labor leaders had feared they might take jobs away from Americans. Green's letter, we hoped, would pull the plug on that argument.

Early Friday afternoon, the delegates, in heavy overcoats, thick gloves, and winter hats, arrived in my office. Led again by Joe Chamberlain, they were Clarence Pickett, executive secretary of the American Friends Service Committee, who had sent the Quaker team to the camp; Judge Nathan Perlman of the American Jewish Congress; Isaiah Minkoff, director of the National Jewish Community Relations Advisory Committee (NACRAC); and Bruce Mohler of the National Catholic Welfare Conference, who had come as the personal representative of Archbishop Spellman of New York. The Archbishop wanted Acheson to know he was deeply concerned for the future of the Catholics in the camp.

In freezing cold, we walked from Interior to State and waited for Acheson in a large reception room.

Exactly at two-thirty, his secretary appeared. "The meeting has been postponed until five-thirty."

We decided to stay where we were. In Washington, the treadmill of government grinds to an early halt. By four, most of the State

Department staff had put on their hats and winter coats and headed for home or dates or a friendly bar. We were alone, growing more apprehensive as the hours dragged by.

In low voices, we tried to analyze the three-hour delay. Perhaps Acheson had slipped out a back door to see the President.

The refugee problem had become a world crisis. The Anglo-American Committee of Inquiry on Palestine was meeting this very day in Washington, taking testimony. Earl Harrison had described the chaos in the DP camps. Witnesses were repeating Truman's request that Britain act magnanimously, that she open Palestine to 100,000 DPs. And here we were, five men and a woman, watching the clock, waiting for Acheson, hoping desperately that our government too would act magnanimously and open America to one thousand DPs.

Acheson himself was an enigma. Ickes had told me that he regarded him as a good friend, but that Acheson was opposed to a homeland for Jews in Palestine. Whether this would influence his thinking about a homeland for the Oswego refugees in America, we could not judge.

At five-thirty, a massive wooden door swung open, and Acheson emerged from his private office.

He shook our hands. "I'm sorry to have kept you waiting. I have nothing to report to you right now. I'm going to see the President tomorrow, and I'll get back to you."

Chamberlain had carefully drawn up a strong legal document; he handed it to Acheson, and we left.

Dusk had already darkened the ice-cold streets. The men looked somber as they said goodbye to me and took the train back to Philadelphia and New York.

I taxied home to my apartment.

There were still doors to be opened, I had promised the refugees in November. The White House door was the last.

Saturday morning, December 22, I worked at my office desk and then turned on the radio for news.

The announcement came quietly: "President Truman will make a major statement from the White House this evening on immigration and refugees."

I tossed papers into desk drawers, pulled on my coat, and walked through the great bronze doors of Interior. The snow-covered streets were crowded with Christmas shoppers; jolly Santa Clauses with fake beards were ringing Salvation Army bells; church bells chimed Christmas carols.

All afternoon my phone kept ringing.

"Ruthie, what does it mean?" Manya asked from the camp.

"I don't know."

"You don't know! Then what should we think?"

"Stay close to the radio. I'll phone you after his talk."

In the evening, I moved the radio next to an armchair, not to miss a single word. The music stopped. The midwestern voice, honest, unadorned, came through the box.

"The war has brought in its wake an appalling dislocation of populations in Europe. . . . The immensity of the problem of displaced persons and refugees is almost beyond comprehension."

I nodded, as if I were watching him at his desk in the Oval Office. I knew how he hated reading speeches, how he read them into a recording machine, listening to himself, repeating words over and over to get the right emphasis. The emphasis now was fine.

"A number of countries in Europe, including Switzerland, Sweden, France, and England, are working toward its solution. The United States shares the responsibility to relieve the suffering. To the extent that our present immigration laws permit . . ."

Could I be hearing right? He was making no recommendations to change the immigration laws.

". . . everything possible should be done at once to facilitate the entrance of some of these displaced persons and refugees into the United States."

Maybe he planned to circumvent the immigration laws, as Roosevelt had done.

"Most of these persons are natives of Central and Eastern Europe and the Balkans." Just like Oswego, I thought. "The immigration quotas for all these countries for one year total approximately thirty-nine thousand, two thirds of which are allotted to Germany. Under the law, in any single month, the number of visas issued cannot exceed ten percent of the annual quota. This means that from now on only about thirty-nine hundred visas can be issued each month to persons who are natives of these countries."

So, 3,900 refugees would enter the United States each month—under the law. The quotas would not be changed!

The words I was waiting for came in the middle of his talk. "There is one particular matter involving a relatively small number of aliens." He recounted President Roosevelt's decision to bring one thousand refugees to America and his message to Congress "that these persons would be returned to their homelands after the war."

"However," he said, his voice buoyant, "surveys have revealed that most of these people would be admissible under the immigration laws."

His words came into the apartment like shafts of light.

"In the circumstances, it would be inhumane and wasteful to require these people to go all the way back to Europe merely for the purpose of applying there for immigration visas and returning to the United States.

"Many of them have close relatives, including sons and daughters, who are citizens of the United States and who have served and are serving honorably in the armed forces of our country.

"I am therefore directing the Secretary of State and the Attorney General to adjust the immigration status of those members of this group who may wish to stay here, in strict accordance with existing laws and regulations."

"We're staying," Manya wept into the telephone. "The camp has gone wild. Everyone kissing and laughing and crying. Are you there? Do you hear me?"

I heard, but my voice was blurred with tears.

Sunday morning's newspapers headlined the story.

TRUMAN ACTS TO AID ENTRY OF REFUGEES, the *Washington Times-Herald* said in a banner headline. TRUMAN REFUGEE PROPOSAL WINS SUPPORT ON "HILL."

Representative E. H. Hedrick (D.) of West Virginia, a member of Dickstein's House Immigration Committee, saw no objection "as long as the quotas are not increased."

Lowell Stockman, the giant rancher from Oregon, told the press he doubted there would be much criticism, since the current quotas were not affected. But he personally believed, he said, that the quotas should be cut in half.

Representative Rankin (D.) of Mississippi said there was still "a good deal of cloakroom sentiment for shutting off immigration for a while." He favored stopping all immigration "till we get our own house in order." But as long as the President did not envisage increasing the quotas, Rankin said, "nothing can be done about it."

"We won," Ickes said Monday morning, exultant. "It was a rough battle with State and Justice and some of those congressmen, but well worth it. You'd better go back to Oswego and help people get ready to leave for a new life."

At Fort Ontario, Adam Munz pumped my hand. "Do you know what it means to wake up in the morning and say, 'I'm free'?"

Once again the camp was inundated with journalists, government officials, and representatives of the private welfare agencies.

The refugees staged a gala Sylvesterabend, to be the happiest New Year's Eve of their lives.

Otto Presser thanked President Truman "for the gift of freedom." Then, rolling his eyes, he said, "I've been in camps for five and a half years, and I don't know what it will be like to sit alone on a toilet seat."

The camp staged an operetta written by Miriam Sommerburg, with music by Charles Abeles, called *The Golden Cage*. It was the saga of Oswego, with Manya and Mirković in the lead roles. Well-dressed women stood outside a fence listening to poorly clad refugees singing:

> We are in a cage without reason,
> We are in a cage, golden cage;
> We're missing nothing but our freedom.

Mirković sang:

> I feel myself a monkey
> In the zoological garden;
> Are we to be on display?
> There's nothing missing but the warden!

The operetta ended in a grand finale. The cast, arms intertwined, laughing, dancing, thanked Roosevelt, "who sent an angel to the world to free us from this farce."

At the stroke of midnight we stood up in the post theater, cheering, blowing horns, kissing each other.

Nineteen forty-six! The first year of freedom. The running was over; the golden cage had swung open; they were free.

In the cold starlit night we left the theater and headed to the Service Club, where tables fringed the walls, laden with food and soft drinks. All of us—refugees, reporters, government officials—joined hands, dancing the hora until the room began to spin.

"Silence!" Presser shouted.

The huge Service Club grew still.

"You all know I have been looking for a girl of seventy-five to marry. I have found my girl. She's not seventy-five. Now, in front of all of you, I want to say, I have proposed marriage and she has accepted."

"Who?" we asked each other.

Presser came across the room and led me to the center of the crowded hall.

In a mock ceremony, one of the men placed a prayer shawl

around my shoulders, held his hand over my head, and married me to the camp comedian. While the audience cheered and applauded, Presser led me in a wild Viennese waltz around the hall.

New Year's Day broke over the camp, cold and clear and free.

Speed was important.

The Oswego refugees would be the first to enter the United States under Truman's directive for 3,900 DPs a month. They had to be processed by immigration inspectors, border patrolmen, and officials of State, Immigration, and the Public Health Service. Seventy communities from New York to California offered to resettle them, find them housing, help them get jobs, and place their children in schools.

Packing the pictures in her little apartment, Magrita Ehrenstamm told me, "My daughter has already leased an apartment for me in New York. I still can't believe this—that I'll have a kitchen of my own and," she said slowly, "privacy."

To enter the United States legally, they had to leave it. On January 17, 1946, the first three busloads, carrying ninety-five refugees, left camp at six in the morning. They drove across western New York State to Buffalo, where the community invited them to a roast-beef lunch in Temple Beth El. Then the buses traveled to Niagara Falls and crossed the Rainbow Bridge to the town of Niagara Falls in Ontario, Canada. There they were greeted by George Graves, the American consul, who gave each refugee the longed-for visa embellished with a red seal and a ribbon.

They drove back across the Rainbow Bridge and at last entered America.

Some traveled in chartered buses directly from the Canadian border to the office of the National Refugee Service in New York, where relatives waited for them. One of the first off the bus was Dr. Hugo Graner, almost smothered by his two children, while his wife, Elsa, waited to embrace him, her eyes filled with tears.

Ivo Lederer, his parents, and his sister Mira were welcomed by

Mr. Lederer's brother, Leo Lenski, who had come to take them to his apartment on West Seventy-seventh Street.

Talking to the press, fourteen-year-old Ivo summed up what he and most of the refugees were feeling. "It was worth everything, just to be here."

Husbands embraced wives, fathers hugged their children, sisters, brothers, cousins, aunts talked and laughed and wept with joy and relief.

Magrita Ehrenstamm, holding her new grandchild tightly, went directly to the apartment her daughter had furnished for her, "with privacy." Henny Notowicz heard her Uncle Aaron in Brooklyn order his daughter, "Move over. Your cousin is sleeping with you."

Immediately after President Truman's Christmas present allowing them to enter America, they had sat in the camp with social workers from the War Relocation Authority and the private Jewish and Christian agencies, learning about towns in America where they might begin their new lives.

Most of them yearned for New York, the fabled city whose skyline they had glimpsed from the deck of the *Henry Gibbins*. But they were gently dissuaded by the social workers, who had swiftly canvassed and received commitments from communities across the country prepared to take in families, help them find homes, jobs, and schools, and give them interest-free loans.

Some of those who had come from Eastern Europe's small towns and villages preferred settling in small towns. They cherished the quiet beat and rhythm of a town where they would soon know their neighbors.

Rena Romano Block's father, Alberto Romano, selected Baltimore because he wanted to be near the sea. The last syllable of the name *Baltimore* means "ocean" in Yugoslavian. Fortunately, as he discovered, Baltimore was on Chesapeake Bay.

In the next days, people dispersed by train to the towns and cities they had selected across America.

Irene Danon, her parents, and her two younger brothers were

warmly welcomed by the Cleveland Jewish community. Her father worked in a zipper factory, her mother in a sewing shop, while Irene and her brother Iċa stuffed envelopes. But after a few years they moved to New York and found an apartment at Forty-second Street and Ninth Avenue. "I loved New York," Irene told me. "I opened my window and I could hear Italian, Spanish, Jewish. I loved everything about being alive in that wonderful town."

Others, too, found their way back to New York. One day in the subway, I met one of Mirković's best friends. "Jellinek!" I exclaimed. "What are you doing in New York? I thought you settled in Pittsburgh?"

"I couldn't stand the provinces," he said.

Of the families destined for New York, most arrived in Grand Central Station, where they were met by Hebrew Immigrant Aid Society and NRS social workers and escorted to dormitories in the HIAS shelter on Lafayette Street, the former Astor Library. It is now Joseph Papp's famous Public Theatre.

Postwar housing in New York was tight, but there were empty cold-water flats on the Lower East Side, tenements that had housed the tempest-tossed from Europe for over a hundred years.

And so they began their new lives.

Part Four

—《 》—

AFTER THEY CROSSED
THE RAINBOW BRIDGE

TWENTY-SIX

THIRTY-FIVE YEARS LATER, some fifty of us, with spouses and children, returned to Oswego to dedicate a monument at the camp.

"Everything I have today I owe to this place." Irene Danon, the vivacious Ljiljana, who had flown in from Los Angeles, flung her arms out. "I love it. It's my America."

The reunion had been set up by the Syracuse Council of Pioneer Women, an organization of American volunteers who help provide education and social services in Israel.* The most famous of the Pioneer Women was Golda Meir, Prime Minister of Israel.

"Geri!" Edith Semjen Starkman shouted to a woman walking toward her. Geraldine Desens Rossiter, the Oswego waitress who had disguised herself as a refugee the first day, wrapped her arms around Edith in a bear hug.

"See, Murray?" Edith Bronner Klein showed an empty site to her husband, then co-owner of Zabar's, one of New York's most famous gourmet shops. "This is where the street of the barracks was, and about here, this was where our barracks was."

Ralph Faust, white-haired but ramrod-straight, was pummeled and hugged by former students who had never forgotten what they owed him and the high school. Oswego schoolteachers, Boy

---

* The Pioneer Women organization has changed its name to Na'amat, but since it was known as Pioneer Women during the events described here, I have continued to use its former name in this chapter.

251

Scout leaders, and old girlfriends searched for the refugees whose pictures they had kept all these years.

It was late October. The color of the trees was muted, the day flooded with sunshine.

Fred Baum and his wife, Jenny, joined my late husband and me as we strolled across the parade ground, greeted townspeople from Oswego and Syracuse, and discovered we were heading, as always, toward the blue-green endless waters of Lake Ontario.

"Doesn't the camp seem smaller to you?" Fred asked.

"Don't all things from the past seem smaller?" I answered his question with another question.

But the camp *was* smaller.

The white wooden barracks had all been torn down. Only a few of the handsome red-brick Georgian buildings with white colonnades still stood: the guardhouse with the jail that had been my office, the post theater, a few warehouses, and the recreation hall where Mirković and Manya and Presser and scores of others had entertained us. Part of the chain-link fence that had meant prison to some and security to others still stood.

After the last of the refugees left in buses on February 6, 1946, the camp had become a temporary housing project for veterans of the war and their families. Then, in 1951, it was decided that Fort Ontario should be turned into a New York State historical museum and park. Its multilayered history from the French and Indian War to World War II was to come to life again with blown-up photographs, letters, and waxwork models of the soldiers who had been stationed here for nearly two hundred years.

Early in the spring of 1981 the Pioneer Women had learned that the restoration was nearly completed, but thus far no markers had been planned to show that Fort Ontario had been a haven for refugees too.

In Syracuse, speaking at a dinner, I was approached by two leaders of the Pioneer Women, Celia Meren and Belle Shiro. "Would it be appropriate for our organization to erect a marker for the refugees?" they asked.

I reacted instantly. Of course it would be appropriate to link this haven in Oswego with Israel, which had become the haven for over a million refugees. I offered to do everything I could to help.

The idea took fire. Within six months enough money had been raised from the community and the refugees themselves to buy a magnificent granite boulder.

Now, on October 25, 1981, with an autumn wind blowing off the lake, the ceremony began. The townspeople crowded around us as we walked toward the boulder, on a slight promontory overlooking Lake Ontario. The color guard of Jewish War Veterans, men in their sixties and seventies, members of Onondaga County Post 131, marched with the flags of the United States and Israel. Their World War II rifles sparkled in the sunlight.

The wind grew fierce, flapping the flags as we sang "The Star-Spangled Banner." Memories of that first Sunday in the camp when the refugees had listened to the anthem solemnly, unable to grasp its words, flooded over me. Now it was their anthem, and they sang it with passion.

Two rabbis from Syracuse recited the prayer: Thank the Lord for sustaining us to this day.

I stepped forward, raised the white cloth, and read the words chiseled into the stone:

FROM 1944 TO 1946 FORT ONTARIO
SERVED AS A HAVEN FOR
982 SURVIVORS OF THE
EUROPEAN HOLOCAUST

The air was still, filled only with the sound of the waves of Lake Ontario beating against the embankment. The Jewish War Veterans stood at attention. Then they cocked their rifles and fired three volleys into the sky.

The wind fought us. Some ran, some lowered their heads and walked, others drove across the empty grounds toward the ramparts of the old fort. Shivering, we entered one of the renovated buildings, where chairs had been set up. Mine was to be the keynote address; I made it brief. The contagious joy of the refugees, meeting again after thirty-five years, was more eloquent than words. Then, in a Syracuse café, Adam Munz rose to speak on behalf of the group.

Adam used his prerogative as a psychologist to discuss a psychological phenomenon where "reality is unacceptable and fantasy takes the place of reality." He turned to me. "Dear Ruth, you tenaciously insist on the reality that you came to us in the Bay of Naples through very conventional means, when all of us from the shelter know that you came down from the heavens on wings."

Somehow Adam and a score of others had convinced themselves that I had landed on the *Henry Gibbins* in a plane "dressed in white—just like an angel." Laughingly, I tried to tell them that a plane landing on that overcrowded deck would have sunk the ship. It was useless. One of them insisted he watched me in the sky through binoculars.

"The fantasy is more powerful than the reality," Adam insisted. "For us, that is as it shall always be!"

He then described what coming to America had meant for him. "I arrived here some thirty-seven years ago, starved for freedom and human warmth, embittered at the human race for allowing and participating in the carnage that was the Holocaust. But then I left through the gates of the shelter on the way to my round trip across the Rainbow Bridge to Canada. On that cold January morning in 1946, I became convinced that the world was not all bad and the human spirit at times prevails."

Adam's was to have been the last speech. But Alice Pearlman rose with another announcement. "Dr. David Hendell has asked to be allowed to say something."

David made his way around the overcrowded tables to the microphone. "We want to make a presentation to the person who brought us to America and who became part of us." He opened a bag, drew out a large plaque mounted with a scroll in brass, and read:

TO

RUTH GRUBER

HUMANITARIAN

For your friendship, love and dedication
to the refugees from Nazi oppression,
and for your determined support in our efforts
to join the mainstream of American life.

YOU HAVE FOREVER BECOME A PART OF US

THE OSWEGO REFUGEES

1944–1946

Presented October 25, 1981

David kissed me. Unashamed, I wiped my eyes, said a few words of gratitude, and then, still shaken, joined my friends, for we had begun the joyous task of catching up with one another's lives.

The reunion in the camp was the beginning of an unexpected chapter in the Oswego story. Soon after that reunion, I began to criss-cross the country to search for more survivors of the one thousand.

Fred Baum, living in Hillsdale, New Jersey, was a walking direc-tory, as was Zlatko Hirschler in San Francisco. Several, like Steffi Steinberg Winters, rediscovered me through my books and wrote letters reestablishing our friendship. Others, like Liesl Neumann in Kansas City and Fortunée Levitch in San Francisco, came to talks I gave in their cities. One person led to another.

There was joy and delight but no order in the way I found them, nor is there any particular order in the way I have recorded what happened to them after they crossed the Rainbow Bridge and began their new lives in America.

Since, like most immigrants, they often clustered together, I have listed them geographically, beginning in California and moving eastward.

CALIFORNIA

ALEX (ACÁ) MARGULIS became chief of radiology at the University of California. He helped develop the CAT scan and the MRI. "Oswego," Alex told me, "was one of my most wonderful experiences. We young people were happy. It was an island of plenty."

RENÉE REISNER MARGULIS,* Alex's wife, whom he had courted on the *Henry Gibbins,* died in 1979.

ROLF MANFRED, who dropped his last name (KUZNITSKI), studied engineering and is one of the creators of both the Polaris and Minuteman missiles. He travels continuously, searching for nonnuclear alternatives to oil.

PAUL ARNSTEIN became a veterinarian in the U.S. Public Health Service. "I feel," Paul says thoughtfully, "that the *Haven* experience should never be forgotten—one small group of people who were supposed to be exterminated, survived and came to America."

WALTER ARNSTEIN, Paul's brother, is a computer designer.

PAUL BOKROS worked as an electronics engineer in defense and the conquest of space. At General Dynamics he was in charge of the design and development of the computer equipment used in maintaining the F-16 aircraft.

EVA KAUFMAN DYE is a teacher and the daughter of KITTY and BRANKO KAUFMAN,* the camp's official photographer.

HENNY NOTOWICZ HAAS* was an art collector with infectious humor. She was skilled at teaching Braille to the blind.

JOSEPH LEVITCH,* a pharmacist and poet, taught his wife, FORTUNEE,* and their three children in Yugoslavia how to hang themselves if they were caught by the Yugoslav fascists. His younger son, LEON LEVITCH, is a pianist and composer of orchestral and chamber music. EDWARD LEVITCH is an architect and builder. Their sister, MANON LEVITCH RAINBOLT, is a potter and painter.

MANYA BREUER is a consultant to major art galleries. Having survived five concentration camps, Manya often bursts into uncontrollable tears. "But when I sing," she assures me, "I stop crying."

* An asterisk follows the names of those who are deceased.

ERNST BREUER, Manya's ex-husband, is self-employed. Their daughter, DIANE BREUER, was one of the twenty-four babies born in the Oswego camp. Versatile and adventurous, Diane was an airline flight attendant and is now a self-employed businesswoman.

IRENE DANON is a painter, poet, and real estate tycoon. "I arrived here with only the clothes on my back. Now I have three beautiful daughters, my own home, a hot tub, and I drive a Mercedes. Who would have believed it?"

MARGARET COHN FRIEDMANN became an aerospace electronics expert and community activist. Her daughter IRENE FRIEDMANN REINSDORF, born in the camp, is in real estate. Another daughter, ANNA ITALA FRIEDMANN, is a teacher of educational administration in the Los Angeles public schools.

FRED Z. HARRIS and MAY M. HARRIS* (formerly ZLATKO and MILIÇA HIRSCHLER) settled in San Francisco. Fred, the retired owner of an appliance repair shop, has written an autobiography called "The Flight," describing his odyssey fleeing from Yugoslavia to America.

ZDENKA RUCHWARGER LEVY, her eyes filled with the tragedies she has endured, is a nurse and administrator in a physician's office. She is married to DAVID LEVY, a salesman, whom she met on the *Henry Gibbins.*

ERIC LEE is a gastroenterologist, director of medical education in the Kaiser Permanente Medical Group in Bellflower, and an associate clinical professor at UCLA.

BRUNO KAISER, electrical engineer, is the owner of Sentry Technology, makers of burglar and fire alarms.

MARGARET SPITZER FISSE worked as a private nurse for children, then became a teacher in the San Francisco schools.

MIDWEST

GLORIA FREDKOVE's mother, EVA BASS*, changed Gloria's birth name, YOLANDA, to Gloria, to show her patriotic love for America. Gloria works as a legal secretary, and, inheriting her mother's unforgettable voice, sings in a synagogue choir.

EDNA SELAN EPSTEIN is a lawyer and educator in Chicago.

EVA ARNSTEIN BOGAR, the sister of Paul and Walter Arnstein, owns an art gallery in Indianapolis.

EDNA TUSAK LOEHMAN, the daughter of GISELLA TUSAK,* teaches environmental economics at Purdue University, and travels to Israel to develop water-sharing projects between Israelis and Palestinians.

JOSEPH LANGNAS is a physician and teacher of pathology at Botsford Hospital outside Detroit. Joseph, the first boy to be bar mitzvahed at the camp, came with his parents, DORA* and IGNAZ,* and his sister, BETTINA LANGNAS LIS. "Oswego," he says, summing up his eighteen months in the camp, "was one of those experiences by which we measure our lives."

NEVA SVECENSKI GOULD is a physician near Chicago.

RALPH (RAJKO) MARGULIS, Alex's brother, is a gynecologist who built his own hospital in Royal Oak, Michigan. He is married to VESNA CULIĆ, whom he courted on our ship.

WASHINGTON, D.C., and BALTIMORE

TAMAR HENDELL FISHMAN, David Hendell's sister, is an art therapist and lecturer.

ESTHER DANON KAIDANOW worked for the federal government.

SIMON KALDERON, a community leader in Baltimore, is president of the Advanced Packaging Corporation, working with the government and private agencies.

FLORA KALDERON FRIEDMAN, Simon's sister, is a homemaker. Their father, AVRAM,* worked as a foreman at an upholstery company.

RENA ROMANO BLOCK worked as a legal secretary.

SONYA FINCI SETREN worked for Baltimore's Department of Public Safety.

PHILADELPHIA

SYLVAN BONI teaches philosophy of religion at Central High School, the honors school of the city. RAYMOND BONI and CLAUDE BONI, his brothers, are in real estate.

ICEK* and SARAH (HELIA CHAYA) FRAJERMAN,* came with their three children: RACHEL FRAJERMAN GOLDFRAD, SAMUEL FRAJERMAN, and JACOB FRAJERMAN. Their youngest son, HARRY FRAJERMAN, was born in the camp.

NELLY BOKROS THALHEIMER, Paul Bokros's sister, returned to school after her three children were grown, and earned a master's degree in gerontology.

NEW YORK and VICINITY

IVO JOHN LEDERER,* author, teacher, and historian, earned a Ph.D. from Princeton and taught Russian and East European affairs at Yale, Princeton, and Stanford. In his last years, he turned from academia to business. "Only a foreign-born," he told me, "can truly understand the nature of the trunk of the tree on which he's grafted. Only a foreign-born can truly appreciate what America is."

ADAM MUNZ* was associate professor of medical psychology at Columbia University and director of psychological services at St. Luke's Hospital in New York. He was an inspiration and mentor to young interns studying to become clinical psychologists. His mother, FRADL MUNZ,* with my mother, escorted the camp's first bride, Manya Breuer, to the chupah on her wedding day.

IRVING SCHILD was chairman of the photography department at New York's Fashion Institute of Technology. A few years ago, at his son Ari's *brith milah* (circumcision), sitting on a gold-painted throne like a white-robed king, Irving put his hand on my head and blessed me. "If not for you, I wouldn't be here and Ari wouldn't be here. At sixty-two, I'm ready to retire and I've just become a father."

FLORENCE SCHILD MILLER, Irving's sister, taught French at the Hebrew Institute on Long Island.

DAVID HENDELL became a dentist and teacher at Columbia University.

ELFIE STRAUBER HENDELL, David's ex-wife, is a social worker and mother.

JETTA HENDEL, David's cousin, became the United Nations representative of the nongovernmental Pan Pacific and Southeast Asia Women's Association.

GISELLE HENDEL SEBESTYEN, Jetta's sister, teaches cultural anthropology at the State University of New York at New Paltz.

LIESL BADER FRIEDMANN became an occupational therapist, working with Dr. Howard Rusk at the Institute of Rehabilitation Medicine.

STEFFI STEINBERG WINTERS—highly organized, multilingual, and thorough—found work in a New York office. For years, she sent warm, newsy, handwritten notes to Ralph Faust, the much-loved principal of Oswego High School.

DORIS BLUMENKRANZ SCHECHTER is a cookbook author and owner of My Most Favorite Dessert Company, a kosher restaurant and café in New York's theater district. She has made her life, like her restaurant and her home, a work of art.

BERTA BADRIAN,* Doris's mother, elegant and beautiful, worked into her eighties selling dresses. RUTH HOFFMAN, Doris's sister, sells designer shoes at Saks Fifth Avenue.

WALTER GREENBERG, who was president of the Boy Scout troop in the camp, is an educator and documentary filmmaker. Walter lectures on the art created by the children who died in Teresin (Theresienstadt).

MAURICE KAMHI is not only a multitalented actor, writer, and director, but is also a passionate fencer.

LEO MIRKOVIĆ,* the operatic star of every performance in the camp, became the cantor at the Brotherhood Synagogue in New York's Gramercy Park.

EDITH SEMJEN STARKMAN,* the "Blond Bombshell" and the "hairdresser with golden hands," owned and operated a hairdressing salon in Manhattan for twenty-eight years. "When I closed my beauty parlor," she told me, "I donated all my equipment and supplies to the prisoners on Rikers Island. I wanted to give them a vocation in gratitude for what America and Oswego gave me."

FRED FLATAU is a physician and medical activist.

LIANA KRAMER BROWN is a schoolteacher.

EDITH BRONNER KLEIN is a homemaker and the wife of Murray Klein, formerly president of Zabar's, the gourmet emporium on New York's Upper West Side.

LIVIA FINGER owns a fine lingerie shop on the Upper East Side.

RAYMOND B. HARDING (formerly BRANKO HOCHWALD), is president of the New York State Liberal Party.

JOHN HUNTER (formerly IVO HIRSCHLER) is the founder of Delta Resources, a computer firm.

GEZA BLEIER, a salesman, whose wife, KAROLINE,* died on the banks of the Barge Canal, raised his two sons to become educators: RONALD became a high school teacher and GEORGE a guidance counselor.

RENÉE CONFORTE MCKEE is the owner with her husband, David, of the McKee Art Gallery.

DORRIT REISNER OSTBERG, sister of Alex Margulis's late wife, is a high school math teacher.

ANNY PICK* was the ebullient star of many of the musical-comedy skits in the camp. Her son, PETER, works in art history in San Francisco, and her daughter GERALDINE CASSENS, born in the camp, is an assistant professor of psychology at Harvard Medical School.

MIRIAM SOMMERBURG* was a sculptress and winner of twenty-one awards. Several of her wooden sculptures are in the permanent collection of the Metropolitan Museum of Art. Four of her children attended Oswego's schools: DMITRI, a carpenter; SONIA RABIN, formerly an art director in a publishing house; PETER, an architecural engineer in Atlanta; and GIOCONDA, a systems analyst.

RHODE ISLAND

TINA KOERNER CHERNICK, after recovering from the loss of two sons to muscular dystrophy, devoted herself to helping find a cure for the disease. She is now vice president of the Rhode Island chapter of the Muscular Dystrophy Association.

CANADA

HARRY MAURER—"International Harry"—who was born in a jeep, worked for several years for NASA and the Air Force in California. He now works in Ontario, Canada, as an electronic data processing manager.

PARIS

ANDRÉ WAKSMAN, whose mother wanted a little girl, is a documentarian and film producer. "Going back for the first time to the reunion in 1999," he wrote me, "was concrete evidence that that war which flowed in my veins from birth had ended for me on a grassy hill overlooking a Great Lake."

Because I had been so much a part of these lives, it was hard for me to form a single view of the total experience.

How to stack up the frustration and anger of some of the old, obsessed by the fence, against the exciting vistas opened by the Oswego schools to the young?

How to weigh the bitterness at the insensitivity of so much of official Washington against the gratitude for the noble and determined caring of people like Harold Ickes and Eleanor Roosevelt?

How to forgive FDR, my idol, for proving to be "a politician first and then a humanitarian"? And how to understand his need to tread carefully, even though this meant anguish and uncertainty, for so long, for so many?

After the search and the rediscovery of the Oswego refugees, however, I felt I had attained that final overview. The people themselves helped me attain it. I was stunned and delighted by the record of their lives.

They had helped give back to America the kind of human values that made it great. Whether it was genes, heritage, an inborn passion for learning, or their strength as survivors, they absorbed with relish and enthusiasm what America offered and, in turn, made their own unique contributions.

How grateful my country can be for having given them haven.

TWENTY-SEVEN

At the June 1999 Safe Haven reunion in Oswego, several people said, "We know now what happened to many of us former refugees, but we don't know what happened to *you* after the camp closed in February 1946." So at eighty-eight, when I looked back at the *Haven* experience, as well as at more than a half century of journalism, I realized that my involvement with the Oswego refugees was the defining moment of my life.

It had made me aware that as a journalist, I would always be both witness and participant. I learned that I must live a story to write about it.

I began to live the Oswego story the moment I climbed aboard the Army Transport Ship *Henry Gibbins* and met the survivors, many still wearing their striped concentration-camp pajamas with newspapers wrapped around their bare feet.

We became a family and have remained one to this day. It delights me to think that from these people I have probably inherited more than five thousand grandchildren and great-grandchildren. How many more we could have saved will always haunt me.

Because of them, and those we lost, I vowed I would fight with every cell of my body to help rescue Jews in danger.

My weapon was words. I had learned to love words in the first grade, listening to a beautiful African-American teacher read poetry. She was the only teacher I had in elementary school who was not Irish or Jewish. Her soft voice reading poetry was like music. I was mesmerized. I knew I was going to be a writer.

As I grew older, I came to learn that words can build and words can destroy. Words—written, spoken, waking me in full sentences from my sleep—were the fuel that drove me.

At war's end, when the State, Justice, and Treasury departments announced they were sending the Oswego refugees back to Europe, I knew there would be a battle. How lucky that the old curmudgeon Harold L. Ickes, secretary of the interior, taught me how to fight the bureaucrats with indignant letters and angry speeches. We pressured editors and columnists, hoping to create a climate of public opinion that would influence President Truman to grant them asylum. It worked.

In 1946, I was asked by the *New York Post* to fly to Europe to cover the plight of an even more desperate group of refugees, the last survivors of the Holocaust.

For four hectic months, I traveled with the Anglo-American Committee of Inquiry on Palestine through Germany, Austria, Palestine, and the Arab world. Even the most hardened judges and lawyers on the committee were shocked to see emaciated survivors still living in former death camps, sleeping on the wooden shelves on which millions had died during the war. Only now the people had a new name in the lexicon of homelessness: displaced persons, DPs.

My body trembled as I listened to their stories. Few people knew about the DPs. It was as if a dark curtain had fallen on them. I wanted to shake the world by the lapels and shout, *You're learning more and more about the Holocaust, but do you know what's happening to the survivors? Take action! Get the DPs out of these godforsaken camps!*

With my portable typewriter and two cameras, I used everything I had learned to try and lift the curtain. I interviewed dozens of survivors and often had to stop writing because tears were blurring the words. Some told me they had gone home and when they knocked on their doors, neighbors greeted them with shotguns. "Are you still alive? Why didn't they turn you into soap?" In Kielce,

Poland, forty-one Jews were murdered when they tried returning to their houses.

Where could they go? No one wanted them—except the Jews of Palestine, who had their arms open for every survivor. But Britain controlled Palestine, and Britain had slammed the doors shut.

Palestine in 1946 was not yet important enough for hundreds of reporters to descend on her. It was easy then to make friends among the people and their leaders, especially Dr. Chaim Weizmann, who in two years would become Israel's first president; David Ben-Gurion, the tough labor and political leader who would shape the country as its first prime minster and commander-in-chief; Moshe Sharett, its first foreign minister, who spoke six or seven languages fluently; and Golda Meir, the American who would become Israel's minister of labor and then prime minister.

Sitting for hours in their homes as they told me of their vision of a Jewish homeland strengthened my own commitment. Later, back in my apartment in Brooklyn, mulling over what I had lived through, I began to discover myself. I did not know what depths of pain and outrage I could experience. Shocked by the indifference around me, I found solace in beginning to write a novel. It was set in Bergen-Belsen, one of the DP camps I had visited in 1946.

I was halfway into the novel when my previous newspaper, the *New York Herald Tribune,* asked me to cover UNSCOP, the United Nations Special Committee on Palestine. It was 1947.

I was torn. Should I continue the novel or travel with UNSCOP? This was the nineteenth committee dealing with the problems of Palestine—but the first one without any Englishmen on it. That could make a difference.

Still undecided, I asked the German-Jewish novelist Lion Feuchtwanger what he thought. (I was interviewing him about his rescue from Gurs, the dreaded concentration camp in southern France, the camp from which Manya Hartmayer Breuer, one of our Oswego refugees, had escaped.)

"Drop the novel," Feuchtwanger said. "You can always go back to writing it. But to travel with this U.N. committee—the most important committee yet—and do something to help the people in those terrible camps is the chance of a lifetime." He was right. In Germany I began to live the very story of my novel.

I found the DPs in the DP camps had changed in this one year. They were no longer victims. Now they were defying the British Empire, defying the world.

They were on the move. With the Haganah, the Jewish Army of Resistance, they were gathering up orphans, climbing snow-covered mountains, trekking across Europe, packing tens of thousands of DPs on a secret fleet comprised of dilapidated fishing boats, obsolete navy vessels, even Teddy Roosevelt's yacht *Mayflower,* determined to break through the British blockade into Palestine.

The most famous of this motley fleet was the *Exodus 1947.* In its former life, named *President Warfield* for the uncle of Bessie Wallis Warfield, the Duchess of Windsor, it was an elegant little steamer sailing between Baltimore and Norfolk. Built to hold 400, it now had 4,500 survivors, squeezed into every available space.

I left UNSCOP to cover its fateful voyage. I stood on the deck in Haifa, Palestine, on July 18, 1947, and watched the battered ship limp into harbor. Rammed by five British destroyers, she looked like a matchbox splintered by a nutcracker. British sailors and marines pulled reluctant people off the *Exodus,* many with their heads bandaged from the fighting. Three had been killed and 120 wounded in the terrifying battle. British marines armed with Sten guns, tear gas, and truncheons had killed the second mate, Bill Bernstein of San Francisco, the most popular member of the crew, and two sixteen-year-old orphans.

On the dock, British soldiers hurried the weary refugees onto three so-called hospital ships (really prison ships) and told me they were sending the Jews of the *Exodus* to the British internment camps on Cyprus, so I flew ahead to wait for them.

Cyprus was a hellhole of desert sand and wind, of drafty tents, and Quonset huts, blistering in the summer sun and freezing in the winter rain. There was no water. No lights. No privacy. You had to smell Cyprus to believe it.

But the DPs never arrived; Britain had decided that Cyprus was too good for them. After several days the prison ships turned up in Port-de-Bouc in southern France. I flew there, still the only journalist covering their story of courage and defiance. "We will not get off!" they shouted to me. "We will come down only in Palestine!"

For eighteen days of insufferable heat, they floated in French waters. Then the British announced they were sending the 4,500 Holocaust survivors to Germany—the deathland. Shocked and outraged, dozens of reporters descended on Port-de-Bouc. Unbelievably, the British selected me to represent the entire U.S. press corps.

As I climbed aboard the prison ship *Runnymede Park,* some of the refugees raised a flag. They had painted the Nazi swastika on the Union Jack to show their contempt. My photo of the flag became *Life*'s Picture of the Week, in the September 8, 1947, issue. It was to become the most famous photo I have ever shot.

I went below to the prison pen. It was a scene out of Dante's inferno. People were half naked, sitting or sleeping on the metal floor. It was their living room, dining room, bedroom. Some held up babies for me to take pictures. I shot blindly—blind because the only light came through prison bars; blinded by their agony. The *New York* and *Paris Herald Tribune* syndicated my stories and photos and sent them around the world.

The British took the *Exodus* Jews to prison camps in occupied Germany, but the refugees escaped and nearly every one of them was in the Holy Land by May 15, 1948, when Israel was born. The novel I had put aside became the true story of these 4,500 Holocaust survivors and the suffering they endured. The book I wrote, then called *Destination Palestine,* was reissued in 1999 as *Exodus 1947: The Ship That Launched a Nation.*

In the summer of 1948, Helen (Mrs. Ogden) Reid, the publisher of the *Herald Tribune,* announced to her staff that she was sending me to cover Israel's War of Independence. One of her top aides protested. "How can you send her?" he demanded. "What kind of military experience does she have? What does she know about covering a war?"

"I'm sending her," Helen Reid answered.

"Before you go," she told me, "I want you to address the annual convention of the Women's Clubs of America, meeting right now at the Waldorf-Astoria. They represent political clubs, university clubs, garden clubs, the whole range of women's activities. Tell them about the DP camps in Germany. Tell them about the British prison camp on Cyprus. They don't know any of this."

On the dais, I saw cold faces, icy stares. The chairwoman introducing me was impatient. I suspected she was annoyed that Helen Reid, the powerful publisher of the country's leading Republican newspaper, had prevailed on her to shuffle her program and include me at the last moment.

I plunged into a description of the DP camps in Germany. I tried to make them see the tents and Quonset huts on Cyprus and the defiant refugees, daring the world to give them justice. The words I wanted didn't come. I saw people shift restlessly on their chairs. Some looked at their watches. I cut my lecture short. A few people applauded. I was a total failure. I felt a clawed hand around my throat. My faith in myself was shaken. Could I really touch readers who might be as impatient or indifferent as those club-women? I would have to learn how to reach an audience that had no interest in me or the subject that was consuming me.

Slowly I regained confidence as I began covering Israel's War of Independence. Traveling in a jeep with a unit of the Israeli army, I heard the commanding officer call out directions. "We are about to enter an Arab village. We will not touch a single mosque."

I cabled the story to the *Herald Tribune,* describing how I had watched the soldiers capture the village without touching the mosque, and a few days later the foreign editor, Joe Barnes, sent me a message. "Your story changed the vote at the United Nations. They were going to censure Israel. But when the Israeli delegate stood up and read your article, the debate ended."

I continued covering the battles with the army, filing stories not only of victories but also of defeats. Israeli forces failed to capture the notorious Latrun prison, but they captured Nazareth without firing a single bullet.

One day, still early in the war, the *Tribune* cabled me: GET AN INTERVIEW WITH DAVID BEN-GURION. I called his aide, Nehemia, whom he loved as if he were his own son. "Nehemia," I said, "can you set up a meeting, today if possible, with BG?" It was the name we all used, as if Ben-Gurion were a big tycoon, though he was only a few inches over five feet. Of all the political leaders I have known, he was the most prophetic. The friendship that had begun in 1946 stood me in good stead. Nehemia called back. "Come now."

Ben-Gurion was in his office in Tel Aviv. It was twilight and the sun was setting on his crown of then-dark hair, laced with white. He motioned for me to sit down facing him across his desk.

"BG," I began, "my paper wants an interview."

His voice was high and strident. "You—you ought to know better. You know I haven't given interviews to anyone. Not *The New York Times*, not *The Washington Post*, not even the Israeli papers."

"I know that. But I'm not going to ask you a single thing about the war. I'm not going to ask you a thing about politics. I just want you to shut your eyes and dream. I want you to tell me what Israel will look like when the blood has stopped flowing and the Jews have come home."

He shut his eyes, and for a moment I could forget that the Arab armies were a few miles away and that the shelling hadn't stopped. He spoke slowly, as if he were envisioning a new landscape.

"There will be no more desert," he said. "There will be no more sand. There will be trees on every hill. The sky will be full of planes. The sea will be full of ships. There will be small towns and villages, not big cities like you have in America. We're a little country. There will be white cottages and lots of children—children are our future."

I jotted his words in my notebook without looking down, using the fingers of my left hand to guide my pen across the page. I am recording his vision, I thought, the way a scribe might have written sitting at the feet of Isaiah.

His eyes were still closed. There was a long silence. I finally broke it. "What will be the philosophy of life of this cottage civilization?"

A smile, unusual for him in these tense days, flickered across his lips. He opened his eyes. "It takes too many words in English." His strident voice was softer. "In Hebrew it takes only three: *Veahavta reekh'a kamoh'a*. They mean: Love thy fellow human being as thyself."

I was to remember that prophecy when the deluge began in the spring of 1949. The doors of Israel had been flung wide open as soon as the five invading Arab armies were defeated. The Law of Return granted every Jew, anywhere in the world, the right to enter the brave new nation.

At the airport, on the docks, I watched them come, great rivers of Jews flowing into the sea which was Israel. They came, young and old, sick and well, blind and sighted, in a migration such as the world had never seen. I helped them down the gangways. Some of the older women kissed me. I hugged the children, not knowing who needed the hugs more. I filed stories filled with joy.

But soon the joy turned to bile. With little time to build housing, Israel was putting them into camps. Tent cities. The largest and by far the worst was outside of Haifa. It was the rainy season. "Look at us," the refugees told me, pulling up their trousers and long skirts. I looked unbelievingly. They were in mud up to their knees. I went to see Ben-Gurion.

"BG." I tried to control my anger and disappointment. "I've just come from visiting your camps. We had a camp in America, in a place called Oswego, New York. For a year and a half, we gave people food and shelter and schools and warm housing." I knew I was talking too fast, but he listened. "We gave them everything a rich country could give. But BG, a camp is a camp is a camp, and those inside deteriorate. Life in a camp can drive some to madness, even suicide. You . . ." I paused and spoke carefully. "You of all nations— you cannot afford to keep people in camps."

"Write me a report," Ben-Gurion said.

I spent the night at my typewriter, describing what I had learned in Oswego and what I had seen in Israel. "If you keep people in a camp," I wrote, "you diminish them. You rip away the fabric of their lives. I learned this the hard way in Oswego. . . . Do you know"—I ended the report—"I checked and found that not a single member of your cabinet has been in one of these camps?"

I took the report to him early in the morning and sat silently in front of his desk, watching him read it, remembering his prophecy: "Love thy fellow human being as thyself."

He stood up; his face was grim, his lips tight. He walked around his desk and shook my hand, "You are a *berrieh*." He used the Yiddish word. "It means you give somebody a job and they do it." He called Nehemia. "I want this report translated right now and sent to every cabinet member with an order that they visit the camps immediately."

"BG," I said, "I'm going to cable the story of the camps to my paper."

He nodded. "Good."

A few months later, I flew back to New York and began a hectic lecture tour that wound up at the annual United Jewish Appeal convention in Atlantic City. Moshe Sharett, the foreign minister, and I were the keynote speakers. Sitting next to me on the dais, Sharett whispered, "Because of you, I had to visit those miserable camps."

"Did you make changes?" I whispered back.

"What do you think? Of course. We're building new development towns all across the country."

At home, my mother was agitating as usual. "When are you going to stop running? Isn't it time you got married and settled down?"

"I will, Mom. I just haven't met the right man."

I met Philip Michaels, an eligible bachelor, in Puerto Rico as 1949 was ending. Many people claim they introduced me to him. Actually, Governor Luis Muñoz Marín was the matchmaker. Muñoz had invited us both to his inauguration as the first elected governor of Puerto Rico in 450 years, and at a picnic on the white sands of Luquillo Beach, he took Phil's hand and mine and drew us together. "You two New Yorkers should know each other."

Philip was vice president of a chain of furniture stores. Trained as a lawyer, he lived his life as a social activist. He turned part of the store he managed in the south Bronx into a neighborhood settlement house. He corralled school principals, priests, ministers, rabbis, police, and a score of others to work together to fight drugs and crime and get dropouts back into school. Each year before Christmas, he brought thousands of schoolchildren into the store's auditorium to watch puppet shows, thrilled to hear children who had never seen a play scream with delight. He was a member of the Youth Board, mediated fights between Puerto Ricans and African-Americans, and ran Saturday-night dances to keep teenagers off streets wrenched by gang violence. Leaders of the Democratic Party urged him to run for the Senate. He refused. He felt he could serve better where he was.

We were married in January 1951. I was thirty-nine and Phil was forty-eight. Both of us were eager for children. Nearly a year later, I announced to our families at dinner in our apartment, "I'm pregnant."

My brother, Harry, a physician, was worried about my age. "The chances of your having a Down's syndrome child are about one in a thousand." I knew most doctors believed this. "I think you should consider having an abortion," Harry said tentatively.

I refused, and gave birth to Celia, an ordinary Jewish genius.

Another year later, I told the family, "Everybody has two eyes, two ears, two legs, two hands. I'm going to have two children."

This time Harry was adamant. "At forty-three, your chances of Down's syndrome are worse than ever. You really must have an abortion." Instead, I gave birth to David, another ordinary Jewish genius.

Celia, mother of two, is an award-winning videotape editor,

whose work includes documentaries and news specials. I began to appreciate my mother's nights spent worrying about me when CBS sent Celia to Lebanon, where she was its only editor during some of the bloodiest battles in the terrible civil war there. One day when the telephone lines weren't broken by gunfire, she phoned me from Beirut and heard the tremor in my voice. I wasn't sleeping well. She tried to reassure me. "I'm safe, Mom. Really, I'm safe. But why are you worried? You were in World War Two when you brought the refugees to Oswego. You covered the wars in Israel. Why should you worry about me?" How do you tell your daughter that being a mother is different from being a foreign correspondent?

During the Gulf War, CBS assigned Celia to London, where she met Stephen Evans, a gifted artist and editor working for the British Broadcasting Company. In 1990, they were married in a torrential downpour in the Secret Garden of Central Park. Now they live near me on the Upper West Side of Manhattan with their two school-age children. I am their prime babysitter. They have only to call. I may have theater tickets, but my answer is always the same: "I'll come right over."

David made his career in preventative medicine and public health. While preparing for his Ph.D. in epidemiology at Columbia University, he worked full-time at the Montefiore Medical Center in the Bronx doing research in occupational health, studying the effects of asbestos, mercury, and other chemicals on human beings. In 1979, he began teaching at the Albert Einstein Medical School and, at twenty-nine, was given an award by the American Public Health Association as the outstanding young health professional in the country. I stood up in the convention with some thousand APHA members, all of us cheering and applauding. Early in the HIV/AIDS epidemic, he developed the mathematical model now widely used to estimate the number of children who have lost their mothers because of AIDS.

David moved on, becoming a full professor at the City University of New York Medical School. In 1990, he married Gail Dratch, a political whiz devoted to helping senior citizens lead a better life.

They also have two young children. In 1998, President Clinton nominated David to the position of Assistant Secretary for Environment, Safety and Health in the Department of Energy. The Senate approved his nomination unanimously.

Phil would have been as proud of our two children as I am, but it was not to be. He had just returned to his first love, law, and was beginning to build a practice when, unable to lick his two-pack-a-day cigarette addiction, his health deteriorated. He developed scleroderma, a disease I had never heard of. It is a hardening of the arteries under the skin. I researched the disease at the main branch of the New York Public Library and learned that, though it has been known since the 1700s, no cure has yet been found.

"Be prepared," Harry warned me. "You must put everything in order. Soon the disease will affect his extremities. His hands and feet will turn purplish black in cold weather. He can survive that, but as soon as it reaches his internal organs, he'll go."

I listened but, foolishly, Phil and I lived in denial. I might have helped him face his mortality, while he might have helped me prepare for life without him. Instead, we would talk blithely of some of Phil's law cases and make plans for our next summer vacation.

We had always shared expenses, but when Phil began his new career, I worked harder than ever, writing articles and books and lecturing. One day, Jerry Spiegel, a dynamic tie manufacturer, telephoned. "We need your help. There's a Polish Catholic man here from my town in Poland, Stanislav. He's a real hero. He hid thirty-two Jews in his cellar two blocks from the Gestapo and kept them alive for nearly two years. Senator Robert Kennedy was so happy to hear that a Polish Catholic had done this, he helped us get a visa for him. His name is Staszek Jackowsky." Jerry pronounced it for me: "Sta-shek Yats-koff-sky."

"How can I help?" I asked.

"Staszek has a wife and three sons. Teenagers. They're in Warsaw and he wants them here, but nobody will help us. You know Washington. Maybe you can help."

Jerry brought Staszek to my apartment. I listened in awe as this man, a skilled carriage maker, small, agile, fair-skinned, with thick dark-blond hair and a dimpled smile, described in Polish, with Jerry translating, how he had built three bunkers in his cellar. He equipped them with bunks and mattresses from his carriage shop, electricity that he tapped, free, from the city's wires, ten small electric stoves, indoor plumbing, and a radio on which they listened each night to speeches by Churchill, Roosevelt, and Stalin. Bartering with leather from his shop and some gold coins, he bought food for the people whose lives he was saving at risk to his own. He amassed a small arsenal of guns and ammunition in case the Gestapo discovered them. His stepmother and two sisters did not even know they were walking over the heads of Jewish men, women, and three little children.

"Tell her about 'bloody Sunday,'" Jerry said.

Staszek talked. The sun set outside my windows, the room grew dark, but I could not move as Staszek described a Sunday massacre on the Jewish holiday of Hoshanah Rabbah, the seventh day of Sukkot, the harvest festival. According to tradition, it is the day when the blessings for the coming year are decreed in heaven (another example of how the Nazis made a point of choosing Jewish holidays for many of their worst *Aktionen*).

"SS Hauptsturmführer Hans Krüger, the head of the Gestapo in Stanislav," Staszek related, "together with hundreds of police and militia, rounded up more than twelve thousand people and marched them through the city to the Jewish cemetery. They forced the people to undress and hand over their belongings to Krüger and his officers. Krüger and his men were sitting at a table in the graveyard eating sandwiches and getting drunk on cognac."

I shut my eyes. I was no longer in a darkened living room; I was in a graveyard in Stanislav, Poland.

Staszek went on. "The people had to dig big graves. 'Shoot!' Krüger kept yelling at his killers. They shoveled all the dead bodies into the graves. Krüger went away for a while, and the shooting went on. Then, about six o'clock at night, he came back, riding a white horse. He shouted, 'Quiet! I have just received a cable. Der Führer has saved your lives. Everyone, together, Heil Hitler! Now run home, all of you who are still alive.'

"The next day, Krüger sent his uniform and boots, all covered with blood, to the Judenrat, the Jewish community council, with orders to clean them and pay for the twelve thousand bullets he had used up."

I realized I was listening to the death of a city. Stanislav, in eastern Poland, was the second largest city in Galicia, a city of 100,000 people, half of them Jews. When the Russians liberated Stanislav in July 1944, sixty-two Jews came out of hiding. Thirty-two of them had been saved by Staszek.

I turned on the light in my living room. I shook Staszek's hand. "I will help in any way I can." A wave of happiness washed over me. "This is, in a way," I told Jerry and Staszek, "an Anne Frank story with a happy ending."

We were able to get visitor's visas for Staszek's wife, Jasia, whom he had married after the war, and their three teenage sons. The grateful survivors set them up in an apartment in the Bronx and gave them $500 a month to live on until Staszek could become self-supporting. But the visas expired, and they were all in danger of being sent back to Poland. I went to Washington and called on Senator Kennedy. His legislative aide told me, "Sorry, the senator has done all he can." I called on Senator Jacob Javits. His legislative aide said, "If Robert Kennedy can't help, neither can we."

On a Saturday morning, I took Staszek to meet Congressman James H. Scheuer of New York in his office in the city. On Monday, Scheuer introduced a private bill to permit Staszek and his family to remain in the United States. As soon as the bill passed, they were granted citizenship.

In October 1966, Krüger and seventeen of his officers were put on trial in Münster in the North Rhineland. They were charged with the murder not only of the 50,000 Jews of Stanislav but with the death of 30,000 more from neighboring villages and shtetls. Two of Staszek's survivors, Max Feuer, a white-haired baker in the

Bronx, and Jack Horn, a taxicab owner in Queens, were called to testify in the war crimes trial. "You must come with us," Max Feuer pleaded. "We need your help."

I did not look forward to leaving Phil, weakened by his illness, or Celia and David, but Phil insisted. "You must go. Help them tell their story. I'll take care of the children."

Once again, as in Oswego, I was witness and participant. Each day, covering the war crimes trial in Münster for the *Saturday Review,* I sat with Max Feuer and Jack Horn, working on strategy as we watched Hans Krüger. He was six feet two, heavyset, with brown sunglasses and graying hair, still acting like the dictator of the city he had destroyed. He kept jumping up from his chair and shouting at the witnesses as if they, not he, were on trial.

"We can't stop him from saying what he wants," the prosecuting attorney told me.

Three judges and seven jurors sat together. The presiding judge asked the questions and directed the trial. Then the state prosecutor and the defense counsel cross-examined the witnesses and the defendants. At the end, the jury would determine the verdict and the judges hand down the sentence. I looked at the jury. Who were they? How could we know if they were former Nazis or present Nazis? A lawyer told me, "Since the amnesty, nobody knows. Any Nazi can serve on a jury."

Max Feuer, who had led many of the people to safety in Staszek's cellar, testified. "We called the cemetery *der heilige Ort,* the holy place," he told the court. The presiding judge asked him, "Did you see the graves in the cemetery on bloody Sunday?" Max explained to the court that he was standing at the rear of the cemetery, and because he was blue-eyed and wore the red pants of Ukrainian mountaineers, a white Ukrainian blouse, and a big cross, he passed as a Christian. "That's why they didn't shoot me. I was a goy."

I found it hard to believe that I was actually in the same room with these murderers: not the Hitlers and Himmlers who gave the orders, but the Krügers who gave their own orders and executed them themselves.

Jack Horn began his testimony, describing how Krüger had shot a pregnant woman from his balcony. Krüger was asked by the president of the court if he wanted to say anything. He didn't deny shooting the woman. He denied there was a balcony.

I left Münster, where Krüger's trial dragged on, to attend the trial of the Mauer brothers in Vienna. They were former SS officers who had served with Krüger and been awarded Austrian citizenship after the war. They were being retried for killing the Jews of Stanislav, after having been found innocent a few months earlier in Salzburg. In November 1966, the new jury in Vienna reversed the trend in Austria of acquitting most war criminals—including Franz Novak, Eichmann's chief deputy. They found the Mauer brothers guilty and sentenced them to eight and twelve years' imprisonment.

Back in Münster, Krüger's trial continued for two more years. In 1968 he was found guilty and sentenced to life in prison. He was released in 1986, but he had little time to savor his return to freedom. He died in 1988.

Meanwhile, little by little, Staszek Jackowski's story of heroism was being revealed to the public. A few years later, a group of us took him and Jasia to Israel, where he was honored at Yad Vashem along with other righteous gentiles who had risked their lives to save Jews.

In 1967, as the Six-Day War was ending, the Ford Foundation gave me a fellowship to research and report on how Israel was absorbing its hundreds of thousands of new immigrants and what could be learned from their experience. I took the whole family to Israel for the summer. We celebrated David's bar mitzvah in Jerusalem, where his portion of the Torah was *Comfort ye, comfort ye, my people* from Isaiah. It had also been Phil's portion at his bar mitzvah. Phil kept himself alive for David's rite of passage. He died six months later, in February 1968.

I became a single mother, raising two teenagers. I had a new title: WIDOW. There would be days when I thought I would never smile again. And I was sure I would never remarry. As our sole breadwinner, I supported us with articles, books, and speeches. Writing and lecturing became two sides of the same coin. The more I lectured, the clearer and more simply I wrote. The more I wrote—and I loved writing—the stronger the speeches became. I tried to do both with passion and truth.

In 1974, Peggy Brooks, a senior editor at Putnam, asked me to coauthor a book with Marjorie Margolies. Marjorie was a television reporter who had adopted a child from Korea and another from Vietnam. Young and determined, she had broken the rule barring single parents from adopting children. Later, married to Ed Mezvinsky, a former congressman from Iowa, she overcame another barrier. In 1992, she was elected as Democratic representative to Congress from Montgomery County, a longtime Republican stronghold in eastern Pennsylvania.

"I admire Marjorie for adopting those children," I told Peggy, "but I would never dream of writing about orphans unless I gave them back their history. To write this book, I would have to go to Korea and Vietnam and find the families of those two little girls, so that when they're eighteen or so they won't wind up on some psychiatrist's couch crying, 'Who am I? What kind of family did I come from?' "

Peggy nodded silently. I went on.

"Oswego taught me about orphans. The children who came with parents were happy, carefree. Some later told me this was the happiest time of their lives. But the orphans were sad, depressed, often bursting uncontrollably into tears. For them, Oswego was a lonely waiting room. Each day, even at school, they hungered for news. Where were their parents? Had they been shot or hanged or gassed? Their nights were interminable. Only after the war, when they learned their parents had been murdered, could they begin to mourn and heal."

"Did any of the children find their parents?" Peggy asked.

"The six Weinstein orphans. They raced around the camp, laughing, weeping, ecstatic, when we discovered their mother was alive in Switzerland. They got back not only their history but their childhood."

"It never occurred to me that orphans should be given back their history," Peggy observed. "Of course you should go to Vietnam and Korea. We'll help you any way we can."

Celia went with me, and together we found the relatives of the two children Marjorie had adopted: Holly's mother in Saigon and Lee Heh's two brothers in an orphanage near Seoul. We then brought ten already adopted orphans from Korea to America. On the plane, Celia, who was not yet twenty-one and had no experience with children, became their surrogate mother, diapering the babies, wiping their tears, playing with the toddlers, and feeding them from tin packages the airline marked (heartlessly, I thought), ORPHAN FOOD.

Stopping in airports in San Francisco, Chicago, and New York, we delivered the children to the families who had gone through the long and convoluted legal process of adopting them. I had fallen in love with a four-year-old who filled his little belly with his dinner and mine and then stood up for two hours on his seat, talking and waving his hand at Zero Mostel riding a horse in a movie. At O'Hare Airport in Chicago, I turned my four-year-old over to a farming family who looked as if they would give him a good life.

My little friend, and the other orphans whom we helped rescue from the hopeless future that many orphans face in Korea, restored my life juices. That same year I married an old friend, Henry Rosner, the Deputy Commissioner of Human Resources for New York City. Like Phil, Henry was both a lawyer and a born social activist. He spent his days and often his nights trying to feed the poor, put clothing on their backs, and provide them with decent housing. He made certain that no New Yorker in medical need was turned away from a public hospital. He liked to jest that marrying me took him from a caseload of one million to a caseload of one.

Love in one's mature sixties, I discovered, could be enriching and ennobling. Every Sunday afternoon, our two families, artists, healers, and activists, got together in our apartment for Chinese food and good talk. Whoever was in town came: my Celia and David and Henry's three daughters: best-selling author and co-founder of the National Women's Health Network, Barbara Seaman; artist and photographer Jeri Drucker with her husband, epidemiologist and social activist Dr. Ernest Drucker; and Elaine Rosner-Jería, owner of the West Side Family Preschool in Manhattan, who came with her husband, Pablo Jería, a political refugee from Chile.

I had just finished writing the book for Putnam about adopting orphans, called *They Came to Stay*, when John Beaudoin, vice president of the Reader's Digest Association, invited me to lunch. "We want you to go to Israel."

"Israel," I repeated, thinking I had not heard right. *The Reader's Digest* was not then known for its passion for Israel.

"We want you to find a woman," he went on, "not Golda Meir, not a political or world-famous figure. We want a typical Israeli so that anyone, man or woman, reading this book would say, 'If I lived in Israel, that is the life I would have led.' "

"I go to Israel every year," I said, "and it never occurred to me that this is the best way to tell the Israel story. You've never been to Israel. How did you get this idea?"

"You gave it to me."

"Not me, I'm not that smart."

"Every time we had lunch while you were writing *They Came to Stay*, you were either going to or coming from Israel on some assignment. Your fascinating stories gave me the idea. But I didn't want an American or a journalist. I wanted an Israeli."

Henry resigned from his job so he could come with me on my search, and in Jerusalem we found the perfect candidate, Raquela Prywes. Regal and beautiful, a ninth-generation Jerusalemite, she was a Hadassah nurse-midwife who had delivered survivors' babies in the British prison hospital in Cyprus and tended to the wounded in Israel's wars.

To give the book a sense of time and place and history, Henry and I lived wherever she had lived. We spent nearly a year with Raquela and with more than a hundred and fifty people whose lives she had touched. She was so frank about a previous lover that her second husband, Dr. Moshe Prywes, was jealous retrospectively. *Raquela: A Woman of Israel* became a selection of the Reader's Digest Condensed Books Book Club and won the National Jewish Book Award as the best book on Israel in 1978.

A year later, I was covering the summit meeting in Alexandria, Egypt, between Egypt's president Anwar Sadat and Israel's Prime Minister Menachem Begin, when Henry had his first stroke. We flew to Israel where, under the care of a woman therapist who came every day, he made a complete recovery. We shared seven good years, never out of each other's sight, until he suffered a massive stroke in New York and died in 1982. I had loved and been loved by two caring and decent human beings.

From the birth of Israel to this day, I have covered every major emigration to Israel—from North Africa, Yemen, Iraq, Romania, the former Soviet Union, and, most recently, Ethiopia, where I was the only correspondent allowed to witness and participate in Operation Moses. Making two trips to Ethiopia in 1985 and 1986, I traveled with Barbara Ribakove, the founder of the North American Conference on Ethiopian Jewry (called NACOEJ); Elsie Roth, a registered nurse from St. Louis; Middie Giesberg, a community leader in Los Angeles; and several other men and women devoted to rescuing Jews from danger in Ethiopia.

We flew to Addis Ababa and Gondar, climbing up and sliding down muddy hills to reach the isolated Jewish villages in the highlands. We brought food and medicine and hope. I became an instant paramedic, putting drops in people's eyes to heal or prevent trachoma. Sitting inside their *tukuls,* huts made of mud and dung and straw interlaced with slats of eucalyptus wood, mothers and fathers studied the photos I had taken of their children in Israel and wept. "I will never see my children again." I tried to console them and failed. Returning to Israel, I brought the children photos of their parents, and the children wept. "I will never see my mother and father again." They were wrong. There are now more than 70,000 Ethiopian Jews in Israel, reunited with their families.

"Israel," I wrote in my 1987 book *Rescue: The Exodus of the Ethiopian Jews,* "is the only country, of all the nations in the world, who sent white men to bring black men, women, and children out of Africa, not to be sold but to be saved."

In these last years, my photos, safely stored for over sixty years in filing cabinets, have taken on a life of their own. I have given the United States Holocaust Memorial Museum in Washington more than one thousand of my negatives of the refugees on the *Henry Gibbins,* life in Oswego, survivors in the DP camps in Germany and Cyprus, the *Exodus 1947,* and the three prison ships that took the *Exodus* Jews back to Germany. The photos play an important part in the film *The Long Way Home,* which won the Oscar as the best documentary feature in 1998. "We couldn't have made this film," Richard Trank, the producer, told Charlie Rose on PBS, "without Ruth and her photos."

Retire? Never. In the late summer of 1995, I flew to China to cover the United Nations Fourth World Conference on Women for *Na'amat Woman* magazine. I greeted each day with exhilaration, watching the mosaic of faces of all colors, excited by the sheer presence of women coming together from 185 nations in the largest gathering of women in history. We went to fight abuses like genital mutilation and burning girl babies, to give women equal rights, and to fulfill not the American dream but the whole world's dream of ending poverty and disease.

Two years later, singing to myself as I walked blithely to the post office with photographs for another paperback edition of *Haven,* I fell in a pothole. Surgeons straightened the bones of my left thigh with an eight-inch stainless steel plate, a useful device that I will live with for the rest of my life (when I go through airport security, I often set off the alarms as if I were a terrorist). Lying in the hospital bed, I thought ruefully, You climbed mountains in Alaska and Ethiopia and never got a scratch, and you walk around the corner and break a leg. Ah, well, it could have been worse. What if I had broken my head?

Celia, who treats her children with homeopathy and is now a distributor of magnetic technology, brought arnica pellets to me in the hospital. The swelling went down, the pain eased, and after five days the resident physician agreed with me that hospitals are hazardous to your health. He signed me out, and David came to take me home.

Now I am never without arnica in my purse in case of an accident. I sleep on a magnetic bed pad and cover myself with a soft white FAR-infrared comforter. FAR-infrared rays, Celia explained to me, are bands of light that cannot be seen but are felt as heat. NASA uses them to keep astronauts warm in space. During the day, I wear magnetic pearls and insoles for energy and balance. After all, Thomas Jefferson believed in magnets too.

Three weeks after my fall, using a cane, I boarded a plane to Miami Beach to give two talks at Hadassah's national convention. "You have to tell those young women about your accident," Marlene Post, Hadassah's national president and a nurse herself, insisted.

"Why make a big deal out of it?"

"What could inspire young women more? But don't be foolish. Just keep using that cane."

After some months, Celia helped me throw the cane away.

In August 1998, with my leg completely healed, I flew to Poland and the Czech Republic. We were some thirty-five men and women of three generations on a mission led by the Museum of Jewish Heritage—A Living Memorial to the Holocaust, based in New York City. Doris Schechter, my surrogate daughter whom I had brought to Oswego when she was five, came with her daughter, Laura Chess. Barbara Ribakove, my traveling companion in Ethiopia, was my roommate. Also sharing the searing experiences was Nancy Fisher, who had interviewed me in the category of "rescuers" for the Survivors of the Shoah Visual History Foundation created by Steven Spielberg.

We relived years of agony as we tried to make our way through a cemetery in Warsaw whose headstones, jammed together with no space between them, stretched to the very horizon. I found the grave of Janus Korczak, the beloved Jewish teacher who refused a Nazi offer to escape from the ghetto. He would not let his orphans walk alone to their deaths in Auschwitz.

We left the cemetery to trudge through the ruins of the huge Warsaw Ghetto in the oldest part of the city. It had been cleaned and sanitized, with only a piece of the original ghetto wall still standing. We saw no evidence of how the people, like the headstones, had been jammed together, thirteen in a tiny room with one bathroom, to starve or die of typhus or to survive just long enough to be deported to Treblinka and other death camps.

We stood in silence at the Umschlagplatz, the huge open transit point separating the ghetto from the Polish part of the city. Here in the summer of 1942 and the spring of 1943, more than 300,000 Jews who had been rounded up in the ghetto were herded onto cattle cars and deported.

Suddenly Regina Finer, a youthful blond septuagenarian surrounded by her daughter and her granddaughter, broke into sobs. In a mixture of Yiddish and English, she told us her story. "In 1942, the Germans made us go down to the street. Whoever didn't go down was shot. My mother hid my little brother Moishele in a drawer between the pots. They took away my father, my mother, and my sister Ruchele, who was fourteen, one year older than me. I was left in the ghetto. I took care of my little sister Leahela—she was six—and Moishele. He was three. There was nothing to eat; we were half dead."

She wiped her eyes and went on. "We were in the ghetto until the last minute. We were hiding in a big bunker in the ghetto with seventy families. It was April 1943, just before Passover. They threw a grenade in the bunker and pulled everybody out. They took us to the Umschlagplatz and put us on a train. Most of those trains went to Treblinka. For some reason, my train didn't go there. It went to Majdanek."

She wiped her eyes again. "I pulled Leahela up on the train, but

I couldn't lift Moishele. With nothing to eat, he couldn't walk. He was lying on the ground. All my life, I cry for him: 'Moishele, forgive me. I couldn't save you, I couldn't lift you on the train. I will never forgive myself.' "

I tried to comfort her. "Regina, this is the time for closure. Today, with all of us around you, you can say goodbye to Moishele."

The Polish sun beat down on us. The thousands of Jews who had left the ghetto from the Umschlagplatz were no longer nameless and faceless. For me, Moishele has given each of them a name and a face.

Warsaw led to Treblinka.

Traveling in a comfortable tour bus, we rode sixty miles across a disturbingly lyrical landscape, with row upon straight row of ripening wheat, barley, and rye, all the way to Treblinka. It was one of six notorious killing centers in Poland—Treblinka, Majdanek, Chelmno, Sobibor, Belzec, and Auschwitz-Birkenau.

Entering Treblinka, we were shocked to find not a trace of the camp where 870,000 Jews had been murdered and shoveled into mass graves. Heinrich Himmler, the head of the Gestapo, had visited Treblinka in February 1943. The Nazis had just been defeated at Stalingrad, and the war was turning against them. Determined to conceal the evil committed here, he issued a grisly order. "Dig up all the corpses and burn them."

Three months later, a courageous Jewish resistance group was captured and shot. They had had a spectacular victory. They had burned all the barracks to the ground. All that was left of Treblinka was a long black pit filled with stones that gleamed like black diamonds.

We ended our visit as Yitzchak Mais, our resident scholar, created an open-air altar from a small mound of dirt. He lit six candles for the six million dead and we recited the Kaddish, the Hebrew prayer of mourning.

Lublin led to Majdanek.

Majdanek lay just outside the city of Lublin. From 1942 to

1943, 130,000 Jews from Poland, Czechoslovakia, Holland, and Greece were sent to Majdanek. More than 60 percent of them—women, children, the aged and infirm—stepped off the cattle cars and were immediately shot or sent to the gas chamber. Near the end of the war, the Russian army reached Majdanek so quickly that the Nazis and their local helpers had no time to destroy the camp. It was exactly as it had been when Regina survived its horrors.

My stomach sickened from the smell of death as we walked through the dark ugly barracks. We walked past huge glass cases, some filled with human hair, others with torn shoes and sandals. One glass case hit me as if I had been kicked by a Nazi's boot. It was filled with baby clothes.

As if we were prisoners ourselves, we followed, step by step, the path on the death walk. First, we entered the area in which victims were told to strip naked and hand everything over to other inmates—who knew their turn would come as soon as they could no longer work. Then we were squeezed together in a tiny room that led to a heavy door supposedly opening into the "shower room." It was, as we know now, a lie. As soon as they entered and the heavy door was bolted behind them, cylinders of Zyklon-B were tossed in. Within minutes, the naked people, jammed together for the last time, were dead from asphyxiation.

A little glass window was framed near the top of the ominous door. Through it the German, Polish, and Ukrainian guards had peered to watch people standing or falling against each other, gassed to death. My roommate, Barbara, whispered to me, "I wonder what these men were doing while they watched? Did they get a high from it?" I did not answer. The words were clamped in my throat.

Our walk on the death path continued. We moved on to a small hospital-like room with a stretcher. Here, each corpse taken from the gas chamber was cut up to extract gold teeth, dentures, and anything else like diamonds or gold coins that victims might have hidden in their bodies.

Moving on in anger and disgust, we entered a huge bright space with four iron ovens that looked like the fancy baker's ovens I had seen in prewar Europe. Only here, I thought bleakly, they were baking one thousand bodies a day. I walked behind the ovens. The floor was still strewn with fifty-five-year-old ashes. I swear I could smell and taste the odor of burned flesh.

Outside, we joined Yitzchak in the Kaddish. Of all the camps we visited, Majdanek, grimly real, unchanged in more than fifty years, left me physically ill.

Cracow led to Auschwitz-Birkenau.

In Cracow, Rosa Strygler, accompanied by her daughter Olivia, showed us the apartment she had lived in. "My mother owned a shop with fabrics. Once this was a good town to live in. Now, what can you say . . . ?" Her voice, always upbeat, full of laughter, trailed away.

We drove to Auschwitz-Birkenau, a huge complex of three camps. Auschwitz I, with permanent brick buildings, was called the "mother camp." It held mostly Polish prisoners. Auschwitz II was Birkenau, the German name for Brzezinka, a neighboring hamlet. Jews and some Gypsies, after March 1942, were imprisoned here in endless rows of wooden barracks. One whole area was set aside for women. Auschwitz III was named Buna for the Buna Works, where Jewish slave laborers were forced to make synthetic rubber.

We entered the huge complex of Auschwitz I, walking the long road that the prisoners had trudged from the railroad tracks. Someone suggested that with my bad leg I should be driven. I refused. The rest of our group decided to walk too. Isaac Herzog took my arm. Isaac, a graduate student at Columbia, was the son of the brilliant Israeli Foreign Ministry official Jacob Herzog and a nephew of Chaim Herzog, the former president of Israel.

I stopped for a few minutes to touch the barbed-wire fence on both sides of the road. It seemed alive as I pressed it between my fingers. Once, I thought, this wire electrocuted anyone choosing to die instantly instead of being gassed. The ghosts of the 3 million Jews walked with us.

We left Auschwitz I and headed toward Auschwitz II—Birkenau, stopping where the cattle cars had spewed out their human cargo. On the railroad siding, often with an orchestra playing classical music, people were selected to go one way to the labor camps, the other way to the crematoria. How ironic, I thought, that the sun should be shining this day. The sky should be crying with pain.

The barracks were still standing, as if they waited for yet more victims. Once again, my throat clamped shut. While Adolf Eichmann, in a few time-squeezing months beginning May 17, 1944, was shipping more than 500,000 men, women, and children on countless cattle cars to these barracks and their deaths, I was taking 1,000 refugees to new life in Oswego.

In the hot sun, Regina, who had been transferred from Majdanek and then spent two years in Auschwitz-Birkenau, led us on again. Hurrying past row after row of barracks, she shouted, "Here it is—the women's barracks." We followed her inside, down a narrow aisle just wide enough to separate tiers of stacked-up shelves that looked like wooden cages.

"Here is my bunk," she said, touching an empty shelf. We saw the purple numbers the Nazis of Auschwitz had tattooed on her left arm. "Here in Block Two," she said, still speaking in a mixture of Yiddish and English, "here I slept with four other women, and now"—she shook her head still in disbelief—"I am alive."

We recited the Kaddish outdoors. Asked to speak, I said, "The greatest lesson I've learned coming here is that these death camps strengthened the survivors and gave them backs of steel, so they could trek across the face of Europe, climb on so-called illegal ships like *Exodus 1947*, defy the British empire, defy the world, and reach a safe haven, refugees no more. These were Jews such as the world had never seen."

We left each killing center in Poland depressed and tormented. But as soon as we climbed back into our tour bus, Regina began belting out songs of joy in Hebrew and Yiddish. The bus shook with laughter as we joined Regina in songs we had grown up singing.

> *Aufn pripachok, brennt a feierel,*
> *un in shtib is hais,*
> *un der rebbe lerent klainer kinderlach*
> *dem aleph bais.*

> On the stove a little fire is burning,
> the room is hot,
> and the rabbi teaches little children
> their ABC's.

A stranger had given Regina a bottle of champagne. We toasted each other, raising little paper cups, singing, "*Loh mir alle trinken a glesele vine*" (Let us all drink a little glass of wine).

On the overnight train taking us from Cracow to Prague, Polish border guards banged on our compartment doors and shouted gruffly, demanding our passports. The moment they left, most of the young women and men on our mission whooped and screamed, "We're out of Poland!" The Czech border guards were polite as they welcomed us to their country. I remembered the people on the *Henry Gibbins*, waving at the Statue of Liberty. "The air smells free," they had told me. Here too the air smelled free.

Prague led to Terezin (Theresienstadt).

The Nazis had built a Potemkin village here, pretending the Jews were living an idyllic life in a country club atmosphere. They had thrown all the townspeople out of the middle-class homes surrounding the camp. They filled every room in every house with Jews. Those who didn't die from typhus or hunger were shipped to Auschwitz.

A woman survivor approached me. "The children were starving," she told me, "but when the Red Cross people came to investigate, the children were made to sit outdoors at café tables with cans of sardines in front of them. I was one of the mothers who was forced to make these hungry children pretend they were full and make them complain in loud voices, 'Was! *Noch einmal sardinen?* (What? Sardines again?).' Don't tell me the Red Cross people, who reported to the world that everything was fine here, didn't see through that farce."

It seems to me on this journey of mingled emotions that my life had come full circle. There was a line that ran from our vibrant camp at Oswego to the death camps in Poland and the Czech Republic.

Often, describing the years I tried to balance my life as wife, mother, and journalist, I am asked by college students, "Did you ever run into sexual harassment? You were out there alone at a time when most women were home having babies."

I tell them, "I know sexual harassment exists, but I never experienced it. I think men have always realized I am as serious as they are. I am no helpless female. I never wanted to be known as a 'girl' or 'woman' reporter. I was a reporter. Period. But I will always see the world as a woman, feel as a woman, and write as a woman. Women see the world differently from men. A man cannot know what it is to give birth and to hold a baby to one's breast."

Instead of harassment on assignments in frontier lands like Siberia and the Soviet Arctic, some of the men would insist on helping me. They tied woolen scarves around my neck and covered my head with woolen hats to keep me from freezing in open cockpit seaplanes. They had never seen an American before, certainly not an American journalist. Some wanted to marry me.

I found there were many advantages in being a woman. Golda Meir often invited me to her kitchen. We would first catch up on our families, then turn to the issues she was working on that were making front-page news. After she retired to a small house outside Tel Aviv, she confided to me that she had not been a very good mother. For a whole year, she had left her two small children, Sarah and Menachem, in Palestine to go to America to work for the Pioneer Women, now called Na'amat. "But I'm a much better grandmother," she said. "I see my grandchildren every day. I bake cookies this high, and by three o'clock they're all gone."

In the early 1950s, Eleanor Roosevelt asked me to take her to a new development town in Israel. She wanted to see for herself how Israel was absorbing the deluge of new immigrants. I chose a small town near Tel Aviv with a mixture of newcomers from various countries in the Middle East. The day before our visit I gathered some of the people together. "Tomorrow," I alerted them, "I am bringing the widow of a great American president to see you."

The next morning, we traveled with an interpreter who spoke many of the languages of the newcomers. As we stepped out of the car, we saw people lined up on both sides of the road, holding platters of food and ululating with joy. It is a unique cry that comes up from the throat while the tongue beats a rhythm against the roof of the mouth. I caught tears in Eleanor's eyes as the people sang out in their few words of English: "The Queen of America has come."

Eleanor then went from one woman to another, tasting exotic food she had probably never seen before, always smiling graciously. Through the interpreter, she asked them where they had come from and how they felt living in Israel.

"Good," they said.

Suddenly I saw her again, visiting the camp in Oswego. There too, with little or no English, our newcomers had made her feel their admiration and love.

As we drove back to our hotel, she looked sad. "Is anything wrong?" I asked.

"I wish I had done more," she said. Her lips were drawn with pain.

I took her hand. "You did what you thought was right. It was government policy—the party line. Nearly every leader in Washington (except the few brave ones like Harold Ickes), insisted, 'First we must win the war. Then we can take care of the refugees.' They didn't realize that if they waited there might not be any refugees to take care of."

She shook her head. "I should have done more."

When I learned she was planning a trip to Moscow, I went to see her in her New York apartment on Washington Square. "You know how the Jews are suffering in the Soviet Union," I said. "You are the most admired woman in the world. Could you ask the leaders to let the Jews go?"

"I wish I could do it," she said, "but that's a diplomatic mission, and Eisenhower would never give me that assignment. He has never invited me to the White House."

I was shocked. "Why?"

"He told one of my friends he had heard that at a dinner party I had said, 'Mamie is a drunkard.' Can you picture me saying something like that?"

A few weeks before David Ben-Gurion died on December 1, 1973, I called upon him. He lay ill and alone in his modest house in Tel Aviv, guarded and cared for only by young soldiers. (His wife, Paula, had died several years earlier.) The room was bare, save for a chair and the narrow bed he lay on, propped up by white pillows. He still had his crown of white hair, but his once-ruddy face had the pallor of impending death. The loneliness I had always sensed in him filled the lonely room.

"I'm glad you've come." He spoke in a weak voice. "I don't get many visitors these days. I wish I was back in Sde Boker. I'm happiest in the desert." He stopped and took a labored breath.

"Why do you love the desert so much?" I asked him.

"The desert is our future. The Negev is our future. In Jewish history the people who wanted to do something for other people had to find themselves first. They went to the desert. The prophets especially went to the desert to purify themselves. That was standard training for prophets. To be a prophet, you had to suffer alone. You had to know pain. You learned it in the desert." He suddenly became aware of my tape recorder. "Put that thing away."

"I just wanted to have your voice—and your words—on tape."

"You don't need it."

I put the recorder in my bag and opened a fresh notebook. I looked at the dying leader. "Master," I said, "will there ever be peace here?"

"Yes."

"When?"

"Not in my time, but in yours and your children's."

"Where will it come from?"

"Egypt."

"Egypt?" I blurted. "That's where the fedayeen, the terrorists, come from. They steal across your borders and throw bombs in day-care centers."

He waved his hand impatiently. He was the old lion again. "A whole generation is rising up in Egypt. They know what we can contribute to them, and what they can contribute to us. They have diseases like trachoma and bilharzia that we cured over fifty years ago. We have so much we can help them with, and they have natural resources that can help us."

In 1979, standing on the south lawn of the White House as Menachem Begin, Anwar Sadat, and President Jimmy Carter shook hands, I could hear Ben-Gurion's words. His prophecy had come true. Peace was coming from Egypt.

The Haven experience is with me every day. On January 27, 1986, the New York State Museum in Albany opened a permanent exhibit called "Bitter Hope: From Holocaust to Haven," in which our Oswego camp is featured. The Safe Haven committee in Oswego, with Scott Scanlon as its president, is now working on a traveling art exhibit and museum honoring the Holocaust survivors we brought to America. With proceeds from *Haven* and other fund-raisers, we are building the museum in the former bakery on the campgrounds, and they are naming the library and research center for me. I am deeply honored.

What, in the end, have the years of journalism meant to me, years of covering the survivors and the displaced? Through journalism, I sought to understand people and politics, to explore new frontiers, to see and feel and taste and touch and try to capture with honesty and compassion what I had seen. I hope I have succeeded.

People often ask me, "How do you do it all?"

I say, "In four simple words: never, never, never retire. If you don't use your brain, you lose it. If you don't use your body, you destroy it."

I hope to go on writing and speaking for many more years. I am still a reporter, but also a woman, a mother, and a grandmother, with four enchanting grandchildren. Looking at them, I think of all the people who came before them, who gave them the color of their eyes, the thrust of their lips, and the bodies and character that shape them. I see them as they are today, Michael and Lucy, Joel and Lila, so beautiful I want to hold them all in my arms. And I do.

And then I wonder what they will be like when they grow up. I pray they will do better than we did and build a world without hunger and fear, a world with no more refugees who require haven, a world at peace.

APPENDIX

DIRECTORY OF FORT ONTARIO EMERGENCY REFUGEE SHELTER,
WAR RELOCATION AUTHORITY, OSWEGO, N.Y.,
FROM THE *CONGRESSIONAL RECORD*

Name	Relationship to head of household	Identi- fication no.	Birth date	Citizenship (or last known)	Address
Alkalaj, Bosa. (See Adanja, Sofija.)					
Alkalaj, Rifka. (See Kamhi, Emica.)					
Alster Lapter, Sigmund J	Head	413	Feb. 14, 1894	Austrian	D.
Altarac:					
Betty	Head	13	Oct. 22, 1913	Yugoslav	164–4AB.
Hana	Daughter		Dec. 4, 1937		
Altarac:					
Estera	Head	14	May 5, 1905	do*	179–1ABC.
Belja	Daughter		Oct. 27, 1932		
Dora	do		Oct. 13, 1936		
Altarac:					
Jacob	Head	16	Jan. 17, 1889	do	169–1ABC.
Hana	Sister	15	Aug. 1, 1905		
Laura	Niece		May 9, 1942		
Altaras, Rene	Head	17	Aug. 25, 1920	do	168–1A.
Antic:					
Joseph	do	18	Jan. 30, 1887	do	181–8AD.
Terezja	Wife	19	Feb. 12, 1891		
Arditti, Adele	Head	20	Feb. 27, 1891	French	153–6A.
Arnstein:					
Lavoslav	do	21	Jan. 30, 1897	Yugoslav	6–10.
Jelka	Wife	22	Dec. 25, 1905		
Pavle	Son	775	Nov. 20, 1928		
Vlado	do		Feb. 25, 1932		
Eva	Daughter		July 14, 1935		
Ackerman, Hermine	Mother-in-law	2	Sept. 9, 1876		

* In government shorthand, "do" stands for ditto.

Name	Relationship to head of household	Identification no.	Birth date	Citizenship (or last known)	Address
Arnstein:					
Leo	Head	23	Apr. 14, 1899	} Czech	174–5BC.
Emilie	Wife	24	Mar. 18, 1901		
Arvay, Richard	Head	25	Jan. 13, 1897	Austrian	203–42.
Ascher, Herman	do	26	June 23, 1882	do	D–1.
Atias:					
Flora	do	27	Apr. 10, 1915	} Yugoslav	172–3A.
Laura	Daughter		Oct. 6, 1937		
Auerbach:					
Jakob M	Head	28	Mar. 22, 1900	} do	203/41/43.
Eva	Wife	29	July 28, 1903		
Aufricht:					
Paul	Head	30	Dec. 22, 1897	Austrian	} 159–5BC.
Marguerite	Wife	31	Sept. 3, 1908	German	
Baden, Fritz	Head	32	Sept. 5, 1884	Danzig	217–15.
Bader:					
Karl	Head	33	June 21, 1900		
Magdalene	Wife	34	Mar. 17, 1901	} Austrian	151–7ABC.
Liesl	Daughter		Aug. 8, 1931		
Baeder:					
Josip	Head	35	Sept. 5, 1887		
Klara	Wife	36	June 25, 1889	} Yugoslav	168–1BC.
Vera	Daughter		July 16, 1932		
Balakan, Dr. David	Head	37	Feb. 8, 1882	Austrian	D–5.
Baravram, Mirjama	do	38	Oct. 7, 1895	Yugoslav	158–2A.
Bardfeld:					
Emil	do	39	Feb. 26, 1889	} Austrian	157–5BC.
Rosa	Wife	40	Sept. 29, 1889		
Barnass:					
Dagobert	Head (deceased Dec. 12, 1944).				
Herta	Wife	42	Nov. 2, 1887	German	176–7BC.
Baruch:					
Isak	Head	43	May 15, 1890		
Eva	Wife	44	June 5, 1896	} Yugoslav	165–7ABC.
Aneta	Daughter	45	Dec. 30, 1922		
Jenny	do	76	Oct. 14, 1926		
Basch, Hugo	Head	46	Sept. 30, 1884	Austrian	D–2.
Bass:					
Eva	do	47	Oct. 5, 1909		
Joachim	Son		Jan. 11, 1932	} Polish	162–1ABC.
Jolanda	Daughter		May 14, 1943		
Susanna	Daughter (born at shelter).		Feb. 10, 1945		
Bass, Norbert I	Head	48	July 17, 1883	Austrian	158–6A.
Bauer:					
Artur	do	49	Sept. 30, 1879	} Yugoslav	174–4AB.
Sida	Wife	50	May 22, 1884		
Baum:					
Filip	Head	51	Dec. 23, 1890		
Frieda	Wife	52	Apr. 26, 1896	} Yugoslav	158–5ABC
Fredi	Son	53	June 14, 1919		

Name	Relationship to head of household	Identification no.	Birth date	Citizenship (or last known)	Address
Becker:					
Joseph	Head	54	Dec. 31, 1879	} Austrian	150–2ABC.
Rosa	Wife	55	Aug. 15, 1882		
David	Son	56	July 5, 1913		
Erna Ester	Daughter	57	Dec. 9, 1922		
Beer, Osiasz	Head	58	Sept. 19, 1899	Polish	D.
Behr, Marianne	do	59	Aug. 2, 1900	German	153–3A.
Berkovic:					
Rudolf	do	61	Sept. 1, 1892	} Yugoslav	153–6BC.
Kitty	Wife	60	Feb. 9, 1910		
Berkowicz:					
Samuel	Head	62	Jan. 9, 1882	} Polish	163–6BC.
Gitla	Wife	63	Nov. 8, 1886		
Bermann:					
Josef	Head	64	Feb. 10, 1878	} Austrian	153–8BC.
Ella	Wife	65	July 21, 1888		
Bernfest, Claudy	Head	66	July 21, 1883	Yugoslav	152–2A.
Birnbaum, Julius	do	67	Apr. 8, 1894	Austrian	D.
Bjelic (Bjelic family departed for Yugoslavia May 31, 1945):					
Alexander	do	68	Dec. 23, 1897	} Yugoslav	169–7ABC.
Gizela	Wife	69	July 2, 1902		
Branko	Son	776	June 8, 1928		
Blatt, Alter	Head	70	Mar. 9, 1891	Polish	D–1C.
Blau:					
Adolf	do	71	Mar. 31, 1888	} Yugoslav	172–7BC.
Gizela	Wife	72	Mar. 26, 1886		
Blaukopf, Leibisch	Head	73	Apr. 8, 1887	Austrian	D.
Blaustein:					
Abraham D	do	74	Sept. 23, 1907	} do	6–12.
Netti N	Wife	75	Mar. 12, 1907		
Susanna	Daughter		Nov. 19, 1933		
Bleier, Ernst	Head	77	Apr. 29, 1899	Yugoslav	203–70.
Bleier:					
Geza	do	78	Dec. 21, 1912	} Yugoslav	1–2.
Karoline	Wife (deceased Dec. 29, 1944).				
Ronald	Son		Nov. 9, 1942		
George	do		Feb. 2, 1944		
Blumberg, Olga	Head	80	Nov. 26, 1871	Austrian	157–2A.
Blumenfeldt, Felix	do	81	Jan. 19, 1898	do	D–1.
Blumenkranz:					
Efraim	do	83	Nov. 2, 1907	} Polish	162–2ABC.
Bertha	Wife	82	May 18, 1908		
Derrit	Daughter		Apr. 25, 1938		
Ruth	do		Nov. 13, 1943		
Boehm:					
Ignan	Head	85	Oct. 4, 1882	} Austrian	157–3BC.
Ester	Wife	84	Sept. 14, 1881		
Bogdanic-Buechler, Leo. (See Buechler-Bodanic, Lee.)					

Name	Relationship to head of household	Identification no.	Birth date	Citizenship (or last known)	Address
Bokros:					
Filip	Head	88	Dec. 16, 1883	} Yugoslav	164–6ABC, 8A.
Alice	Wife	87	Mar. 13, 1897		
Paul	Son	778	July 13, 1928		
Nelly	Daughter	777	Oct. 4, 1929		
Mira	....do....		Dec. 13, 1935		
Bonacic:					
Perica	Head	89	June 3, 1915	} ....do....	152–8BC.
Ana	Daughter		July 26, 1936		
Boni:					
Bellina	Head	90	Dec. 13, 1904	Bulgarian	} 176–8ABC.
Raymond	Son	779	Dec. 2, 1928	French	
Silven	....do....		Nov. 12, 1931	....do....	
Claude	....do....		May 15, 1933	....do....	
Boss:					
Georg	Head	92	Dec. 8, 1879	} Danzig	174–3BC.
Dorothea	Wife	81	May 20, 1890		
Brandweiner, Heinrich	Head	94	Mar. 16, 1889	Austrian	153–8A.
Braun:					
Alfred	....do....	93	Nov. 29, 1890	} ....do....	177–6A.
Pauline	Wife	96	July 19, 1892		
Braun, Ernest	Head	95	July 17, 1914	Austrian	203–79.
Brenner:					
Moses Aron	....do....	98	Apr. 6, 1897	} Polish	162–5ABC.
Bertha	Wife	97	Nov. 13, 1897		
Jakob	Son	780	Feb. 23, 1927		
Breuer:					
Ernst	Head	100	Apr. 2, 1916	Austrian	} 151–5ABC.
Marianna	Wife	102	Sept. 14, 1922	Polish	
Alice Lisa	Sister	99	Aug. 31, 1912	Austrian	} 209.
Diana Kay	Daughter (born at shelter).		Apr. 6, 1945	....	
Breuer, Lilly	Head	101	Apr. 15, 1895	Yugoslav	9–22.
Bronner:					
Heinrich	....do....	104	Aug. 27, 1885	} Polish	163–6A.
Eleonora	Wife	103	Apr. 12, 1897		
Lilly	Daughter	105	Feb. 7, 1925		
Edith	....do....	781	Sept. 6, 1926	} ....do....	163–8ABC.
Margarete	....do....	782	Apr. 6, 1929		
Jakob	Son		Oct. 20, 1931		
Brotz:					
Hugo Israel	Head	107	May 19, 1898	} German	155–8BC.
Emma	Wife	106	Dec. 19, 1892		
Bruck, Hermann	Head	108	Apr. 14, 1873	....do....	203–61.
Buechler-Bogdanic, Leo	....do....	86	Jan. 28, 1892	Yugoslav	173–6A.
Buchler:					
Arpad	Head (deceased at shelter Feb. 19, 1945).		....	....	
Renee	Wife	111	July 10, 1912	} ....do....	No. 18.
Pavao	Son		July 28, 1935		
Blanka	Daughter		Dec. 26, 1936		
Dan	Son		July 31, 1938	....do....	9–22.

Name	Relationship to head of household	Identification no.	Birth date	Citizenship (or last known)	Address
Hanna	Daughter		Apr. 29, 1942	} ------do -----	9–22.
Emilia	Mother	110	Mar. 28, 1881		
Charasch:					
Jakob	Head	113	June 6, 1888	} Polish--------	158–1ABC.
Fanny	Wife	112	Jan. 25, 1889		
Chernitza, Luba	Head	114	Aug. 2, 1894	Russian------	156–5A.
Cicarelli, Angelina	------do------	115	Sept. 5, 1890	} Yugoslav-----	168–3BC.
Culic, Vesna	Daughter	121	Dec. 1, 1920		
Cohen:					
Isaac	Head	117	Apr. 25, 1864	} Spanish------	175–4AB.
Dona	Wife	116	July 30, 1876		
Cohen:					
Richard	Head	120	May 21, 1898	}	
Rebeca	Wife	118	Dec. 10, 1912	------do -----	175–2ABC.
Walter	Son		July 22, 1935		
Cohn, Dorothea	Head	119	Apr. 6, 1877	German -----	176–2A.
Culic, Vesna. (See Cicarelli, Angelina.)					
Cygelman:					
Majlich	Head	123	Dec. 13, 1892	Polish_____	}
Frymeta	Wife	122	Feb. 27, 1895	------do -----	162–6ABC.
Ginette	Daughter	783	Mar. 5, 1928	French-------	
Isidore Andre	Son		May 30, 1937	------do -----	
Czeczer, Abraham	Head	124	Aug. 3, 1892	Polish_____	202–39.
Danon:					
Josip	------do------	127	June 1, 1901	}	
Hana	Wife	785	June 2, 1902		
Isak	Son	126	June 24, 1929	} Yugoslav-----	168–8ABC.
Sari	Daughter		Jan. 5, 1931		
Ester	------do -----		Oct. 30, 1935		
Danon:					
Rafael	Head	129	Apr. 12, 1899	} ------do -----	154–3BC.
Erna	Wife	125	Jan. 17, 1901		
Danon:					
Sima	Head	132	May 2, 1900	}	
Rasela	Wife	130	Dec. 12, 1909		
Irena	Daughter	784	June 6, 1929	} ------do -----	167–8ABC.
Ica	Son		Mar. 8, 1933		
Mika	------do -----		Apr. 1, 1944		
Danon:					
Zadik	Head	133	May 7, 1886	} ------do -----	168–2BC.
Matilda	Wife	128	July 6, 1893		
Danon:					
Zadik	Head	134	Feb. 2, 1881	} ------do -----	161–4BC.
Sara	Wife	131	Mar. 15, 1887		
Danziger:					
Salamon	Head	136	Apr. 25, 1900	} Polish--------	202–2/3.
Isidor Meyer	Son	135	Sept. 20, 1923		
David:					
Wilhelm	Head	138	June 1, 1895	} German -----	21.
Hedwig	Wife	137	Sept. 5, 1878		

Name	Relationship to head of household	Identification no.	Birth date	Citizenship (or last known)	Address
Deutsch:					
Alexandra	Head	139	Mar. 19, 1894	Yugoslav	168–7ABC.
Elsa	Daughter	140	June 19, 1919		
Milinovic, Gordona	do	498	Jan. 2, 1922		
Deutscher:					
Efraim	Head	142	Aug. 18, 1887	Polish	160–8BC.
Beile Ides	Wife	141	May 12, 1895		
Diamant:					
Eisig	Head	143	Jan. 5, 1875	do	158–4AB.
Golda	Wife	144	May 1, 1880		
Dick, Leib	Head	145	Dec. 3, 1874	Austrian	217–14.
Dirnbach:					
Ernest	do	146	July 1, 1901	Yugoslav	172–5BC.
Franzi	Wife	147	Jan. 21, 1914		
Dodeles:					
Josef Hirsch	Head	149	May 14, 1902	Polish	160–8AD.
Hana	Wife	148	Mar. 20, 1908		
Drab:					
Karl	Head	150	Feb. 24, 1889	Austrian	157–7BC.
Augustine	Wife	151	Oct. 7, 1893		
Drahline, Abraham	Head	152	May 21, 1902	Russian	203–77.
Dresdner:					
Jakob	do	155	Feb. 14, 1901	Rumanian	No. 17.
Ellena	Wife	154	Sept. 10, 1903		
Elisabeta	Daughter	153	July 29, 1925		
Abraham	Son	786	Dec. 29, 1928		
Isidor	do		Apr. 14, 1930		
Rudolf	do		Sept. 3, 1931		
Salomon	do		May 13, 1933		
Rosena	Daughter		Oct. 1, 1934		
Josef	Son		July 4, 1936		
Paula	Daughter		May 1, 1938		
Franka	do		Aug. 7, 1940		
Dromlewicz (Freund):					
Ignatz	Head	156	June 7, 1881	Polish	163–4AB.
Cecelia	Wife (married Mar. 17, 1945).	206	Nov. 4, 1904		
Drucker, Peter S	Head	157	May 6, 1880	German	202–7.
Drucks:					
Chaim	do	159	July 17, 1898	Polish	162–3ABC.
Ada	Wife	158	Dec. 14, 1911		
Herbert	Son		Apr. 1, 1937		
Dugalic, Maria	Head	160	Nov. 21, 1883	Yugoslav	168–3A.
Dutka, Julius	do	161	Nov. 23, 1886	Austrian	154–7C.
Ebel, Schewe	do	162	Apr. 20, 1875	Polish	172–1A.
Ebenspanger, Hugo	do	163	Mar. 1, 1897	Yugoslav	172–7A.
Edelstein:					
Sender	do	165	Oct. 1, 1887	Austrian	153–3BC.
Sara	Wife	164	Feb. 7, 1890		
Ehrenkranz, Ginda	Head	166	Mar. 15, 1876	Polish	156–2A.
Ehrenstamm:					
Moritz	do	168	June 14, 1883	South German	6–10.
Magrita	Wife	167	May 31, 1887		

Name	Relationship to head of household	Identi- fication no.	Birth date	Citizenship (or last known)	Address
Eisen, Moses	Head	169	Jan. 20, 1887	Austrian	D.
Eisenberg, Friedrich	do	170	June 25, 1889	do	D.
Elias, Victor	do	171	Nov. 7, 1879	German	217–2.
Ernst, Dr. Artur	do	172	July 3, 1885	Austrian	203–47.
Fajnzylberg:					
Jakob	do	173	Sept. 1, 1904	Polish	⎫
Sara	Wife	174	May 1, 1913	do	⎬ 162–7ABC.
Karl	Son		Feb. 7, 1930	French	⎭
Feffer, Chaim H	Head	175	June 26, 1910	Polish	202–19.
Feilbogen:					
Robert	do	177	Sept. 26, 1898	⎫	
Bertha	Wife	176	July 2, 1904	⎬ Austrian	155–4AB.
Peter	Son		Nov. 15, 1940	⎭	
Feinstein, Moses	Head	178	May 6, 1914	do	217–1.
Feldmann, Ludwig	do	181	Dec. 25, 1887	do	151–8A.
Feuermann-Sonnenschein, Frederick-Karoline. (See Sonnenschein Federmann, Frederick-Karoline.)					
Finci, Jakob	Head	187	Mar. 14, 1898	Yugoslavia	D–4.
Finci:					
Silvio	do	191	Dec. 26, 1911	⎫	
Rikica	Wife	190	Nov. 19, 1911	⎬ do	179–2ABC.
Mika	Son		June 24, 1935	⎪	
Sonja	Daughter		Aug. 25, 1938	⎭	
Finger:					
Oskar	Head	183	Jan. 3, 1898	⎫	
Livia	Wife	182	Oct. 25, 1908	⎬ Czech	154–8ABC.
Arnon	Son		Apr. 5, 1940	⎭	
Fink, Baruch	Head	186	Sept. 16, 1883	Polish	202–37.
Finzi:					
Moso	do	188	Sept. 5, 1906	⎫	
Bianca	Wife	185	May 15, 1915	⎬ Yugoslav	164–7ABC.
Iso	Son		June 30, 1938	⎪	
Ria	Daughter		May 11, 1940	⎭	
Finzi:					
Nelly	Head	189	Oct. 16, 1906	⎫ do	169–4AB.
Alfonso	Son	184	Jan. 12, 1925	⎭	
Fischer, Ignatz	Head	192	Mar. 25, 1881	Austrian	D–1.
Fischer, Dr. Oskar (departed for Yugoslavia May 31, 1945).	do	194	Dec. 31, 1891	Yugoslav	202–15.
Fishhof, Moritz	do	193	Aug. 14, 1891	Austrian	156–6A.
Flasner, Anna. (See Novovic, Milorad.)					
Flatau:					
Dr. Ernst	Head	197	Oct. 31, 1885	⎫	
Anni	Wife	196	Apr. 29, 1903	⎬ German	154–2ABC.
Fred	Son		July 26, 1931	⎪	
Rolf	do		July 26, 1931	⎭	
Fliegler, David	Head	198	Apr. 14, 1884	Polish	161–1A.

Name	Relationship to head of household	Identi- fication no.	Birth date	Citizenship (or last known)	Address
Flink:					
Naftali	do	199	Dec. 31, 1880	} do	161–1BC.
Rywa	Wife	200	Feb. 25, 1878		
Frajerman:					
Icek	Head	204	Apr. 27, 1904		
Hella Chaje	Wife	203	Apr. 7, 1911		
Rachael	Daughter		Sept. 28, 1938	} do	152–6ABC.
Salomon	Son		Nov. 29, 1940		
Jakob	do		Oct. 14, 1942		
Franco:					
Victor	Head	202	Jan. 3, 1910		
Lidia	Wife	201	Feb. 18, 1916		
Rachele	Daughter		Jan. 22, 1937	} Libian	177–2ABC.
Davide	Son		Apr. 23, 1939		
Miriam Mary	Daughter (born at shelter).		Sept. 29, 1933		
Frank, Margarette. (*See* Aufricht, Margarette.)					
Freudenfeld, Herman (departed for Yugoslavia May 31, 1945).	Head	205	Apr. 26, 1895	Yugoslav	172–5A.
Freund, Irene. (*See* Drom- lewicz, Ignatz).	do	207	Oct. 2, 1924	Polish	158–3A.
Fried:					
Franjo	do	208	July 16, 1905		
Irena	Wife	209	Apr. 20, 1915	} Yugoslav	165–1ABC.
Anita	Daughter		Feb. 25, 1938		
Aleksandar	Son		Aug. 12, 1942		
Friedlaender, Elli	Head	210	Aug. 17, 1897	German	176–7A.
Friedman-Mirkovic, Leo. (*See* Mirkovic-Friedman Leo.)					
Friedmann:					
Alexander	Head	211	Jan. 30, 1903		
Margit	Wife	214	Aug. 13, 1913	} Czech	209.
Anna	Daughter		Mar. 20, 1943		
Friedmann, Eisig	Head	213	Dec. 1, 1874	Austrian	177–5A.
Friedmann:					
William	do	215	July 4, 1910	} Hungarian	179–8BC.
Charlotte	Wife	212	Dec. 29, 1913		
Frischwaser, Schloimi	Head	216	Oct. 25, 1888	Austrian	D.
Froehlich:					
Oton	do	218	Jan. 31, 1877	} Yugoslav	161–2BC.
Elsa	Wife	217	Jan. 10, 1887		
Fros:					
Ferdinand	Head	219	Sept. 28, 1896	} do	173–6BC.
Lilly	Wife	220	May 4, 1907		
Fuchs, Chaim	Head	221	Dec. 13, 1885	Austrian	171–5A.
Fuchs:					
Osias Jakob	do	222	Dec. 5, 1899	} Polish	158–8AD.
Jetti	Wife	224	Jan. 1, 1904		

Name	Relationship to head of household	Identification no.	Birth date	Citizenship (or last known)	Address
Fuchs:					
Dr. Theodor	Head	225	May 10, 1870	} Austrian	157–1BC.
Marianne	Wife	223	Jan. 12, 1897		
Fuerth, Martha	Head	227	Dec. 24, 1889	do	154–7A.
Furmanski, Abe	do	226	June 28, 1909	Polish	203–59.
Gabba, David	do	228	Sept. 8, 1896	Russian	203–71.
Gal:					
Rywka	do	229	Sept. 9, 1909	Polish	} 163–3ABC.
Charlotte	Daughter		Aug. 17, 1935	French	
Albert	Son		Sept. 27, 1937	do	
Gaon:					
Salomon	Head	231	May 12, 1905		
Klara	Wife	230	Apr. 24, 1913	} Yugoslav	169–5ABC.
Zanko	Son		Feb. 20, 1938		
Gedroic, Nichola	Head	232	Nov. 6, 1898	Russian	D.
Gerstner:					
Moses Hirsch	do	235	Jan. 28, 1875		
Lieber	Son	234	Nov. 29, 1900	} Polish	163–2ABC.
Jenny	Daughter	233	Oct. 29, 1906		
Glaser, Emil	Head	236	Oct. 2, 1884	Austrian	203–64.
Goldberg, Oskar	do	237	Aug. 22, 1900	do	203–51.
Goldberger:					
Hanus	do	238	Feb. 25, 1897	} Czech	178–3BC.
Jolan	Wife	239	July 11, 1897		
Goldberger, Sigmund	Head	240	June 17, 1896	Austrian	D.
Goldmann:					
Oskar	do	242	Sept. 13, 1887	} do	153–1BC.
Isolde	Wife	241	Sept. 7, 1896		
Goldman-Lapajowker:					
Rifka	Head	242	Aug. 23, 1906	Polish	} 162–4BC.
Liana	Daughter		Dec. 12, 1939	Italian	
Goldschmidt:					
Fritz	Head	244	May 4, 1907	German	} 156–2BC.
Suzanne	Wife	245	Aug. 12, 1916	Czech	
Goldstein:					
Ernst	Head	247	Apr. 9, 1890	} Danzig	177–7BC.
Erna	Wife	246	Mar. 7, 1901		
Gottlieb:					
Mendel M.	Head	249	Jan. 13, 1886	} Austrian	157–6BC.
Baschie (deceased May 24, 1945).	Wife	248	Apr. 27, 1893		
Grajewska, Rosa	Head	250	Sept. 9, 1893	Polish	178–7A.
Graner, Dr. Hugo	do	251	Mar. 10, 1894	Austrian	D–2.
Greif, Gisela	do	252	July 5, 1906	Polish	173–53.
Grin:					
Dr. Alexander (departed for Yugoslavia, May 31, 1945).	do	253	July 1, 1902	} Yugoslav	154–1ABC.
Dusanka	Wife	254	Jan. 1, 1918		
Paul	Son		June 28, 1938		

Name	Relationship to head of household	Identi-fication no.	Birth date	Citizenship (or last known)	Address
Gross:					
Alexander	Head	255	Jan. 25, 1897	} Yugoslav	179–7ABC.
Jolanda	Wife	256	Sept. 15, 1909		
Vera	Daughter		May 15, 1935		
Gruber:					
Julius	Head	261	Dec. 12, 1903	} Austrian	153–5BC.
Margit	Wife	262	Mar. 5, 1905		
Grun:					
Leopold	Head	264	Apr. 5, 1901	} _____do	150–7ABC.
Franziska	Wife	263	July 13, 1909		
Heinz M	Son		Apr. 30, 1936		
Offenberg, Hermine	Mother-in-law		Nov. 14, 1880	_____do	151–3A.
Grunberg:					
Jacob	Head	258	Dec. 12, 1893	} _____do	151–1ABC.
Irma	Wife	257	Apr. 10, 1908		
Walter	Son		Jan. 24, 1933		
Guillemin, Bernard	Head	260	Sept. 7, 1898	German	203–66.
Gunsberger, Berthold	_____do	259	Feb. 23, 1901	Austrian	D–2.
Gutmann, Joseph	_____do	266	July 29, 1879	German	176–3A.
Guttman:					
Richard	Head	267	Mar. 2, 1899	} Austrian	151–2ABC.
Adele	Wife	265	Nov. 9, 1898		
Renate	Daughter		May 14, 1937		
Haas, Pinkas	Head	268	Apr. 5, 1884	_____do	217–D.
Hacker:					
Pinkas	Head	270	Dec. 18, 1883	} Polish	162–8AD.
Paula	Wife	249	Oct. 10, 1887		
Hahn:					
Josif	Head	241	Feb. 22, 1904	} Yugoslav	203–62/65.
Julia	Wife	242	Mar. 5, 1901		
Hajon:					
Rosa	Head	273	Oct. 18, 1896	} _____do	171–4BC.
David	Son	273	Dec. 14, 1931		
Haipern, Martin (departed for Yugoslavia May 31,1945).	Head	274	Sept. 12, 1893	_____do	D.
Hamburger, Daniel	_____do	275	Mar. 19, 1902	German	202–31.
Hammer-Helsinger, Lieb Leo.	_____do	276	Apr. 2, 1887	Polish	D.
Hanf:					
Zlata	_____do	278	Sept. 6, 1893	} Yugoslav	172–3 B and C.
Lea	Daughter	277	July 4, 1925		
Hartmayer, Marianna. (See Breuep, Marianne.)					
Hazan:					
Hajim	Head	279	July 11, 1903	} Yugoslav	158–5ABC.
Rika	Wife	280	Oct. 20, 1908		
Josef	Son		Dec. 1, 1934		
Jack	Son (born at shelter).		June 1, 1945		
Heller, Fanny. (See Rosenbaum, Moses.)					

Name	Relationship to head of household	Identification no.	Birth date	Citizenship (or last known)	Address
Hellner:					
David	Head	282	Mar. 12, 1883	} Polish	175–3BC.
Dina	Wife	283	May 10, 1890		
Hellsinger, Leib Leo. (See Hammer-Helsinger, Lieb Leo.)					
Hendel:					
Eisig	Head	284	Apr. 3, 1903	} Yugoslav	167–6ABC.
Hana	Wife	285	Nov. 30, 1908		
David	Son	287	Sept. 11, 1928		
Ruth	Daughter	287	Apr. 26, 1935		
Jeta	Niece	286	Sept. 30, 1925	do	} 209.
Gisela	do	286	Aug. 18, 1935	do	
Henle, Alfred	Head	287	Jan. 17, 1890	German	19.
Herzberg, Dora	do	288	Jan. 17, 1884	do	162–2ABC.
Herzfeld:					
Marcell	do	289	Oct. 23, 1882	} Austrian	159–6BC.
Stefanie Magdalena	Wife	290	May 13, 1897		
Herzog, Albert	Head	291	Mar. 25, 1884	Yugoslav	202–6.
Himmelreich, Max	do	292	Apr. 20, 1890	Austrian	D.
Hirschel:					
Herman	do	293	Sept. 6, 1885	} do	157–4AB.
Ida	Wife	294	May 3, 1877		
Hirschler:					
Julio	Head	296	July 2, 1894	} Yugoslav	169–3 ABC.
Ella	Wife	295	June 16, 1906		
Ivo	Son	295	Mar. 27, 1934		
Hirschler:					
Zlatko	Head	298	Apr. 15, 1911	} do	169–8AD.
Milica	Wife	297	Aug. 17, 1918		
Hirschsohn:					
Leo	Head	299	Feb. 1, 1899	} do	169–7C.
Olga	Wife	300	Nov. 19, 1906		
Ivo	Son	----	Nov. 17, 1935		
Hirt:					
Artur	Head	304	Mar. 31, 1896	} Polish	163–5ABC.
Amalia	Wife	302	Oct. 12, 1903		
Joseph Bernard	Son	807	July 10, 1930		
Michael Leonard	do		Feb. 19, 1934		
Hochwaldd:					
Mane	Head	304	Oct. 16, 1903	} Yugoslav	169–2ABC.
Jelica	Wife	303	June 19, 1905		
Branko	Son	303	Jan. 31, 1935		
Hoefler, Samuel	Head	305	Nov. 5, 1890	Austrian	217–D.
Iconomu, Athanasia. (See Kouzouca, (?) Athanasia.)					
Israel, Ella. (See Market, (?) Vilma.)					
Jacob:					
Alfred	Head	308	Apr. 1, 1905	} German	155–7ABC.
Ilse	Wife	310	May 7, 1902		
Herbert	Brother	309	Feb. 21, 1904		

Name	Relationship to head of household	Identification no.	Birth date	Citizenship (or last known)	Address
Jakovljevic, Zora (departed for Yugoslavia May 31,1945).	Head	311	Feb. 12, 1907	Yugoslav	159–2A.
Jancovici:					
Karolina	Head	313	Sept. 10, 1880	} Rumanian	177–3ABC.
Betty	Daughter	312	Mar. 16, 1910		
Weissenberg:					
Fanny	do	754	July 26, 1905	} do	
Adolf	Grandson		Dec. 2, 1938		
Jawetz:					
Baruch	Head	314	Feb. 10, 1890	} Austrian	151–8BC.
Mindel	Wife	315	Sept. 12, 1889		
Jellinek, Slavko	Head	316	Mar. 31, 1893	Yugoslav	D–4.
Jellinek, Theodor	do	317	June 9, 1885	Austrian	D–1.
Joachim, Fritz	do	318	May 17, 1897	do	D–6.
Josefowitz, Egon	do	319	Apr. 21, 1879	German	173–2A.
Jouravieff, Anastasia	do	320	Dec. 22, 1899	Russian	154–5A.
Jungmann:					
Heinrich	do	321	June 10, 1896	} Austrian	157–8BC.
Martha	Wife	322	Apr. 21, 1898		
Jurat, Marko (departed for Yugoslavia May 31, 1945).	Head	323	May 31, 1890	Yugoslav	161–8A.
Kabiljo, Abraham I	do	324	Jan. 1, 1901	do	D–4.
Kabiljo:					
David	do	326	June 15, 1911	} do	171–5BC.
Berta	Wife	325	Jan. 5, 1914		
Luna	Daughter		May 23, 1939		
Kabiljo, Irene. (See Neufeld, (?) Erna.)					
Kabiljo (Mr. and Mrs. Kabiljo departed for Yugoslavia May 31, 1945):					
Jakov	Head	328	Apr. 23, 1911	} do	157–4AB.
Caterina	Wife	329	Aug. 9, 1915		
Kabiljo:					
Leon	Head	330	Mar. 8, 1898	} do	172–6BC.
Seri	Wife	331	July 11, 1918		
Silvia	Daughter (born at shelter).		May 19, 1945		
Kahl, Artur	Head	332	Jan. 31, 1888	German	D.
Kahn, Ernst Jakob	do	333	May 9, 1887	do	156–3A.
Kaiser:					
Eduard	do	334	Aug. 9, 1895	} Yugoslav	174–2ABC.
Margita	Wife	335	Feb. 18, 1905		
Bruno	Son	788	Nov. 25, 1928		
Kalderon:					
Avram	Head	336	Mar. 18, 1902	} do	165–5ABC.
Berta	Wife	337	Apr. 7, 1912		
Simon	Son		Sept. 15, 1935		
Flora	Daughter		May 15, 1938		

Name	Relationship to head of household	Identification no.	Birth date	Citizenship (or last known)	Address
Kamhi:					
Benveniste M	Head	339	May 2, 1877	------do-----	172–2BC.
Beja	Wife	338	Jan. 21, 1888		
Kamhi:					
Emica	Head	340	Dec. 28, 1913	------do-----	164–8ABC.
Moric	Son		Mar. 11, 1932		
Alkalaj, Rifka	Mother	12	Dec. 15, 1888		
Kampos:					
Albert I	Head	341	July 26, 1908	------do-----	173–3ABC.
Sara	Wife	343	Sept. 29, 1909		
Lela	Daughter		Aug. 6, 1938		
Kampos:					
Josef I	Head	342	Jan. 4, 1903	------do-----	165–2ABC.
Sol	Wife	344	Sept. 21, 1907		
Jakov	Son		Jan. 13, 1936		
Luna	Daughter		May 30, 1938		
Karasch. (See Charasch.)					
Karmona:					
Celebon	Head	346	Aug. 1, 1906	Turk	175–8BC.
Dudu Coen	Wife	345	July 26, 1907		
Kaska, Ferdinand	Head	347	Oct. 15, 1902	Austrian	D–3.
Kastl, Milan	------do-----	348	May 14, 1888	Yugoslav	21.
Kattan, Estera. (See Levi, Rafael.)					
Katz:					
Artur	Head	350	Feb. 23, 1891	Austrian	177–4AB.
Ottilie	Wife	351	July 2, 1893		
Katzenell, Max	Head	352	Jan. 3, 1895	------do-----	D.
Kauert:					
Dora	------do-----	353	June 25, 1900	Danzig	154–6BC.
Lola	Daughter	354	June 22, 1923		
Kaufmann:					
Branko	Head	355	Feb. 6, 1909	Yugoslav	174–6ABC.
Kathe	Wife	357	Mar. 15, 1909		
Eva	Daughter		July 8, 1936		
Kaufmann:					
Karl	Head	356	Aug. 15, 1897	German	179–5BC.
Recha	Wife	358	Dec. 19, 1908		
Klein, Eugen	Head	359	June 4, 1891	Yugoslav	D–4.
Kleinmann, Josef	------do-----	360	July 12, 1880	Austrian	D–13.
Klimpl, Rahela	------do-----	361	Apr. 27, 1901	Yugoslav	175–6A.
Knopf, Kalman	------do-----	362	June 11, 1885	Austrian	D–1.
Koen:					
Stevan	------do-----	364	Aug. 31, 1886	Yugoslav	156–6AB.
Helen Elena	Wife	363	Apr. 8, 1886		
Koeppler, Dagobert	Head	378	Jan. 4, 1896	German	D.
Kohane:					
Moses	------do-----	366	Nov. 3, 1886	------do-----	156–7BC.
Helene	Wife	365	May 8, 1887		
Kohn, Anna	Head	367	Apr. 14, 1873	Czech	202–22/23.
Reinisch, Sofie	Sister	572	Feb. 9, 1879		
Kohn, Ernst	Head	368	Sept. 2, 1895	Austrian	202–8.
Kohn, Markus	------do-----	369	Dec. 9, 1901	------do-----	156–8A.
Konforte, Blanka	------do-----	370	Apr. 15, 1880	Yugoslav	171–3ABC.

Name	Relationship to head of household	Identification no.	Birth date	Citizenship (or last known)	Address
Konforte:					
Isaac	......do......	371	Mar. 1, 1907		
Solika	Wife	372	July 20, 1917	......do......	165–3ABC.
Renee	Daughter		Oct. 5, 1940		
Konig:					
Moritz	Head	373	Mar. 3, 1879	Czech	178–1BC.
Rosa	Wife	374	Feb. 22, 1886		
Kopp:					
Eduard	Head	375	Mar. 28, 1912		
Rosa	Wife	376	Sept. 11, 1912	Yugoslav	172–8ABC.
Theodor	Son		July 21, 1943		
Koppelmann, Feibish	Head	377	Oct. 28, 1882	Austrian	179–5A.
Korein:					
Stefan Edward	......do......	380	Nov. 16, 1897	......do......	153–2BC.
Rosa	Wife	379	Dec. 8, 1897		
Kornbluth, Jakob	Head	381	Dec, 16, 1889	Polish	202–4.
Koener:					
Schlome	......do......	383	Dec. 21, 1880		
Schewa	Wife	384	Oct. 13, 1884		
Regina	Daughter	383	Nov. 4, 1908	Austrian	150–8ABC.
Mina	......do......	382	May 21, 1911		
Tina	......do......	386	Sept. 16, 1921		
Kouzouca:					
Atanasia	Head	306	Jan. 14, 1907		
Stella	Daughter		Jan. 18, 1939		
Meropi	......do......		Sept. 16, 1939	Greek	175–1ABC.
Evangela	......do......		Jan. 1, 1941		
Kranz:					
Chana	Head	387	Apr. 20, 1904	Polish	162–8BC.
Edith	Daughter		Apr. 16, 1936		
Kraus, Alfred	Head	388	Mar. 13, 1887	Austrian	D.
Krauthamer:					
Naftali	......do......	389	Jan. 4, 1902	Polish	
Resel	Wife	390	Apr. 6, 1903	......do......	
Simon	Son		Aug. 6, 1932	......do......	175–6ABC.
Julius	......do......		Oct. 21, 1933	......do......	
Susanna	Daughter		May 22, 1939	French	
Kremer:					
Berta	Head	391	Jan. 3, 1911		
Hermann	Son	808	Jan. 2, 1930	Yugoslav	167–5ABC.
Vilko	......do......		July 22, 1934		
Kricer, Mihajlo	Head	392	Aug. 1, 1884	......do......	203–78.
Kron, Theodor	......do......	393	July 13, 1994	Austrian	217–13.
Krycler, Josef	......do......	394	July 27, 1994	Polish	202–36.
Kupfer, Augustine. (See Salem, Augustine.)					
Kuppermann, Laya	......do......	396	June 20, 1901	......do......	171–1A.
Kurz, Benno	......do......	397	Oct. 20, 1900	......do......	D.
Kurzmantel, Benjamin	Head	398	Dec. 7, 1882	Polish	173–1A.
Kuttner:					
Siegfried	......do......	400	June 21, 1903		
Charlotte	Wife	399	Aug. 20, 1910	German	179–3ABC.
Peter	Son		Dec. 18, 1933		

Name	Relationship to head of household	Identi-fication no.	Birth date	Citizenship (or last known)	Address
Kuznitzki:					
Berthold	Head	401	Dec. 6, 1891	} _____do _____	161–7ABC.
Felicitas	Wife	402	Aug. 27, 1894		
Rolf Manfred	Son	677	May 12, 1929		
Lammel, Alfred	Head	403	Jan. 8, 1886	Austrian	202–9.
Landau, Edmund	_____do_____	404	Jan. 20, 1895	Polish	203–45.
Landau, Samuel	_____do_____	405	Oct. 28, 1882	German	178–8A.
Landsberg:					
Dr. Paul	_____do_____	407	Apr. 5, 1892	} _____do _____	167–1BC.
Margarete	Wife	406	Dec. 22, 1894		
Lang:					
Geza	Head	409	Oct. 10, 1900	} Yugoslav	166–7ABC.
Garabela	Wife	408	Mar. 23, 1906		
Vladimir	Son		July 21, 1938		
Miroslav	_____do_____		Nov. 26, 1934		
Lange, Betti Rita	Head	410	June 2, 1894	Austrian	153–7A.
Langnas:					
Ignaz	_____do_____	412	Oct. 18, 1909	} _____do _____	150–6ABC.
Dora	Wife	411	May 23, 1912		
Josef	Son		June 23, 1931		
Bettina	Daughter		Aug. 6, 1936		
Lapajowker, Riwa and Liane. (See Goldman-Lapajowker, Rifka and Liana.)					
Lapter-Alster, Sigmund Joseph. (See Alster-Lapter, Sigmund Joseph.)					
Lederer:					
Georg	Head	415	Jan. 20, 1888	} German	176–2BC.
Erna	Wife	414	Oct. 21, 1887		
Lederer:					
Dr. Otto	Head	416	Feb. 11, 1897	Yugoslav	} 267–2ABC.
Ruza	Wife	418	Mar. 11, 1901	_____do _____	
Mira	Daughter	417	Oct. 2, 1924	_____do _____	} 209.
Ivo	Son	788	Dec. 11, 1929	_____do _____	
Leer, Oskar	Head	419	June 22, 1892	Austrian	203–46.
Lehman, Abraham Arthur	_____do_____	420	Aug. 23, 1877	German	217–8.
Lehr:					
Jakob	_____do_____	422	July 12, 1892	Austrian	} 159–8BC.
Friederike	Wife	421	Feb. 12, 1905	Dutch	
Leicht:					
Ernest	Head	423	Aug. 21, 1892	} Austrian	152–5BC.
Matilda	Wife	424	Jan. 27, 1900		
Leitner, Victor	Head	425	July 9, 1879	_____do _____	217–12.
Lepehne, Eva Ruth	_____do_____	426	Apr. 22, 1927	German	166–8ABC.
Levi, David	_____do_____	427	Apr. 12, 1922	Yugoslav	168–1A.
Levi:					
Flora	_____do_____	428	Apr. 7, 1908	} _____do _____	170–8BC.
Netti	Daughter		Aug. 1, 1937		

Name	Relationship to head of household	Identi- fication no.	Birth date	Citizenship (or last known)	Address
Levi:					
Josef D	Head	430	Mar. 3, 1904		
Maria	Wife	433	Sept. 13, 1911		
Rikica	Daughter		Apr. 29, 1937	------do -----	168–4BC.
Rachela Ella	Daughter (born at shelter).		Mar. 12, 1945		
Levi, Josef Herz	Head	429	Apr. 23, 1890	German -----	D.
Levi:					
Josef S	------do------	431	Nov. 5, 1904		
Zlata	Wife	437	Jan. 11, 1921	Yugoslav-----	174–1ABC.
Sara	Daughter		July 1, 1941		
Levi:					
Juda	Head	432	Feb. 26, 1909	------do -----	173–8A.
David	Son		Nov. 23, 1937		
Levi:					
Stella	Head	435	May 5, 1910	------do -----	164–3BC.
Jakov Zika	Son		Mar. 11, 1935		
Levi:					
Rafael	Head	434	June 23, 1891		
Vida	Wife	436	June 28, 1906	------do -----	167–3ABC.
Kattan, Estera	Sister-in-law ---	349	Oct. 10, 1907		
Levitch:					
Josip	Head	439	May 5, 1897		
Fortenee	Wife	440	Aug. 15, 1900		
Edward	Son	789	Sept. 5, 1924	Yugoslav-----	168–6ABC.
Leon	------do------	790	July 10, 1927		
Manon	Daughter		Aug. 29, 1931		
Levinson:					
Boris	Head	441	Feb. 26, 1903	Russian------	
Vera	Wife	443	Mar. 1, 1908	------do -----	174–8ABC.
Ellena	Daughter		Apr. 20, 1939	French--------	
Fanny	Mother	442	Jan. 13, 1875	Russian------	
Levy:					
Dr. Leon	Head	438	Dec. 20, 1898		
Irene	Wife	444	May 9, 1906	Yugoslav-----	166–5ABC.
Silvio	Son	791	May 8, 1928		
Erik	------do -----		Mar. 27, 1931		
Lewin, Ludwik	Head	445	May 2, 1883	Polish--------	202–30.
Lewin:					
Max Isidor	------do------	447	Feb. 17, 1873	German -----	176–1BC.
Else	Wife	445	Dec. 6, 1881		
Liban:					
Dawid	Head	448	Aug. 27, 1884	Austrian -----	6–12.
Rela	Wife	449	Mar. 6, 1890		
Lichtmann, Max	Head	450	June 11, 1904	------do -----	D.
Loewenthal, Frieda	------do------	453	Dec. 11, 1885	German -----	176–1A.
Loewenthal, Walter	------do------	454	Aug. 20, 1901	------do -----	203–54.
Loewinger, Sigmund	------do------	455	June 23, 1889	Austrian -----	D–1.
Loewit, Regina	------do------	456	Apr. 2, 1902	------do -----	151–3BC.
Wadler, Leie	Mother	722	Nov. 8, 1874		
Loewy, Wilhelm	Head	460	Sept. 10, 1893	------do -----	172–2A.
Low, Wilhelm	------do------	451	July 2, 1897	------do -----	203–72.
Lowenkron, Hersch	------do------	452	July 14, 1890	Polish--------	202–5.

Name	Relationship to head of household	Identification no.	Birth date	Citizenship (or last known)	Address
Lowy:					
George	do	457	Feb. 22, 1894	} Czech	178–4AB.
Juliana	Wife	458	Apr. 15, 1915		
Maria Ruth	Daughter		Mar. 13, 1935		
Lowy, Rosa	Head	459	Nov. 5, 1899	Yugoslav	156–7A.
Luftig:					
Leopold	do	461	Oct. 27, 1903	} Polish	158–8BC.
Rosa	Wife	463	Dec. 27, 1909		
Lustig, Alfred	Head	462	Apr. 8, 1888	Austrian	D.
Lustig, Margarete	do	464	Oct. 17, 1892	Yugoslav	152–3A.
Macliach					
Dr. Henri	do	466	Sept. 16, 1900		
Greta	Wife	465	Sept. 22, 1913	} do	167–4AB.
Silva	Daughter		Feb. 26, 1938		
Margoniner, Hilda Meyer. (See Meyer, Hilda.)					
Magrisso:					
Rudolf	Head	468	June 30, 1898	} do	179–6BC.
Lili	Wife	467	July 1, 1908		
Mandl:					
Emanuel	Head	469	May 10, 1897	} Austrian	152–5A.
Maria	Wife	470	Apr. 10, 1906		
Mandler:					
Fritz	Head	472	Sept. 16, 1891		
Margarete	Wife	473	June 22, 1898	} do	152–7ABC.
Alice	Daughter	471	Dec. 15, 1927		
Mandler, Wilhelm	Head	474	May 24, 1897	do	D.
Margulis:					
Dr. Rafailo	do	477	Sept. 26, 1885		
Olga	Wife	476	Aug. 28, 1889	} Yugoslav	167–7ABC.
Rajko	Son	478	Feb. 15, 1919		
Aca	do	475	Mar. 31, 1921		
Marinkovic:					
Simun	Head	479	Mar. 4, 1894		
Vinka	Wife	480	July 21, 1903		
Katica	Daughter	792	June 5, 1927	} do	165–6ABC.
Vicko	Son	793	Feb. 15, 1929		
Nikola	do		May 25, 1935		
Market:					
Vilma	Head	481	Nov. 21, 1921		
Mario	Son		July 17, 1942	} do	169–6BC.
Israel, Ella	Sister	307	Aug. 12, 1927		
Mass:					
Rudolph	Head	483	Aug. 27, 1889	} Austrian	159–7BC.
Katharina	Wife	482	Feb. 2, 1888		
Maurer:					
Leon	Head	484	Apr. 26, 1896		
Olga	Wife	485	June 30, 1902	} Austrian	163–1ABC.
Walter	Son	794	May 29, 1927		
Harry	do		July 11, 1944		
Melcer, Cacilia	Head	486	Oct. 28, 1902	Czech	175–3A.
Merksamer, Max	do	487	Mar. 11, 1891	Austrian	D–6.

Name	Relationship to head of household	Identi-fication no.	Birth date	Citizenship (or last known)	Address
Merzer:					
Jakob	_____do_____	488	Nov. 7, 1904	} Polish_____	160–3ABC.
Sonja	Wife _____	489	June 21, 1907		
Ivonne	Daughter_____		Sept. 16, 1932		
Lilian	_____do_____		Feb. 15, 1942		
Beatrice	Daughter (born at shelter).		Dec. 9, 1944		
Messer, Herman	Head _____	490	Jan. 4, 1896	Austrian _____	217–5.
Messerschmidt, Martin Adolf.	_____do_____	491	Mar. 10, 1890	German _____	203–65.
Metzger, Salo	_____do_____	494	Nov. 6, 1902	Austrian _____	D.
Meyer:					
Joseph	_____do_____	493	Jan. 20, 1882	} German _____	156–9BC.
Hilda	Wife _____	492	Mar. 5, 1895		
Mikhailoff:					
Michele	Head _____	495	Nov. 1, 1891	} Russian _____	175–5–ABC.
Olga	Wife _____	496	Nov. 27, 1893		
Vadim	Son _____	497	Nov. 21, 1924		
Milman, Schia	Head _____	499	June 9, 1880	Austrian _____	D.
Milinovic, Gordana. (See Deutsch, Alexandra.)					
Mirkovic-Friedmann, Leo	_____do_____	500	Jan. 31, 1904	Yugoslav _____	21.
Montiljo:					
Josef	_____do_____	501	Apr. 27, 1890	} _____do _____	151–6–ABC.
Sida	Wife _____	506	Jan. 26, 1894		
Sara	Daughter _____	505	Apr. 2, 1925		
Montiljo:					
Moric	Head _____	503	Aug. 18, 1909	} _____do _____	152–8–BC.
Maria	Wife _____	502	Aug. 28, 1916		
Elia	Daughter (deceased Aug. 3, 1944, on ship to United States).				
Rosica	Daughter (born at shelter).		May 6, 1945		
Montiljo, Relly	Head _____	504	Oct. 3, 1913	_____do _____	154–6A.
Mosauer, Rosa	_____do_____	507	Sept. 15, 1884	Austrian _____	6–12.
Moschev:					
Albert	_____do_____	508	Feb. 19, 1890	} Bulgarian____	176–6–ABC.
Bella	Wife _____	509	Feb. 19, 1904		
Rosa	Daughter _____	795	Dec. 22, 1929		
Moser:					
Louis	Head _____	510	May 23, 1882	German _____	176–3BC.
Maria	Wife _____	511	Oct. 27, 1886	Austrian _____	
Mrduljas:					
Franzesca	Head _____	512	Nov. 10, 1913	} Yugoslav_____	170–1 ABC.
Jose	Son _____		July 19, 1931		
Ivo	_____do_____		Feb. 4, 1934		
Maria	Daughter_____		Feb. 20, 1944		
Munz:					
Pesach	Head _____	515	Apr. 29, 1898	} Polish_____	160–6 ABC.
Fradl	Wife _____	514	Aug. 28, 1900		
Adam	Son _____	513	Mar. 9, 1927		
Leon	_____do_____		Feb. 5, 1930		

Name	Relationship to head of household	Identification no.	Birth date	Citizenship (or last known)	Address
Hafusi:					
Rafael	Head	516	Nov. 29, 1895	} Yugoslav	173–1BC.
Rusa	Wife	517	June 15, 1902		
Neubauer, Henrik	Head	518	Aug. 14, 1881	Czech	174–3A.
Neubrunn, Albert	......do	519	July 7, 1902	Austrian	D.
Neufeld:					
Erna	......do	520	Dec. 5, 1911	} Yugoslav	171–2ABC.
Georgie	Son	....	Mar. 8, 1938		
Kabiljo, Irene	Mother	327	May 15, 1889		
Neumann, Elsa. (Departed for South Africa Feb. 28, 1945.)	Head	521	July 3, 1884	Austrian	153–5A.
Neumann, Feliz	......do	523	July 10, 1887	......do	202–18.
Neumann:					
Karl	......do	524	May 19, 1896	} ......do	150–4–AB.
Liesl	Wife	522	Dec. 20, 1907		
Peter	Son	....	July 26, 1938		
Neumann, Maria	Head	525	Mar. 30, 1890	Austrian	153–5A.
Nitsch, Matilde	......do	526	June 23, 1894	Czech	157–7A.
Notowicz:					
Osias	......do	529	Feb. 20, 1900	} Polish	160–7ABC.
Maria	Wife	527	Apr. 14, 1908		
Henny	Daughter	....	Apr. 3, 1930		
Novovic:					
Dr. Milorad	Head	530	Jan. 29, 1999	} Yugoslav	6–10.
Berta	Wife	528	Apr. 17, 1906		
Smiljka	Daughter	....	Feb. 14, 1930		
Senka	......do	....	June 20, 1931		
Sergije	Son	....	Oct. 8, 1932		
Flaschner, Anna	Mother-in-law	195	Apr. 15, 1876		
Nurmberg, Saul	Head	531	Feb. 20, 1900	Polish	202–32.
Nussbaum, Max	......do	532	Jan. 19, 1885	German	217–4.
Nussbaum:					
Sarika	......do	533	June 12, 1900	} Yugoslav	172–1BC.
Mirko	Son	....	July 24, 1930		
Offenberg, Hermine. (See Grun, Leopold.)					
Oriel, Benjamin	Head	535	Nov. 26, 1898	Yugoslav	178–3A.
Ouroussoff:					
Peter	......do	537	Dec. 28, 1899	} Russian and Italian.	179–8AD.
Emilia	Wife	536	Aug. 14, 1913		
Ovadia:					
Moise	Head	539	Apr. 1, 1874	} Turk	160–1ABC.
Lucia	Wife	538	Jan. 25, 1879		
Rachele	Daughter	540	Mar. 31, 1921		
Ovadia, Selda. (See Roditi, Selda.)					
Papo:					
Mose	Head	542	Apr. 15, 1883	} Yugoslav	173–2BC.
Lenka	Wife	541	1886		
Pechner:					
Erich	Head	543	Mar. 1, 1896	} German	155–5 BC.
Hertha	Wife	544	July 17, 1898		
Hans	Son	....	Apr. 18, 1930		

Name	Relationship to head of household	Identi- fication no.	Birth date	Citizenship (or last known)	Address
Pesah:					
Sarika	Head	545	Oct. 8, 1914	} Yugoslav	166– BC.
Albert	Son		June 30, 1940		
Penzias Karoline. (See Sonnenschein-Feruermann, Karoline.)					
Pfingst:					
Arnold	Head	546	Oct. 18, 1888	} German	156–6 BC.
Erna	Wife	547	June 1, 1905		
Pick:					
Cilika	Head	549	Sept. 26, 1886	Yugoslav	157–3A.
Ani	Daughter-in-law	548	Feb. 2, 1918	......do	
Peter	Grandson		Jan. 11, 1940	......do	} 209.
Geraldine	Daughter (of Ani, born at shelter).		Mar. 2, 1945	......do	
Pick:					
Joseph	Head	550	Aug. 9, 1879	} Czech	178–2BC.
Valerie	Wife	552	Apr. 4, 1887		
Pick, Oskar	Head	551	Feb. 17, 1896	......do	203–44.
Pillersdorf, Joseph	......do	553	Apr. 11, 1887	Austrian	D.
Pinto, Avram	......do	554	Jan. 15, 1890	Yugoslav	202–26.
Pinto, Bertha	......do	555	Dec. 19, 1909	......do	164–3A.
Pohorilles, Dr. Noah	......do	556	Nov. 24, 1885	Austrian	202–13.
Polivka:					
Adolf	......do	557	Jan. 26, 1884	} ......do	156–3BC.
Ida	Wife	558	Nov. 28, 1888		
Poljokan:					
Sarafina	Head	559	July 28, 1907	} Yugoslav	170–6BC.
Milan	Son		July 14, 1936		
Pollak, Sandor	Head	560	May 6, 1883	......do	169–2ABC.
Popper, Fritz	......do	561	Apr. 2, 1892	Austrian	D.
Porges, Arthur	......do	562	Dec. 27, 1888	......do	202–33.
Porjesz:					
Jacob	......do	564	Sept. 7, 1880	} ......do	6–12.
Elsa	Wife	563	Apr. 1, 1883		
Praeger, Elias	Head	565	Mar. 23, 1883	......do	D–1.
Presser, Otto	......do	566	Sept. 23, 1902	......do	21.
Rappel:					
Hersz	......do	567	Mar. 27, 1896	} Polish	158–7BC.
Recha	Wife	568	Sept. 20, 1891		
Regenhardt, Elsi	Head	569	Dec. 22, 1876	Austrian	153–2A.
Reiner, Michael	......do	570	Sept. 25, 1913	......do	202–34.
Reiner, Zlatko	......do	571	Feb. 9, 1899	Yugoslav	159–7A.
Reinisch, Sofie. (See Kohn, Anna.)					
Reis, Ludwig	Head	576	July 14, 1883	German	175–8A.
Reisner:					
Fritz	......do	573	Aug. 4, 1887		
Stella	Wife	574	Mar. 6, 1892	} Yugoslav	150–5ABC.
Renate	Daughter	796	Nov. 2, 1926		
Dorit	......do	578	Sept. 29, 1929		
Reiss, Hermann	Head	573	Sept. 16, 1897	Austrian	D.

Name	Relationship to head of household	Identi-fication no.	Birth date	Citizenship (or last known)	Address
Rinl, Max	do	577	Sept. 26, 1892	do	D.
Roditi:					
Mose	do	579	July 7, 1900	} Turk	153–7BC.
Selda	Wife	580	Apr. 19, 1910		
Roesler, Oskar	Head	593	Jan. 10, 1892	Yugoslav	D.
Romano:					
Albert	do	581	June 15, 1900	} do	173–8BC.
Ema	Wife	582	Jan. 12, 1908		
Rena	Daughter		Aug. 15, 1935		
Romano:					
Sima	Head	584	Jan. 15, 1893	} do	170–5ABC.
Clara	Wife	583	Feb. 20, 1900		
Samuilo	Son	797	Oct. 8, 1923		
Zarie	do	798	Jan. 21, 1927		
Rosenbaum, Moses	Head	585	Feb. 15, 1896	Polish	} 202–9/10.
Cheller, Fanny	Wife	281	June 23, 1898	German	
Rosenberg, Chaja	Head	586	July 27, 1883	Polish	153–1A.
Rosenberger, Gisela	do	587	Aug. 31, 1910	Yugoslav	159–5A.
Rosenthal:					
Julius	do	589	Dec. 20, 1879	} German	156–1BC 9–22.
Meta	Wife	590	Feb. 4, 1894		
Rosenthal:					
Lida	Head	588	Oct. 8, 1900	} Yugoslav	170–7ABC.
Alfred	Son		Jan. 18, 1932		
Heinrich	do		Apr. 28, 1934		
Edith	Daughter		Nov. 7, 1936		
Rosenzweig, Josef	Head	591	Oct. 8, 1898	Austrian	202–12.
Rosenzweig, Josefine	do	592	Mar. 11, 1903	do	176–5A.
Rothschild:					
Israel	do	594	Apr. 23, 1907		
Netti	Wife	595	Feb. 11, 1915		
Renata	Daughter		Feb. 6, 1942	} German	155–1ABC.
Grazia	do		July 4, 1944		
Fanny	do		Mar. 25, 1939		
Rothstein:					
Josip	Head	596	May 8, 1893		
Sara	Wife	597	July 9, 1909	} Yugoslav	170–2ABC.
Lavoslav	Son		May 31, 1938		
Mirjam	Daughter		Jan. 11, 1940		
Ruchwarger:					
Abraham	Head	598	Sept. 1, 1912	} do	166–4AB.
Zdenka	Wife	599	Sept. 15, 1925		
Rujder, Max	Head	600	Sept. 18, 1897	Austrian	202–25.
Sabniewicz:					
Nechuma	do	601	Apr. 17, 1913		
Manuel	Son		Mar. 15, 1939	} Polish and French.	177–6BC.
Paul	Son (born at shelter).		Mar. 29, 1945		
Salem:					
Augustine	Head	395	Jan. 21, 1909		
Sonja	Daughter		Sept. 29, 1930	} do	163–7ABC.
Helene	do		Oct. 19, 1935		
Salom, Blanka	Head	602	Dec. 13, 1889	Yugoslav	171–7ABC.

Name	Relationship to head of household	Identification no.	Birth date	Citizenship (or last known)	Address
Salom:					
David	do	603	Sept. 13, 1908	} do	171–7ABC.
Erna	Wife	604	Apr. 6, 1910		
Salzstein:					
Abramo	Head	605	Sept. 1, 1912	}	
Ester	Wife	606	Jan. 21, 1912	Polish	160–5ABC.
Elizabeta	Daughter		Sept. 28, 1939		
Scharge, Simon	Head	607	July 16, 1887	do	177–7A.
Scheinfeld, Isaqc	do	608	Dec. 12, 1898	do	202–27.
Scherzer, Cipre	do	610	Mar. 8, 1887	do	157–1A.
Scheyer, Friederich	do	609	Nov. 24, 1889	German	D.
Schild:					
Adolf	Head	611	July 4, 1890	}	
Fanny	Wife	612	June 7, 1905	Russian and	175–7ABC.
Florence	Daughter	804	Jan. 21, 1929	Belgian.	
Ignacio	Son		Apr. 26, 1931		
Schimel:					
Albert	Head	613	May 15, 1911	} Austrian	151–4AB.
Amalia	Mother	614	July 20, 1883		
Schlamm, Josef (deceased Mar. 28, 1945).	Head	615	Apr. 20, 1869	do	176–5B.
Schlesinger, Jolanda	do	616	Nov. 1, 1886	Yugoslav	203–52.
Schlomowitz:					
Chaim	do	617	Dec. 22, 1887	} Austrian	166–8ABC.
Julia	Wife	618	Oct. 22, 1891		
Schlussler, Rudolf	Head	619	Feb. 22, 1892	do	203–80.
Schmeier, Pauline	do	620	Sept. 23, 1883	Czech	178–1A.
Schmutzer, Dragutin (departed for Yugoslavia May 31, 1945).	do	621	Feb. 25, 1902	Yugoslav	217–6.
Schnaymann:					
Sally	do	623	Apr. 4, 1888	} Polish and	158–6BC.
Marta	Wife	622	Jan. 20, 1887	German.	
Schnurer:					
Josef	Head	624	July 10, 1901	} Czech	177–8BC.
Priska	Wife	625	Feb. 26, 1911		
Schoenbaum:					
Richard	Head	627	Jan. 18, 1876	} Yugoslav	171–1BC.
Louise	Wife	626	Apr. 18, 1885		
Schoenwald:					
Ferdinand	Head	628	Nov. 22, 1871	}	
Nada	Daughter	629	Apr. 28, 1904	do	170–3ABC.
Vili	Son	630	May 2, 1910		
Schwarz, Camillo	Head	632	Nov. 17, 1881	Austrian	217–3.
Schroeter:					
Elsa	do	631	Apr. 16, 1918	} German	156–5BC.
Steven	Son		Mar. 28, 1941		
Schwarz:					
Salomon	Head	634	July 22, 1885	} Austrian	159–3BC.
Rosa	Wife	633	Apr. 28, 1880		
Schwarzenberg:					
Ziga	Head	636	July 28, 1902	}	
Anna	Wife	635	July 16, 1905	Yugoslav	170–4AB.
Slavko	Son		Apr. 11, 1932		

Name	Relationship to head of household	Identi-fication no.	Birth date	Citizenship (or last known)	Address
Seif:					
Rachmiel	Head	638	Mar. 16, 1893	} Austrian	152–3BC.
Berta	Wife	637	Aug. 12, 1890		
Seifter:					
Abraham	Head	639	Apr. 7, 1885	} ------do------	159–1BC.
Anna	Wife	640	Nov. 1, 1887		
Selan:					
Carl	Head	642	June 21, 1900	Yugoslav------	
Lotta	Wife	643	Nov. 17, 1915	------do------	} 166–6ABC.
Edne	Daughter		July 26, 1938	------do------	
Mira	------do------		Oct. 23, 1940	------do------	
Serafina	Mother	646	Aug. 11, 1877	------do------	177–1A.
Selan:					
Rudolf	Head	645	Feb. 6, 1902		
Nada	Wife	644	Jan. 1, 1919	------do------	174–7ABC.
Branko	Son		Nov. 4, 1939		
Semel, Rudolf	Head	647	Sept. 3, 1895	Austrian	203–55.
Semjen:					
Elisabeth	------do------	649	Feb. 1, 1898	} Yugoslav------	173–5BC.
Edit	Daughter	648	Apr. 17, 1923		
Sidon:					
Marko	Head	651	Dec. 31, 1911	} ------do------	152–1BC.
Enrica	Wife	650	Nov. 22, 1922		
Siegmund, Helene	Head	641	May 19, 1905	Austrian	159–6A.
Silberbusch, Maxmilian	------do------	652	Aug. 24, 1890	------do------	159–8A.
Silberman:					
Samuel	------do------	657	May 5, 1910	} Polish------	158–3BC.
Breindel	Wife	653	July 28, 1912		
Silbermann, Michael	Head	655	Nov. 12, 1885	Russian	D.
Silbermann:					
Rudolf	------do------	656	Mar. 30, 1910	} German	6–12.
Charlotte	Wife	654	Dec. 5, 1905		
Silberstein:					
Konrad	Head	658	Feb. 23, 1898	} Danzig------	204.
Irma	Wife	659	Aug. 10, 1905		
Simon, Florentine	Head	660	Aug. 15, 1894	German	156–1A.
Singer:					
Edmund	------do------	661	Oct. 23, 1874	} Austrian	209.
Jelka	Wife	662	June 25, 1883		
Singer, Robert	Head	663	Apr. 12, 1876	------do------	154–3A.
Sipser:					
Max	------do------	665	July 14, 1895	} ------do------	152–4AB.
Frieda	Wife	664	Jan. 20, 1900		
Smotricz, Cipre. (See Scherzer, Cipre from Feb. 28, 1945.)					
Sochaczewska, Hadesa	Head	666	Feb. 16, 1900	Polish------	158–7A.
Sommeburg:					
Miriam	------do------	667	Oct. 10, 1900		
Dimitri	Son	799	May 10, 1928		
Sonia	Daughter	800	Aug. 11, 1929	} German	155–6ABC–8A.
Peter	Son		Oct. 26, 1930		
Gioconda	Daughter		July 30, 1935		

Name	Relationship to head of household	Identi-fication no.	Birth date	Citizenship (or last known)	Address
Sonenschein-Feuermann:					
Frederik	Head	179	Feb. 12, 1910	} Polish	178–7BC.
Caroline	Wife	180	July 10, 1901		
Spira, Benno	Head	668	Apr. 30, 1895	Austrian	217–6.
Spitz:					
Fritz	do	670	June 10, 1894	} do	150–3ABC.
Amalia	Wife	669	May 2, 1901		
Ingoborg	Daughter		Mar. 9, 1930		
Silvia	do		Nov. 5, 1940		
Spitzer:					
Filip	Head	672	June 12, 1897	} Yugoslav	166–3ABC.
Maria	Wife	673	June 10, 1901		
Margarita	Daughter	802	Apr. 27, 1926		
Ernest	Son	801	Feb. 10, 1928		
Spitzer, Richard	Head	674	Sept. 13, 1881	Austrian	203–50.
Splitter, Leo	do	671	June 29, 1888	do	D.
Spritzer:					
Wolf	do	675	Feb. 16, 1882	} do	159–4AB.
Lea	Wife	676	June 16, 1892		
Stajn:					
Philip (deceased at shelter, Sept. 31, 1944).	Head				
Margita	Wife	678	Apr. 6, 1905	Yugoslav	170–6A.
Stein, Margit	Head	679	May 4, 1883	Austrian	153–1A.
Steinberg:					
Gertrud	do	680	Apr. 3, 1895	} German	179–4AB.
Steffie	Daughter	681	Apr. 6, 1924		
Steiner, Carl	Head	682	Mar. 23, 1877	Austrian	173–2A.
Steiner, Kurt	do	683	Nov. 4, 1897	do	202–20.
Steinhardt:					
Dr. Dragutin	do	684	Sept. 6, 1886	} Yugoslav	171–8BC.
Marguita	Wife	685	Aug. 6, 1889		
Steinweis, Heinrich	Head	686	Mar. 19, 1890	Austrian	172–6A.
Sterensis, Rene. (See Wolken, Erich.)					
Stern, Max	Head	688	June 21, 1892	Austrian	D.
Stern, Milan	do	689	Jan. 30, 1889	do	202–1.
Stern, Oskar	do	690	Jan. 5, 1886	do	D.
Stern:					
Richard	do	691	June 23, 1881	} do	152–2BC.
Julie	Wife	687	May 10, 1880		
Sternberg:					
George	Head	692	Aug. 20, 1873	} Czech and German.	155–3ABC.
Hedwig	Wife	693	Nov. 12, 1888		
Wollner, Elsa	Cousin	764	Sept. 9, 1879	Czech	155–3ABC.
Sternberg, Heinrich	Head	694	Mar. 25, 1890	Austrian	159–8A.
Sternthal, Rosa	do	695	July 5, 1904	Polish	169–8A.
Stiasny:					
Emil	do	696	Dec. 25, 1881	} Austrian	159–2BC.
Gertrud	Wife	697	Jan. 4, 1903		
Storch, Sara	Head	698	Aug. 12, 1909	Polish	157–8A.
Strasburg, Chana	do	699	July 23, 1886	do	167–1A.

Name	Relationship to head of household	Identification no.	Birth date	Citizenship (or last known)	Address
Strauber:					
Herman	do	700	Nov. 20, 1901	} do	160–2ABC.
Suzanna	Wife	701	Sept. 25, 1905		
Elfrieda	Daughter		Nov. 20, 1932		
Marian	do		Feb. 24, 1937		
Strauss, Samuel	Head	702	Feb. 1, 1891	German	159–3A.
Strichewsky, Vladimir	do	703	Nov. 12, 1892	Russian	203–67.
Striks:					
Fanny	Head	704	Oct. 7, 1909	} Polish	161–8AB.
Gertrude	Daughter		Jan. 29, 1937		
Svecenski, Ernest	Head	706	Dec. 17, 1887	Yugoslav	203–53.
Svecenski:					
Dr. Eugen	do	707	Mar. 30, 1897	} do	166–1ABC.
Dr. Lenka	Wife	705	June 29, 1899		
Ivan	Son	805	Nov. 20, 1928		
Nevenka	Daughter		Feb. 3, 1931		
Sztorch, Sara. (See Storch, Sara.)					
Ternbach:					
Matilda	Head	708	Sept. 10, 1908	} Yugoslav	171–3ABC.
Lea	Daughter		May 18, 1935		
Thewett, Alfred	Head	709	Nov. 22, 1880	Austrian	174–5A.
Trinczer, Jakob	do	710	June 8, 1884	German	203–48.
Trost:					
Michael	do	712	July 29, 1868	} Polish	178–8BC.
Eugenie	Wife	711	Oct. 20, 1872		
Tusak:					
Makso	Head	714	Oct. 6, 1901	} Yugoslav	173–4AB.
Gizela	Wife	713	Apr. 17, 1907		
Edna	Daughter		Sept. 7, 1943		
Twiasschor, Pinkas	Head	715	Dec. 1, 1883	Polish	D.
Tzechoval:					
Mosco	do	717	Jan. 1, 1907	} Rumanian	177–1BC.
Mindla	Wife	716	May 24, 1914		
Ullman, Hugo	Head	718	May 25, 1885	Austrian	D–1.
Vogel, Julius	do	720	Aug. 1, 1887	Polish	100.
Wadler, Lea. (See Loewit, Regina.)					
Wajc, Icek	Head	724	Apr. 17, 1897	Polish	203–68.
Wajsbrot:					
Azriel	do	752	Oct. 8, 1901	do	} 161–3ABC.
Rywa	Wife	753	Mar. 12, 1912	do	
Paul	Son		Nov. 7, 1938	French	
Josef	Son (born at shelter).		May 18, 1945		
Waksman:					
Jakob	Head	719	Feb. 5, 1910	} Polish	161–6ABC.
Suzzane	Wife	721	Dec. 1, 1911		
Samuel	Son		Oct. 20, 1935		
Andre	do		June 12, 1943		
Wallach, Jakob Isak	Head	723	Dec. 15, 1882	Polish	D–7–4AB.

Name	Relationship to head of household	Identi-fication no.	Birth date	Citizenship (or last known)	Address
Wallentin:					
Paul	do	726	Jan. 3, 1896	} Austrian	154–4AB.
Elisabeth	Wife	725	Oct. 14, 1901		
Wallerstein:					
Max	Head	728	Dec. 13, 1884	} German	177–5BC.
Elizabeth	Wife	727	Sept. 2, 1894		
Wantoch, Hugo	Head	729	June 17, 1883	Austrian	203–49.
Wasservogel:					
Marcel	do	732	Aug. 14, 1882		
Clara	Wife	731	Sept. 4, 1893	} do	155–2ABC.
Dorrit	Daughter	730	June 15, 1923		
Weil, Hugo	Head	733	Feb. 17, 1887	do	154–7B.
Weinfeld, Rudolf	do	734	Mar. 31, 1901	Czech	D.
Weingarten, Regina	do	735	Feb. 23, 1907	do	157–5A.
Weininger:					
Hugo	do	736	July 6, 1887		
Margareta	Wife	738	Dec. 9, 1995	} Austrian	178–5ABC.
Gerta	Daughter	737	Jan. 4, 1925		
Weinstein:					
Marcella	Head	739	Aug. 20, 1925		
Miriam	Sister	803	Dec. 1, 1926		
Bernard	Brother		July 4, 1930	} Czech	No. 18.
Lea	Sister		Aug. 1, 1932		
Jack	Brother		May 30, 1934		
Nathan	do		June 4, 1935		
Weinstein:					
Wilhelm	Head	741	June 25, 1884	} Austrian	176–4AB.
Margarethe	Wife	740	May 27, 1891		
Weiss, David	Head	742	Jan. 24, 1899	do	203–58.
Weiss:					
Gustav	do	746	Apr. 17, 1895	Hungarian	154–5BC.
Edeltrud	Wife	743	July 11, 1899	German	
Weiss, Jeanette	Head	747	Dec. 23, 1887	Yugoslav	161–2A.
Weiss:					
Otto	Head	748	Apr. 14, 1896		
Friederike	Wife	745	Jan. 13, 1900	} Yugoslav	173–7ABC.
Edith	Daughter	744	Oct. 31, 1924		
Weiss:					
Sandor	Head	749	May 10, 1887		
Wilhelmina	Wife	750	Oct. 14, 1891	} do	165–4AB.
Tea	Daughter	751	Nov. 27, 1924		
Weissenberg, Fanny and Adolf. (See Jankovoci, Karolina.)					
Weissmann, Josef	Head	755	Mar. 8, 1889	Austrian	202–14.
Willner:					
Israel Jan	do	756	Mar. 14, 1907	} Polish	158–2BC.
Stefania	Wife	757	Feb. 10, 1911		
Windmuller, Josef	Head	758	Dec. 7, 1886	German	159–1A.
Wischnia, Edeltrud. (See Weiss, Edeltrud.)					

Name	Relationship to head of household	Identi-fication no.	Birth date	Citizenship (or last known)	Address
Wittenberg:					
Erich	Head	759	May 2, 1901	} Czech	178–6ABC.
Julie	Wife	760	Sept. 22, 1909		
Paul	Son		Mar. 27, 1933		
Wilhelm	do		June 18, 1934		
Wolff, Dr. Ernst	Head	761	Mar. 21, 1884	Austrian	177–8A.
Wolken:					
Erich	do	762	May 9, 1904	} do	153–4AB.
Ida	Wife	763	Sept. 4, 1907		
Sterensis, Renee	Son		Sept. 9, 1933		
Wollner, Elsa. (See Stern-berg, George.)					
Zabotin:					
Vladimir	Head	766	July 19, 1884	} Polish	161–5ABC.
Adelheid	Wife	765	Mar. 28, 1889		
Konstantin	Son	806	Sept. 30, 1928		
Zalc, Srul	Head	767	Sept. 10, 1896	do	202–21.
Zeitlin, Ida. (deceased Mar. 16, 1945.)	do	768	May 20, 1875	Russian	152–1A.
Zindorf:					
Berta	do	769	Jan. 8, 1915	} Yugoslav	171–6BC.
Ernica	Daughter		Aug. 20, 1938		
Zindwer, Dr. Nathan	Head	770	July 21, 1883	Austrian	203–60.
Zuckerbaecker, Richard	do	771	May 6, 1887	do	202–28.
Zylberstajn:					
Mordochej	do	773	Oct. 16, 1875	} Polish	160–4AB.
Dwoira	Wife	772	Dec. 4, 1883		

《 》

EXHIBIT 18

THE FOURTH R

(By Naomi Jolles, reporter, *New York Post*)

Reading, 'riting and 'rithmetic may have been good enough in the days when "going west" meant Ohio. But the three R's alone aren't enough today. There's a big new lesson to be learned called how to live with your neighbors in an air-age world.

In Oswego, N.Y., a generation of youngsters who never looked beyond Main Street before are learning the new lesson smartly, thanks to the help of a fourth R. Refugee is the fourth R for them—embodied in the daily companionship of 189 children from a dozen different countries of Europe.

The European children arrived last August, to be settled for the duration at the emergency refugee shelter, Fort Ontario, near Oswego. They went to school in September, just like the other Oswego children, and now that the school year is up, everybody agrees they were as vitalizing as plasma.

If the local youngsters had ever noticed place names like Ljubljana, Charleroi, or Lwow on the map they hadn't paused long enough to pronounce them. But soon these towns and cities were vividly next door, places where the people live who are the friends of their new friends.

And what a surge of new interest in American history the refugees created. "Great stuff," said one Oswego 12-year-old to me, his eyes shining. I knew what he was trying to say, and why.

Our history certainly is "great stuff," and its gold and scarlet strands must glow with splendor in the eyes of boys and girls from Austria, Poland, Belgium, and Yugoslavia who know what freedom means because they have lived in slavery. My American 12-year-old had seen with their eyes.

It is not easy for adults, let alone children, to assimilate many strangers all at once. So a number of the children went to school the first day expecting the newcomers to be—well, what? Not quite trustworthy? Perhaps a little laughable? They didn't really know, but they were suspicious.

Then, just before Thanksgiving, the situation cleared up. A class was discussing the Pilgrims and one Austrian boy asked who they were.

"They were people who came here to find freedom of religion," he was told.

"Oh, them," he exclaimed, "we're just like the Pilgrims."

That set the Oswego youngsters to thinking. If Karl was like a Pilgrim, that would make the Pilgrims our first refugees. Everyone likes the Pilgrims, so what's wrong with refugees? The answer was obvious.

Not that the refugees didn't have some friends from the start. Before the opening of school there had been limited meetings. During their first month here, the refugees were completely restricted to the grounds of Fort Ontario—children as well as the seven hundred adults. Curiosity brought many townspeople to the fence to stare.

But the few kids who went to the fence could see that the children on the other side were not freaks, but kids like themselves. Through the country people began to remark that it was a shame to keep the refugees in camp, that they should be allowed out to share the American way of life. But the Oswego children anticipated this thought and from the beginning were buying chocolates, yo-yos and comic books to thrust through the wire mesh openings as gifts.

The division line between camp and city—irksome to the refugees—became more and more irksome to the Oswego children too. Americans don't like being shut in or shut out. The break came one day when seven Oswego boys rushed under the fence carrying a football. Heck, there were a couple of fellows there who looked as if they could really run. The game that followed was hardly the brand of football that would command respect. Directions were shouted in English, German, Slovenian and Italian, but everybody had fun and the bars were down.

Later, after school opened, the city librarian was startled to see her little-used foreign dictionaries going out on loan. The Oswego children had learned another lesson.

It seems slim attractive Mary Di Blasi, art teacher in the school, had started repeating instruction in Italian for some of the refugee pupils. At first there was tittering at the unintelligible sounds. Then the Italo-American children pricked up their ears, trying to catch a word here and there. It was a fascinating new game. How much could you get? And it became a matter of pride to know what the teacher said in Italian. The other students, anxious not to be left out of anything, begged for words so they too could come in the morning with a "*Buon Giorno, Signorina Di Blasi.*"

According to Oswego teachers, the refugees' serious attitude toward study is having a corresponding good effect on their competitive-minded American classmates. Instead of trailing along, handicapped by language difficulties, some of the newcomers are taking honor grades, even in American history.

"At first a lot of kids laughed at them for being grinds," one high-school senior told me. "But it certainly made you feel small."

When they taunted large-eyed 13-year-old Ignace from Belgium, he answered, "It is not a good thing to grow up and know nothing. In 3 years I did not go to school, now I want to know something."

When they joked with Ernest Spitzer, 17, who was a Partisan with Tito 4 years ago, he said: "In prison camp I was too hungry to study. I have forgotten much. Don't mind me, but I must make it up."

After a short while a kid trying to get good marks just didn't seem like the funniest joke in the world any more.

Luckily adult approval hasn't spoiled the children's liking for their new friends. Or perhaps it wouldn't matter. Their liking is too strong.

For example, who do you think the pupils in 7B1 in the Fitzhugh Park School elected president of their class? You know how clannish children of the seventh grade can be, the cliques they form. Well, it's no small tribute to the refugees that the president of 7B1 this year is Joseph Langnas—you know, Joe who used to live in Vienna.

(Originally published in *Women's Home Companion*)

——《 》——

EXHIBIT NO. 19
DEPARTMENT OF THE INTERIOR,
Washington.

CASE HISTORIES OF THE REFUGEES AT FORT ONTARIO

Memorandum for Secretary Ickes:

Here are some of the outstanding case histories* of the refugees at Fort Ontario as they were told to me on the ship bringing us to America, or as they were written at the shelter. For the most part, these stories are literal translations from

---

* The case histories appearing in the *Congressional Record* have been woven into the contents of this book.

the German, which we spoke. I have tried to keep the flavor of the words, as well as the meaning.

Except for those who still have relatives in Germany and Austria, they all told their stories willingly. Men who had been in concentration camps in Dachau and Drancy spoke in whispers when they described the horrors of what they had seen and lived through. Many of them would apologize, "You must forgive me for speaking to you about these things, you are a woman," before they described the way the Nazis and the French gendarmes had kicked and tortured them. Even on the ship, when we were absolutely alone, walking up and down the deck, some of them spoke furtively with an occasional glance over their shoulder. It was inevitable. The ruthlessness, the humiliations, the terror had left an indelible mark.

The pattern underlying most of these stories is a pattern of bombings, of flight across mountains and frontiers, of hunger and filth, of imprisonment under men whose purpose was largely to break the human spirit. These thousand people came from 18 countries; some have been refugees since 1939, some since 1933 when Hitler first took power. The path of their emigration and escape was the path of Hitler's march across Europe. He came to Germany. They fled to Austria. He came to Austria. The Germans and Austrians fled to Czechoslovakia. He came to Czechoslovakia. They fled to Poland. He came to Poland. They fled through the Balkans to Yugoslavia and from there they fled to Italy. On August 3, 1944, they landed in New York Harbor. Middle-class people for the most part, they are a cross-section of Europe's thinking, Europe's occupations, Europe's nationalisms, and, most of all, of Europe's indestructibility. You realized when you talked to them, when you lived with them, that the most indestructible thing in the world is man. He survives the Gestapo; he survives hunger and long fierce wanderings and crippling torture. And yet, he knows, as all men know, that he will live. These people lived because they scratched and tore and hit and bought false passports, and never for one moment believed in their own death.

Playing Hitler's game, various people are beginning to denounce atrocity stories as war propaganda, deliberately blurring the issues so that the guilty may never be brought to justice. The crimes recorded in this report are not second- or third-hand stories; they are not just the eyewitness accounts of trained observers visiting a crematorium and reconstructing the crime. They are personal histories; and the victims are available to prove the crimes.

Their stories, showing the routes and patterns of escape, revealing Nazi, Vichy, and Fascist guilt, might be of value to UNRRA, the Allied Commission, the War Crimes Commission in London, and other agencies concerned with displaced persons and war crimes. The thousand refugees to whom the President offered the refuge of America can help us break through to justice.

RUTH GRUBER, *Special Assistant*

INDEX

Abeles, Charles, 99, 155, 237, 243
Acheson, Dean, 239–40
Ackerman, Leonard, 53, 64
Agudath Israel, 148, 190
Alaskan Development Bill, 5
Alexander, Robert, 228
Alien Registration Law, 147
Allen, Maj. Judson W., 57, 61, 62, 64–65, 69, 110, 121
American Committee for Christian Refugees, 190
American Federation of Labor, 239
American Friends Service Committee, 190, 216, 239
American Jewish Committee, 216
American Jewish Congress, 239
Arnstein, Paul, 124, 179, 256
Arnstein, Walter, 256
Attlee, Clement, 235

Badrian, Berta, 260
Barnes, Joe, 268
Bar Shmorah, Major, 55
Baruch, Anita, 231–32
Baruch, Jennie, 194
Bass, Eva, 102, 114, 257
Bass, Joachim, 102, 133
Bass, Yolanda (Gloria Fredkove), 102, 257
Bates, Florence, 165, 175
Battle of the Bulge, 196
Baum, Filip, 162
Baum, Fredi/Fred, 63, 105, 143, 163, 194, 209, 252, 255

Baum, Jenny, 252
Beaudoin, John, 281
Ben-Gurion, David, 265, 269–71, 293–94
Bergson, Peter, 15, 27, 28
Berlin, U.S. attack on, 108
Bialik, Rabbi Sidney, 144, 157–58
Biddle, Francis, 28–29, 200–201
Bisgeyer, Mr. (B'nai B'rith), 216
"Bitter Hope" (exhibit), 294
Blau, Commodore, 109
Bleier, George, 197, 198, 261
Bleier, Geza, 197–98, 261
Bleier, Karoline, 197–98, 202, 261
Bleier, Ronald, 197, 198, 261
Block, Rena Romano, 246, 258
B'nai B'rith, 153, 191, 216
Bogar, Eva Arnstein, 258
Bokros, Nelly (Thalheimer), 259
Bokros, Paul, 256
Bondy, Curt, 200
Boni, Claude, 258
Boni, Raymond, 258
Boni, Sylvan, 178, 224, 258
Braun, Eva, 210
Breuer, Diane, 193, 210, 221, 257
Breuer, Ernst, 131–32, 257
    marriage of Manya and, 145–47, 155–58, 259
Breuer, Manya Hartmeyer, 256, 265; see also Hartmeyer, Manya
Bronner, Edith (Klein), 180, 194, 251, 261
Bronner, Lilly (Glass), 180

Brooks, Peggy, 279–80
Buchler, Arpad, 202
Buchler, Emilia, 202
Buchler, Renée, 202
Byrnes, James F., 238–39

Campbell, Mr. (camp guard),
    169–70
Cassens, Geraldine, 261
Catholic Welfare Committee, 190
Catholic Welfare Conference, 239
Celler, Emanuel, 25–26
Chamberlain, Joseph, 192, 200, 203,
    214, 216, 217, 239, 240
Chernick, Tina Koerner, 201, 261
Chess, Laura, 284
Churchill, Winston, 8, 20, 159
Clark, Gen. Mark, 210
Clark, Gen. Tom C., 238
Club of the Lonesomes, 191, 207
Cohen, Isaac, 59
Cohen, Jack, 153
Cohen, Mr. (American Jewish Com-
    mittee), 216
Congress, U.S.:
    isolationists in, 5, 27, 28, 174
    President's message to, 29
    see also House of Representatives,
    U.S.; Senate, U.S.
Cooley, Thomas M. II, 222, 224–25
Cowles, Betty, 164–65
Cowles, John, 164
Crabtree, Thomas, 182
Culić, Vesna, 194, 258

Danniker, Captain, 70–71
Danon, Esther (Kaidanow), 233, 258
Danon, Ića, 247
Danon, Irene, 177, 246–47, 251, 257
Desens, Geraldine (Rossiter), 138–41,
    251
Dickstein, Samuel, 215, 219–22,
    224–25, 227–29, 243
Donovan, Susan, 176
Dreikurs, Rudolf, 202, 204–7
Drucker, Jeri and Ernest, 281
Dubin, Bernard, 191, 192, 215, 216

DuBois, Josiah E., Jr., 22–28, 54, 217
Dye, Eva Kaufman, 133, 256

Economou, Athanasia, 109–10
Economou, Evangelina, 109–10
Economou, Meropi, 109–10
Economou, Stella, 109–10
Ehrenstamm, Magrita, 186, 191,
    192–93, 198, 207, 237, 245, 246
Eichmann, Adolf, 29, 160
Eisenhower, Gen. Dwight D., 29,
    212–13
Eisenhower, Milton, 11, 12
Eisenstaedt, Alfred, 159, 181
Epstein, Edna Selan, 257
Ernst, Arthur, 210–11
Europe, displaced persons in, 223,
    234–35
Evans, Stephen, 273
Evian Conference, France (1938), 8
Exodus (ship), 266–67, 283

Faust, Ralph, 175–76, 178–79,
    180–81, 227, 231, 232, 251–52
Feuchtwanger, Lion, 71, 265–66
Feuer, Max, 276–77
Finci, Alfons, 231–32
Finci, Silvio, 202
Finci, Sonya (Setren), 258
Finer, Regina, 285–86, 289–90
Finger, Livia, 102, 261
Fisher, Clark, 220–21, 222–26, 228,
    229
Fisher, Nancy, 284
Fishman, Tamar Hendell, 176, 258
Fisse, Margaret Spitzer, 124, 136, 257
Flatau, Fred, 261
Flink, Joseph, 150, 175
Flink, Naftaly, 150
Forman/Furmanski, Abe, 70–72, 160,
    202–3, 204
Fortas, Abe, 214
Fort Ontario, Oswego, 138
    advisory council of, 161–63, 169
    citizenship and, 208, 223, 229, 235,
    237, 238–43, 245
    closing of, 211–14

clubs and social activities in, 191, 207

congressional decision about, 217–29, 243

conjugal visits in, 232

contributions to refugees in, 144, 147–50, 153, 165, 190–92

Coordinating Committee of, 190–92, 201, 202

death and, 197–98, 202

directory of, 297–323

entertainment in, 155, 187, 226, 236–37, 243–45

illness in, 199–200, 202, 205–7

legal limbo of refugees in, 147, 186, 189, 190, 193, 199, 221, 236

NBC broadcast about, 196–97

official welcome to, 142–44

open house in, 175

plaque in, 252–53

Quaker camp in, 232–34, 239

quarantine of, 145–47, 150–52, 154, 193, 232

refugees' arrival in, 132–36

religious services in, 154–55, 167–70, 183–84, 203–4

reunion in, 251–55, 262

romance in, 194

schooling and, 166–67, 175–82, 186, 191–92, 201–2, 225, 227, 231–32, 323–25

work policy for, 194–95, 207

Frajerman, Harry, 259

Frajerman, Icek, 259

Frajerman, Jacob, 259

Frajerman, Rachel (Goldfrad), 259

Frajerman, Samuel, 259

Frajerman, Sarah (Helia Chaya), 259

Franco, Lydia, 189

Franco, Miriam Mary, 189

Frank, Lea Hanf, 180, 231–32

Fredkove, Gloria (Yolanda Bass), 102, 257

Friedman, Flora Kalderon, 258

Friedmann, Anna Itala, 257

Friedmann, Irene (Reinsdorf), 257

Friedmann, Liesl Bader, 260

Friedmann, Margaret Cohn, 257

Frischwasser, Schleume, 173

Furmanski/Forman, Abe, 70–72, 160, 202–3, 204

Geher, Captain, 66

Germany, surrender of, 213

Girl Scouts, 233

Glass, Lilly Bronner, 180

Goldberg, Capt. Joshua, 121

Goldberger, Hans, 112–13, 131

Goldberger, Jolan, 112–13

Goldfrad, Rachel Frajerman, 259

Goldman, Mr. (Jewish Labor Committee), 216, 218

Goldsmith, Maj. Sam, 43–44, 46

Goldstein, Charlie, 165

Gomberg, Ephraim, 192

Gossett, Ed, 229

Gould, Neva Svecenski, 258

Grafton, Samuel, 27–28

Graner, Elsa, 151, 245

Graner, Hildegarde, 151, 245

Graner, Hugo, 150–51, 245

Graner, Otto, 151, 245

Graves, George, 245

Green, William, 239

Greenberg, Walter, 260

Grin, Dušanka, 185, 231

Gripsholm (ship), 230–31

Gruber, Ruth:

aftermath for, 263–95

plaque awarded to, 255

Haas, Henny Notowicz, 177, 194, 246, 256

Hadassah, 190

Haltiwaner, Caroline, 58, 96

Hanf, Lea (Frank), 180, 231–32

Harding, Raymond B. (Branko Hochwald), 176, 261

Harris, Fred Z. and May M., 257

Harrison, Earl G., 234–35, 240

Harrison, Leland, 18–19, 22

Hartmayer, Manya, 131–32

and baby Diane, 193, 210, 221

Hartmayer, Manya *(cont'd)*:
  and entertainment, 97, 98, 101–2,
    155, 243, 252
  escape from Nazis of, 89–92, 94–95
  in Fort Ontario, 135, 154, 161, 221,
    241, 242
  on *Henry Gibbons*, 64, 81, 97, 98
  marriage of Ernst and, 145–47,
    150, 155–58, 259
Hazan, Rabbi Hajim, 168–69
Heathcote-Smith, Sir Clifford, 64, 67
Hebrew Immigrant Aid Society
  (HIAS), 190, 247
Hecht, Ben, 15
Hedrick, E. H., 243
Hendel, Giselle (Sebestyen), 176, 260
Hendel, Jetta, 201, 259–60
Hendel/Hendell, David, 193, 194,
  254–55, 259
Hendel/Hendell, Tamar (Fishman),
  176, 258
Hendell, Elfie Strauber, 194, 259
Henry Gibbons (ship), 56–115
  activities on board, 110–11
  arguments and insults on, 104–7
  boarding, 56–58, 252, 263
  docking of, 119–22
  entertainment on, 97–103, 109
  food and meals on, 61–62
  rules, 65–66, 78
  threats to, 78–79, 80–82, 83–84,
    95–97
Herzog, Isaac, 288
HIAS (Hebrew Immigrant Aid Society), 190, 247
Hirschler, Ivo (John Hunter), 176,
  261
Hirschler, Milića (Harris), 257
Hirschler, Zlatko (Harris), 124, 126,
  175, 255, 257
Hirschmann, Ira, 27
Hirt, Artur, 105–7, 133, 134, 161–62,
  207, 236
Hiss, Donald, 23
Hitler, Adolf:
  assassination attempt on, 47
  death of, 210
  and *Vernichtung*, 12, 16–17, 160

Hochwald, Branko (Raymond B.
  Harding), 176, 261
Hodel, Florence, 212, 213
Horn, Jack, 277–78
Horthy, Adm. Miklós, 160
House of Representatives, U.S., 29
  Committee on Foreign Affairs, 25
  Committee on Immigration and
    Naturalization, 215–16, 217,
    219–28, 239, 243
Hull, Cordell, 21, 26
Hunter, John (Ivo Hirschler), 176, 261

Ickes, Harold L., 9, 262, 264
  and author's assignment, 4–8,
    10–12, 29, 33–35, 40–41, 175,
    188, 235
  author's reports to, 60, 123, 144,
    167, 173–74, 188, 193, 195, 208
  and congressional investigations,
    215–16, 217, 219, 243
  Interior Department, U.S., *see*
    Ickes, Harold L.
  and media, 123
  message to refugees from, 143
  and refugee agencies, 28
  and refugees' postwar status, 201,
    208, 214–17, 219, 238–39, 240,
    243
  and WRA, *see* WRA
International Committee on
  Refugees, 8

Jackowsky, Jasia, 276
Jackowsky, Staszek, 274–78
Jellinek (refugee), 247
Jeria, Pablo, 281
Jewish Labor Committee, 190, 216, 218
Jewish War Veterans, 253
Jolles, Naomi, 225–26, 323
Jones, Miss (American Friends Ser-
  vice Committee), 216
Justice Department, U.S., 147, 189,
  200, 214, 215, 216, 218, 229, 231,
  235, 238, 243

Kaidanow, Esther Danon, 233, 258
Kaiser, Bruno, 257

Kalderon, Avram, 258
Kalderon, Flora (Friedman), 258
Kalderon, Simon, 258
Kállay, Miklós, 160
Kamhi, Maurice, 260
Kaufman, Branko, 133, 136, 256
Kaufman, Eva (Dye), 133, 256
Kaufman, Kitty, 133, 136, 256
Klein, Edith Bronner, 180, 194, 251, 261
Klein, Murray, 251, 261
Koehler, Joseph, 86–87
Koerner, Tina (Chernick), 201, 261
Korczak, Janus, 285
Korn, Capt. Lewis, 53, 57, 66–67, 105, 108, 155
Kostelanetz, André, 37
Kramer, Liana, 261
Krüger, Hans, 277–78
Kuznitzki, Rolf Manfred, 81, 124–25, 180–81, 194, 256

La Guardia, Fiorello H., 12
Landau, Edmund, 210–11, 212
Landau, Samuel, 99
Langnas, Bettina (Lis), 258
Langnas, Joseph, 154–55, 182, 258
Laughlin, Anne, 143
Lazarus, Emma, 120
Lederer, Ivo/John, 181, 245–46, 259
Lederer, Mira, 201, 245–46
Lederer, Otto, 184, 210–11
Lee, Eric, 257
Lefkoe, Harold, 191
Lenski, Leo, 246
Levi, Juda, 104, 105–7, 143, 161–63, 186
Levitch, Edward, 179, 256
Levitch, Fortunée, 179, 255, 256
Levitch, Joseph, 179, 256
Levitch, Leon, 179, 237, 256
Levitch, Manon (Rainbolt), 179, 256
Levy, David, 84, 186–87, 190, 201, 257
Levy, Rosa Moschev, 179–80
Levy, Zdenka Ruchwarger, 257
Life, 159, 181
Lis, Bettina Langnas, 258
Loehman, Edna Tusak, 258

Long, Breckinridge, 24–26, 29, 174, 214, 228
Long Way Home, The (film), 283
Lowrie, Rev. A. S., 143–44

McCaffrey, Joseph T., 143
McKee, Renée Conforte, 261
McKellar, Ken, 217
Macliach, Henry, 72–74
Mais, Yitzchak, 286, 288
Manfred, Rolf (Kuznitzki), 81, 124–25, 180–81, 194, 256
Margolies, Marjorie, 279–80
Margulis, Aća/Alex, 107, 166, 194, 201, 226–27, 230, 256
Margulis, Rafailo, 107, 128–29, 169–70, 230
Margulis, Rajko/Ralph, 107, 166, 194, 201, 227, 230, 258
Margulis, Renée Reisner, 107, 194, 256
Marinković, Visko, 197
Marks, Ed, 220, 221, 222
Martin, Lt. Donald M., 57
Martin, Lt. Don C., 110
Mauer brothers, 278
Maurer, International Harry, 121, 221, 262
    birth of, 85–87, 131
    circumcision of, 152–53
Maurer, Leon, 153
Maurer, Olga, 85–87, 121, 135, 153, 221
Maurer, Walter, 201
Meir, Golda, 251, 265, 291–92
Meren, Celia, 252
Mezvinsky, Ed, 279
Michaels, Celia, 272–73, 280
Michaels, David, 272, 273–74, 278
Michaels, Gail Dratch, 273–74
Michaels, Philip, 271–72, 274, 278
Mikhailoff, Vadim, 201
Milinović, Gordana, 231–32
Miller, Florence Schild, 259
Miller, George P., 225
Minkoff, Isaiah, 239
Mirković, Leo:
    and entertainment, 97–99, 103, 155, 187, 209, 226, 243–44, 252
    escape from Nazis of, 88

Mirković, Leo (cont'd):
  in Fort Ontario, 159, 187, 193, 230
  on Henry Gibbons, 63–64, 87–88,
    110
  life in America of, 260
Mizen, Ralph, 166–67
Mohler, Bruce, 239
Montgomery (Red Cross), 110
Montiljo, Elia, 115
Montiljo, Maria, 115, 231
Montiljo, Morris, 115
Montiljo, Rosica, 231
Morgenthau, Elinor, 184, 217
Morgenthau, Henry, Jr., 19, 22,
    23–24, 26, 28, 216–18
Morrison, Esther, 232–33
Moschev, Rosa (Levy), 179–80
Moscovitz, Captain, 54, 55
Muñoz Marín, Luis, 272
Munz, Adam, 108, 157, 180, 193
  escape from Nazis of, 91–95
  in Fort Ontario, 141–42, 194, 243
  on Henry Gibbons, 60
  life in America of, 259
  at reunion, 254
Munz, Fradl, 157, 158, 259
Murphy, Robert, 4, 35, 40–41, 42, 66
Mussolini, Benito, 47, 91, 210
"My Day" (E. Roosevelt), 185, 187, 188
Myer, Dillon, 6–8, 9–12, 37, 58, 123,
    135, 143, 144, 166, 195, 232

National Broadcasting Company,
    196–97
National Catholic Welfare Confer-
    ence, 239
National Council of Jewish Women,
    147–48, 190, 192
National Honor Society, 227
National Jewish Community Rela-
    tions Advisory Committee
    (NACRAC), 239
National Jewish Welfare Board, 190
National Refugee Service (NRS), 190,
    191, 192, 216, 247
Neumann, Elsa, 135–36, 231
Neumann, Liesl, 255
Neville, Bob, 45–46

Nitsch, Mathilda, 76–78, 83, 126, 131,
    143, 231
Notowicz, Henny (Haas), 177, 194,
    246, 256
Novak, Franz, 278
Novović, Milorad, 170–71
NRS (National Refugee Service), 190,
    191, 192, 216, 247

O'Dwyer, Gen. William, 200, 203,
    212, 216, 218–19, 222–23
Ontario Chronicle, 209, 210, 212–13
ORT (Organization for Rehabilita-
    tion and Training), 190, 191, 192
Ostberg, Dorrit Reisner, 261
Oswego, New York, 137–38
  Fort Ontario in, see Fort Ontario,
    Oswego
  friendly citizens of, 138–42, 153,
    175, 193–94, 227
  open hearings in, 215–16
  refugees' arrival in, 132–36
  Safe Haven Committee, 294
  schooling in, 175–82, 225, 323–25
  unfriendly citizens of, 165, 179
Oswego Palladium-Times, 158, 165,
    207, 227
Oswego State Teachers College,
    186–87, 190, 201–2, 226
OWI (Office of War Information), 137

Paul, Randolph E., 23–24
Pearlman, Alice, 254
Pegler, Westbrook, 236
Pehle, John, 10–11, 24, 26, 28, 128,
    143, 194, 216–17
Pentcho (ship), 112–13, 131, 237
Perlman, Max, 53–55, 85
Perlman, Nathan, 239
Petacci, Clara, 210
Piaf, Edith, 102
Pick, Anny, 102, 155, 261
Pick, Peter, 261
Pickett, Clarence, 239
Pioneer Women, 251, 252
Pitts, Malcolm, 221
Poljakan, Milan, 130
Poljakan, Serafina, 130

Pons, Lily, 37
Post, Marlene, 284
Powers, Clyde H., 235
Presser, Otto:
    and entertainment, 98–99, 102,
        155, 193, 236–37, 244–45, 252
    at Fort Ontario, 155, 236–37, 243
    on *Henry Gibbons,* 60, 63, 98–99
Prywes, Raquela, 281–82

Quakers:
    American Friends Service Com-
        mittee, 190, 216, 239
    camp run by, 232–34, 239

Rabin, Sonia Sommerburg, 177–78,
    261
Rainbolt, Manon Levitch, 179, 256
Rankin, John E., 243
Rayburn, Sam, 217
Reid, Helen (Mrs. Ogden), 163–64,
    267–68
Reinsdorf, Irene Friedmann, 257
Reisner, Dorrit (Ostberg), 261
Reisner, Renée (Margulis), 107, 194,
    256
Ribakove, Barbara, 282, 284
Riegner, Gerhart, 16–19, 20
Romano, Alberto, 246
Romano, Samuilo, 201
Roosevelt, Eleanor, 184–88, 190, 201,
    211, 217, 231, 235, 262, 292–93
Roosevelt, Franklin Delano, 9–12, 60,
    64, 203
    and admission of refugees, 3, 4, 8,
        9–10, 12, 16, 29, 43, 59, 66, 229,
        241, 242, 244
    death of, 209
    and elections, 188
    Fort Ontario chosen by, 138
    as politician vs. humanitarian, 8–9,
        14–15, 21, 28, 59, 262
    and postwar refugee status, 67,
        201, 216–17, 223
    and WRA, 11
    and WRB, 7, 26–27
Rose, Charlie, 283
Rosner, Henry, 280–82

Rosner-Jeria, Elaine, 281
Rossiter, Geraldine Desens, 138–41,
    251
Roth, Elsie, 282
Rothenberg, Flora, 148

Saunders, Susan, 138
Saxon, Jimmy, 42–43, 44
Schechter, Doris Blumenkranz, 260,
    284
Scheuer, James H., 276
Schild, Florence (Miller), 259
Schild, Irving, 259
Schuelke, Frieda, 182
Schulte, Eduard, 16
Seaman, Barbara, 281
Semjen, Edith (Starkman):
    and entertainment, 98, 101
    in Fort Ontario, 139–41, 181, 194,
        230, 251
    as hair stylist, 192, 260
    on *Henry Gibbons,* 87–88
    Life photos of, 159
Senate, U.S., 217, 239
Setren, Sonya Finci, 258
Sharett, Moshe, 271
Shaw, Colonel, 127, 130–31
Shea, Capt. John, 57, 98, 109, 114
Shiro, Belle, 252
Silberman, Breindel, 74–76
Silberman, Samuel, 74–76
Silverman, Sydney, 16–17
Smart, Joe:
    and Advisory Council, 161–63,
        165, 169–70, 210–11
    and Eleanor Roosevelt, 185,
        186–87, 235
    and Fort Ontario, 134–35, 143,
        146, 189–90, 194–95, 200, 203
    and Oswego Advisory Committee,
        165, 166–67, 192, 235
    and religious services, 168, 169–71,
        204
Smart, Stanley, 181, 194
Sochaczewska, Dolly, 111–12, 114
Sommerburg, Dmitri, 261
Sommerburg, Giaconda, 261
Sommerburg, Miriam, 221, 243, 261

Sommerburg, Peter, 261
Sommerburg, Sonia (Rabin), 177–78, 261
Spellman, Archbishop Francis, 239
Spiegel, Jerry, 274–76
Spielberg, Steven, 284
Spitzer, Ernest, 101, 182
Spitzer, Margareta (Fisse), 124, 136, 257
Starkman, Edith Semjen, 251, 260; see also Semjen, Edith
State Department, U.S., 9, 14, 17–19, 21–26, 40–41, 43, 58, 174, 214–17, 228, 229, 235, 238–40, 243
Stauber, Ralph, 11, 58–59, 66–67, 83, 105, 107, 108, 127
Stauffenberg, Col. Klaus von, 47
Steinberg, Steffi (Winters), 175–76, 180, 231–32, 255, 260
Stimson, Henry, 26
Stockman, Lowell, 220–21, 224–26, 228, 243
Stop Hitler Now, 18, 19–21, 155
"Storm in the Shelter" (Wolff), 199
Strauber, Elfie (Hendell), 194, 259
Strygler, Olivia, 288
Strygler, Rosa, 288
Sutton, Capt. L. C., Jr., 48–49
Svecenski, Eugene, 207–8
Svecenski, Neva (Gould), 258
Swetman, Ralph Waldo, 226

Taft, Robert A., 235
Talbot, Col. Daniel, 66
Tauber, Abe, 67–69, 82–83, 98–103
Thackrey, Ted, 225
Thalheimer, Nelly Bokros, 259
Thompson, Dorothy, 196–97
Tito (Josip Broz), 159
Toum, Mary, 58, 96
Tozier, Morrill, 123, 126, 127, 128
Trank, Richard, 283
Treasury Department, U.S., 22, 23–24, 42–43, 195, 200
Truman, Harry S, 211, 214, 218, 219, 234–35, 241–43, 245, 246
Tuck (bos'n), 61, 69, 110
Tusak, Edna (Loehman), 258

Tusak, Gisella, 258
Tzechoval, Mindla, 188–89, 231
Tzechoval, Rabbi Mossco, 119–20, 149–50, 152, 154, 158, 183, 203–4

UJA (United Jewish Appeal), 190
Unitarian Service Committee, 190
UNRRA (United Nations Relief and Rehabilitation Administration), 223

Wajs, Ićak, 93, 94
Waksman, André, 262
Wallenberg, Raoul, 27
War Department, U.S., 26, 43, 147
War Information, Office of (OWI), 137
War Refugee Board, 7–8, 26–27, 28, 64, 138, 143, 145, 193, 194, 208, 212, 213, 216–17, 219
War Relocation Authority (WRA), 3–4, 6, 9, 11, 135, 153, 166, 200, 214, 219, 220
Waterbury, Edmund, 207, 227
Weill, Rabbi Julien, 70–71
Weinstein, Margaret, 197
Weinstein, Miriam, 151–52
Weinstein orphans, 279–80
Weiss, Edith, 180, 231–32
Weizmann, Chaim, 19–20, 265
Welles, Sumner, 17–19
Willner, Israel, 207
Winters, Steffi Steinberg, 175–76, 180, 231–32, 255, 260
Wise, Louise Waterman, 155
Wise, Rabbi Stephen S., 16–18, 21, 155, 167
Wolff, Ernst, 105–7, 169, 199, 238
World Jewish Congress, 16
Wydra, Miriam, 215, 219

Yellin, Louis, 191

Zabotin, Kostia, 181, 194, 231
Zabotin, Baron Vladimir von, 181, 221
Zatkin, Mr. (National Refugee Service), 216
Zhukov, Georgi, 200, 210

About the Author

RUTH GRUBER was born in 1911, earned her Ph.D. at age twenty, and soon became a foreign correspondent. At twenty-three, writing for the *New York Herald Tribune,* she was the first journalist—man or woman—to report from the Soviet Arctic. In 1944, while working for Secretary of the Interior Harold L. Ickes, Gruber was sent by President Roosevelt on a covert mission to escort one thousand World War II refugees in a secret convoy across the Atlantic to America. The mission resulted in her book *Haven.* Gruber has published fifteen books, including *Raquela,* which won the National Jewish Book Award in 1978. Her *Exodus* photographs appeared in the 1997 Oscar-winning documentary *The Long Way Home.* In 1998, Gruber received a lifetime achievement award from the American Society of Journalists and Authors. She lives in New York City, has two children and four grandchildren, and speaks frequently around the country.